The Limits of
Competence

The Limits of Competence

Knowledge, Higher Education and Society

Ronald Barnett

The Society for Research into Higher Education
& Open University Press

Published by SRHE and
Open University Press
Celtic Court
22 Ballmoor
Buckingham
MK18 1XW

and
1900 Frost Road, Suite 101
Bristol, PA 19007, USA

First published 1994
Reprinted 1996

A catalogue record of this book is available from the British Library

ISBN 0 335 19341 2 (pb)   0 335 19070 7 (hb)

Library of Congress Cataloging-in-Publication Data

Barnett, Ronald, 1947–
    The limits of competence : knowledge, higher education, and
society / Ronald Barnett.
        p.   cm.
    Includes bibliographical references (p.   ) and index.
    ISBN 0–335–19070–7   ISBN 0–335–19341–2 (pbk.)
    1. Education, Higher—Social aspects. 2. Education—Philosophy.
3. Education, Higher—Aims and objectives.   4. Knowledge, Theory of.
I. Title.
LC189.B39   1994
378′.001—dc20   94–22170
                                                                  CIP

Typeset by Graphicraft Typesetters Limited, Hong Kong
Printed in Great Britain by St Edmundsbury Press Limited,
Bury St Edmunds, Suffolk

For Terry Moore

The question (overt or implied) now asked by the professionalist student, the State, or institutions of higher education is no longer 'Is it true?' but 'What use is it?' . . . This creates the prospect for a vast market for competence in operational skills.

(Jean-François Lyotard (1984) The Postmodern Condition: A Report on Knowledge, pp. 48, 53)

'Is a new type of university responsibility possible?'

(Jacques Derrida, 1992, Mochlos; or The Conflict of the Faculties. In R. Rand (ed.) Logomachia: The Conflict of the Faculties, p. 11)

Contents

Acknowledgements

I am grateful to the Macmillan publishing company for allowing me to reproduce (in Chapter 7) a lengthy quotation from R.K. Elliott's contribution to S.C. Brown (ed.) (1975) *Philosophers Discuss Education*. I should also like to record my thanks to a number of colleagues who looked at the manuscript and gave me comments on it: Pat Ainley, Mary Henkel, Diana Laurillard, Nicholas Maxwell, Peter Scott and David Smith. The manuscript has benefited, too, from the careful editorial scrutiny of Upma Barnett. Naturally, I am entirely responsible for any blemishes that remain.

Introduction

Higher education is in the knowledge industry, although in a special sense. It manufactures not knowledge as such – that is the business of the university's research arm – but knowledge competences. It produces graduates with abilities to handle knowledge in definite ways.

However, what seems definite and desirable in one age comes to be questioned in another. The forms of knowing and competence considered worthwhile give way surprisingly easily to new definitions. This book, accordingly, is an exploration of the changing definitions of knowledge competence held to be valuable in our universities.

The *territory* of this book is the overlap between knowledge, higher education and society. The *method* adopted is principally that of an analysis of contemporary ideas in public debate about higher education (such as competence, skill and transferability). An assumption here is that ideas influence the shaping of our practices in higher education, as in social affairs more generally. We shall also examine ideas that are much less in evidence or even downright neglected, such as understanding and wisdom. The *plot* is about changing ideologies and their associated practices, particularly in the curriculum but also in the organization of our universities. The central *argument* is that one ideology, that of academic competence, is being displaced with another ideology, that of operational competence. And the concluding *proposition* is that a third conception, offering not a compromise but a distinct alternative definition of human being, may be more appropriate and even attainable in the modern age.

Approach

The general approach here is that of social philosophy. Social philosophy is an approach to analytical thinking particularly appropriate to the realm of social institutions (and has, for example, been recently advocated by

Nicholas Maxwell). Social philosophy, as deployed here, has the following features:

1. An appreciation of the object of study as a social practice; of its being constituted by social actors playing out social projects, interests and intentions. Vice-chancellors, lecturers and students are not just individuals with their own psychologies but are groups, even if divided, with separate claims and interests.
2. A sense of the social practices at issue being set within the wider society, which exerts its changing claims on those practices. This is particularly significant for higher education as contemporary society comes to have increasing hopes, and more refined expectations, of it.
3. A view that ideas are revealing of what is held to be important and that an exploration of key ideas can tell us much about the changes taking place. However – and this is crucial – that analysis, if it *is* to tell us anything of substance, cannot be conducted in a purely abstract way. There is no pure thought available. The ideas we are exploring do not appear in public debate just out of the ether, but are representative of certain social forces and interests at work. The use of philosophy, therefore, has to be sociological in this additional sense of being sociologically informed. It has to be grounded in an awareness of the contemporary and changing currents; not just a sense of the contours of the banks but of where the mainstream is flowing.

   For example, higher education cannot be understood apart from its relationships with the labour market, with its patterns of employment, since they enter into both the planning of higher education (at macro and micro levels) and into programme choices of students. But those relationships neither are simple (being different across subjects) nor have much degree of stability; even law courses change, as the lawyers come to want new kinds of 'transferable skill' from their degree courses. So ideas in contemporary debate about higher education are anchored, as a pragmatic necessity, in societal interests; pure thought about higher education is a fiction nowhere to be found.
4. A view that conceptual exploration can be critical in character. By examining our concepts, such as 'education', we remind ourselves of their potential scope. Then clear and broad in scope, our concepts become a means of comparing our actual social practices with the potential offered *by* those concepts. We can ask, against the context of the full possibilities identified in a concept, whether (for example) our universities are really 'educational' in character.
5. What is sauce for the goose . . . If contemporary understandings may be shown to be partial in character and to spring from identifiable interests, our own analyses cannot be immune from interests and aspirations. Again, this note is important in higher education which is a human activity easily susceptible to the pursuit of definite human projects. So the account offered here has to withstand scrutiny as to its validity: validity not just in formal terms but also as a meaningful and plausible story.

6. Social philosophy cannot stop even at meaningful and plausible stories. If they are to be taken seriously, the stories will not just be possible readings but will appear to be realizable as projects. This is a severe injunction and again returns the philosopher to the hard world of social realities. Realizability has two sides. The story must have some degree of face validity as a description of what might be. Secondly, there has to be some plausibility that the story as a project might be brought about. Social philosophy is, if not *the* art, at least one art of the possible.

Social philosophy, therefore, is an interweaving of the philosophical with the sociological, of the conceptual with the empirical, of the descriptive with the recommendatory, and of the what-is with the what-might-be. Far from being a mishmash of thought, the kind of analytical approach that some hoped we had long escaped from, it is testable against the standards of all the relevant discourses on which it draws (educational, philosophical, sociological, political, ethical, aesthetic and so on).

'Higher education': a changing idea

Part of the conceptual background to this book is that the idea of higher education is changing. That 'higher education' stands for a species of educational experience distinctive and apart from the rest of the educational system promotes increasing feelings of unease; linkages, continuities and similarities are now actively sought, tying higher education with and into the larger system. That change is part of the notoriously named élite-to-mass change in its form that higher education is undergoing. (The reading of 'élite' was always ambiguous, as between a value-laden 'élitist' and a descriptive 'for élites', and *both* were debatable, while the reading of 'mass' suffers a parallel fate.) However, the 'élite-mass' shift is not an explanation but is a social phenomenon requiring explanation. Both the changes – in the meanings given to 'higher education' anc reflective of much more fundamental (althoug changes in the relationship between higher ed

Those changes are the subject of the first sec several lines of influence can be detected, the central point is quite simple. Higher education is increasingly being incorporated into the mainstream of society. It can be argued that higher education, with its fragmenting forms of thought, of cognitive style and of intellectual orientation, is a postmodern institution, seemingly intent on abandoning any pretence of holding onto sure foundations of right thinking. Some mileage can be had along those lines, but it is a diversion from the main point which is its polar opposite. Higher education is changing from being a *premodern* to a *modern* institution. Indeed, this book could be described as an analysis of the tensions of that shift, from premodernity to modernity.

The detail will await the analysis which follows but what we are seeing is the last stage in a process in which higher education is brought in from the margins of society. The Robbins Report (1963) is often said to be the last great liberal statement of higher education. One reading of that claim is as a commentary on higher education rather than on Robbins. The Robbins Report – with its belief in general education, in a common culture and in a higher education system still largely ruled by the academics – was possible because higher education was (in the UK, in the 1960s) marginal to society and was susceptible to the definitions of the high intelligentsia. Robbins was a symptom of a higher education for a post-rural society rather than for a modern society. Unwittingly, Robbins marked the end of a transitional era, in which higher education was seen as a cultural or positional good. Post-Robbins, higher education was to be seen as an economic good, not only by the individuals concerned but more importantly by society at large. Higher education, through its knowledge functions, was to be treated as a means of economic investment. In Marxist terminology, higher education was to become one of the dominant forces of production, rather than – at most – part of the maintenance of the relations of production. From here on, a new Robbins could no longer be possible.

Accordingly, the characteristic flavour of higher education today is one of modernity. In the shift from marginality to incorporation in the social mainstream, we have seen arise concerns with planning, quantification, accounting of revenues, outcomes, performance review, productive capacity and societal contribution. All these are symptoms of modernity, not of postmodernity and not of the post-rural era of cultural acquisitiveness marked by Robbins. Higher education provides one good case study, therefore, of the durability of modernity. Postmodernity does not yet rule over this part of society.

Nevertheless, the shift to modernity is not easily accomplished. In the first post-war phase of growth in higher education, the academic class had grown and yet had maintained significant pools of 'academic freedom'. Not surprisingly, as society now calls in its debt and seeks to bring the academic class more into the service of societal ends, tensions arise (evident in the appearance of Russell's recent plea (1993) to preserve *Academic Freedom*). Such pleas can be dismissed as the cries of the dispossessed. But there are real and profound losses felt deeply in the definitions of human development appropriate to higher education.

Pessimistically, Adorno and Horkheimer (in their *Dialectic of Enlightenment*, 1989) saw the new order of modernity as one of impoverished conceptions of human being, dominated by instrumental rationality. Higher education is now taking on some of that character. Their analysis was 'pessimistic' because no get-out was felt possible in the total embrace of this technological ordering which penetrated deeply not only into systems and institutions but also into ways of thinking and feeling. Subsequently, that analysis has been taken up by the contemporary German theorist, Jurgen Habermas, who has striven to locate a foundation for a more optimistic view of human development and many of his ideas inform the analysis and the concluding propositions offered here.

Yes, higher education is being locked into a Weberian iron cage of over-prescriptive rationality, of given ends and of operationalism. But the academic community still has the key to the cage. The way forward does not lie in any attempt to retrieve the past, either as a form of common cognitive culture or as a higher order academicism. Instead, an entirely new form of human development has to inform our curricular aims. Whether in the vocabulary of competence, outcomes, skills and transferability (the new) or of intellect, knowledge, truth, objectivity and disciplines (the old), we are faced with limiting ideologies. The one serves a closed conception of the relationship of higher education with the economy; the other has served a closed conception of higher education with cognitive culture. The question is whether a more open conception of curriculum is possible, which is appropriate to a higher education for a more open-ended relationship with society and for more open-ended conceptions of human being. I shall end by arguing that it is.

Proceedings

We begin by exploring the relationships between higher education, knowledge and society. These three constitute a triangle of independent forces, each interrelating with the other. Accordingly, we have three relationships, each of which is examined in turn in the opening three chapters that form Part 1.

In Part 2, we turn to an examination of ideas now coming to constitute the dominant ideology of curriculum at the turn of the century. Only a few are picked out as representative of the genre: competence and capability are here; experiential learning and problem-based learning are not. The criterion of selection is that of the power base from which the ideas arise.

As it happens, both experiential learning and problem-based learning have a powerful backer. They are both finding support from the state because each addresses issues on the state's agenda. Both promise to reduce the monopoly over learning exerted by the academic community. Experiential learning looks to validate (literally approve as valid) learning gained outside academe. Problem-based learning can be a means of appearing to give learners control over their learning while power over the formation of the learning experience lies with the academic, but it also renders the learning task open to external influence with the problems on which the students work being increasingly taken from 'real-life' (that is, work) situations. Further, both experiential learning and problem-based learning carry the promise of reducing the costs of higher education, since the one sanctions off-site learning while the other appears to sanction a heavily reduced role for the lecturer.

Both experiential learning and problem-based learning – and other innovative forms of learning and curriculum not explored in depth in this book such as work-based learning, peer tutoring and open learning – are all receiving interest from the state, not serendipitiously, but because they appeal to one or another element of the state's agenda in orientating higher education to the claims of the world of work. However, a selection has to be made here in identifying contemporary ideas being taken up widely in higher education. Those that have been chosen – competence and outcomes, capability, credit accumulation, transferable skills and enterprise – are the blockbusters of curriculum reform. For the most part, they are sponsored by the government or government agencies or (as with capability and the Royal Society for Arts, or credit accumulation and the former Council for National Academic Awards) receive the imprimatur of national agencies. At the same time, some of those omitted for examination here are sub-elements of the programmes centrally in view; for example, problem-based learning and work-based learning are both encouraged within the Enterprise in Higher Education initiative. The selection made, therefore, sweeps up some of those other debates and ideas, even if it gives them less prominent attention.

In part 3, I turn to examine some ideas either disappearing from public debate or defunct as apparently unworthy of serious attention. Again, a selection has had to be made and those chosen are understanding, critical thought, interdisciplinarity and wisdom. As Kevin Harris once observed (1979), silences are as much constitutive of educational ideologies as their explicit components. So the reasons for the disappearance of these ideas or their neglect are examined as well. En route, relevant ideas currently in vogue are embraced. For example, I observe that while interdisciplinarity appears to have fallen out of the higher education lexicon, its place has been taken by ideas of modular systems which are, in practice, linked to attempts to develop systems of credit accumulation. This ideological infilling is hardly surprising. Silences in general patterns of thought and ideas are easily overlooked because of their *displacement* by other ideas receiving support from the dominant forces.

The last section of two chapters, Part 4, pulls the threads of the argument together by summarizing and placing against each other the two ideologies of competence – operational and academic – revealed in our explorations through the book. As implied, we do not have to leave things there; indeed, philosophically speaking, we have a responsibility to explore other possibilities. The final chapter concludes accordingly by sketching an alternative definition of human being to carry us into the next century.

Prospectus

It has become fashionable for 'academic' authors explicitly to give their readers carte blanche in choosing the order in which their text might be read. After all, in the wake of poststructuralism, the text is the reader's. And so with this book; well, almost. The order offered here is not arbitrary; it has a logic to it. But it is not an utterly compelling logic.

Readers may find it profitable to come at the book in different ways. Those of an argumentative turn of mind, or who are sceptical of current trends in higher education, may prefer to start with Part 2. Those who find most comfort in remembrance of disappearing ideas may wish to begin with Part 3. Those who prefer a synoptic view of things – or like to know at the outset who done it – could turn directly to Part 4. Those who like executive summaries (or, at least, the nearest thing to it here) had better turn to the conclusion. And those who like to get their bearings before wading in will be most comfortable starting with Part 1, which offers a scene-setting analysis of our contemporary context.

The jigsaw can be put together in different ways. Ultimately, however, all the pieces need to be assembled for the entire picture to be revealed, even if the reader's picture is not the author's. Directions to the author's endpoint can be given easily enough.

If the central argument of the book is that the two dominant contemporary ideas of competence – academic and operational – are reflective of narrow interests and limited worlds (the world of academe and the world of work), the question before us is whether we can derive an idea of human being which is relatively unconstrained by sectional interests, which contains a sense of knowing not derived from mere instrumentality, and which looks to promote human beings in situations and conditions unimaginable because the human beings concerned will be doing the imagining. Precisely this prospect is sketched out in the final chapter and so enables us to go beyond the limits of competence.

Part 1

Knowledge, Higher Education and Society

1

The Learning Society?

The learning triangle

What is it to know and to learn in the university? What forms of knowledge does the learning society look to higher education to promote? A serious attack on these questions requires an assault on different fronts simultaneously.

Three large terms have to be confronted: knowledge, higher education and society. The forces represented by these terms are intertwined with and influence each other; indeed, in the modern age, they are partly constitutive of each other. Their relationships and the possibilities that they open up will occupy much of our attention in the chapters that follow, but we can make a start.

Knowledge is an essential feature of modern society. We cannot hope to understand the modern society unless we find some place for knowledge in our account. In Gidden's terminology, knowledge is part of the 'project' of modern society. Such is the message from the corporate world (Drucker, 1992), from sociology (Bell, 1976) and from anthropology (Gellner, 1991).

Higher education, too, is inescapably bound up with knowledge, both in advancing our understanding through research and in its acquisition through teaching (Clark, 1983). The megaversity (Thompson, 1991) might be engaged in all sorts of business but, whatever else, as a university it has to be in the knowledge business.

Furthermore, the forms of knowledge characteristically to be found in higher education are typically those that the advanced society values. There is no simple correspondence between the knowledge capacities sought by modern society and those favoured in higher education; but the general point still holds. Formalized knowledge is prized both by higher education and by the modern society. Higher education, not surprisingly, has become a pivotal institution in and for society.

So, then, higher education, knowledge and society stand in a set of relationships with each other. We cannot understand any one term without

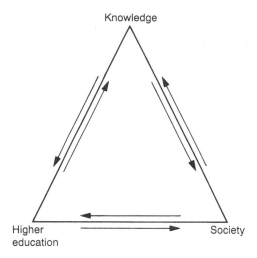

Figure 1.1 The learning triangle

paying some attention to the other two. We might be tempted to conceive of this triple relationship in a linear form, thus:

Higher education → Knowledge → Society.

In this depiction, higher education produces its own definitions of knowledge which it imposes on society as its graduates develop their careers and as its research findings are taken up in various ways.

This won't do, however, for modern society is able to generate and transmit highly technical knowledge outside the academy (Hague, 1991). The many thousands of scientists employed in laboratories within the large corporations constitute an obvious example, being so visible. Those corporations, too, have often developed high level training facilities, and are increasingly seeking academic credit for the knowledge and skills transmitted. So the university is no longer, if it ever was, the monopoly supplier of high level expertise for society. It is not just knowledge, therefore, that is spawned outside the university; higher education itself – in some forms at least – is created outside the university.

We have, then, not a linear relationship but a triangular relationship between knowledge, higher education and society, with each element in some kind of relationship with the other two. In each relationship, the traffic is two-way.

For example, in the higher education and society relationship, higher education takes account of the signals it receives about the knowledge capacities society seeks. And the wider society absorbs in a rough and ready way the graduates who come to it, often in an unpredictable fashion. Not all historians are able to embark immediately on their preferred career, although most do establish themselves in some kind of career within five years or so. Not all law graduates look for careers in the legal profession.

Consider one of the other axes, that between society and knowledge. The interest of society – if not the academy – is weighted in favour of forms of knowledge having a use value in the labour market. This generates an interest in forms of knowledge which can be described in very general terms as operational, computational or strategic. Not only technological, mathematical and computer-based forms of knowledge are favoured, but also those forms of knowledge that facilitate accounting, planning and management.

Certainly, in the liberal democracies of the west, old-fashioned critical and cultural discourses are tolerated. For the moment, the pools of knowledge which are offered in the universities still serve to remind society of the potential range of forms of knowing.

Lastly, in the higher education and knowledge relationship, the formation of knowledge – narrowly termed 'research' – has a more or less direct impact on the character of the higher education curriculum. We have here a particular feature of higher education compared with other parts of the education system. This is not to make a strong point about the often assumed relationship between research and teaching or about the definitions of research as distinct from scholarship. It is simply that the teaching enterprise loosely takes up the contemporary research agenda; indeed, there has to be a research agenda for a new discipline to be admitted to academe. Equally, and often forgotten, the teaching enterprise, in many disciplines at least, colours or even produces the topics taken up for research and for scholarly purposes.

So, knowledge, higher education and society constitute three separate forces, each acting on the other two, with greater or lesser autonomy. With each axis in that triangular set of relationships, we find interactions in both directions. In the rest of this opening chapter, we shall concentrate on the society–knowledge relationship and attend to the other two relationships in the succeeding chapters.

One-dimensionality

Turning then to the society-knowledge relationship, modern society is not even-handed in the encouragement it gives to forms of knowledge as reflected in universities. One modern emphasis is the shift from knowledge as process to knowledge as product (Scott, 1984). The university has become less a place of broad educational and personal development, through an interactive process deemed valuable in itself, and more a place in which knowledge is viewed as a commodity, picked up by those who pass through in acquiring the latest technical competences and analytical capacities. Tellingly, graduates are often described without discomfort as 'products' of higher education.

This sense of higher education becoming a technical business has been pressed forward in the charge of one-dimensionality. That charge has taken different forms. Gunnar Bergendal (1983), for example, has argued that in widening the higher education curriculum to embrace newer professional fields, such as physiotherapy and midwifery, higher education has been bewitched by a sense that real knowledge is scientific knowledge. This scientism, consequently, has neglected the tacit forms of knowing bound up in the professional's concrete activities.

A separate critique of one-dimensionalism has come very recently from Ben Aggar (1991: 130), who argues that intellectual life in general and higher education in particular 'reinforce[s] a one-dimensionality of thought and action [characteristic of "late capitalism"]'. In this society, 'the more we rely on canned computer knowledge and culture, the less we can think, speak and write critically about the social totality'. As the computer and other forms of electronic communication become widespread, 'the medium becomes the message' (in McCluhan's aphorism) and the conceptual universe homogenizes. The educational industry is simply an accomplice in this project.

A yet further diagnosis of one-dimensionality comes in the form of the charge of reductionism. Peacocke (1985) puts it nicely: the essence of reductionism is a 'nothing-buttery' approach, the belief that an understanding of complex phenomena – such as human action and interaction – can be reached by seeing the phenomenon in question as *nothing but* discrete entities understandable in relatively simple conceptual schemas. This approach to understanding is liable to be pervasive, and to invade understanding of quasi-scientific fields with psychological phenomena being reduced to biological entities, and social action being denied the application of sociological concepts but instead being relegated to psychological techniques.

Reductionism is not, however, confined to intellectual life as such but is to be found in its organization. Goodlad, for instance, offers examples of bureaucratic reductionism in universities, where possible interactions between disciplinary groupings – in which sociology and philosophy might have been expected to play a part – are thwarted by being subject to simple bureaucratic and financial constraints: educational possibilities are ruled out because they would run against the 'logic' of the system (Goodlad, 1985). To quote a chapter title from Feyerabend (1970), it might seem at least that here are 'consolations for the specialist'. For those voicing the reductionist charge, however, the point is that it is the specialists of particular persuasions who are getting a hearing.

Despite their differences, the general force of these one-dimensional charges is broadly similar. Higher education (especially through its services to society but also as a result of being hijacked by an uneven balance of forces within academe) has turned to favour some forms of knowing and marginalized others. As a result, those forms of knowledge that might have offered a counter-balance have often succumbed to the dominant cognitive interests of the age. The humanities turn to information technology and quantification while programmes directed at the caring professions seek to derive an academic legitimacy by allying themselves to scientific and positivistic forms of knowing. In turn, the organizational culture of the university reflects its cognitive culture: one-dimensionality rules OK.

Operationalism: a new one-dimension

Modern society is calling on higher education to develop in all students the capacities to be able to *operate* effectively in society. But this observation can mean different things. It can be offered as a recommendation, that higher education ought to be in the business of developing operational capabilities in its students (Birch, 1988). After all, if modern society has an essentially operational character, then higher education had better fall in with its requirements.

A counter view (and one reflected in the title of this book) is that the operational capacities sought by society betoken an attempt to reconstitute human beings and desirable forms of knowing in an unduly limited way. This is not to say that the forms of knowing offered by the academy to society hitherto have been full and satisfactory. On the contrary; they, too, have been marked by a different set of limitations. We are abandoning one form of closure for another. Essentially, the shift in question is from knowing as contemplation to knowing as operation. But to talk of knowing-as-operation begs the question as to whether operations per se can be said to constitute a form of knowing. The problem is that, currently, the question *is* being begged, and often.

As society becomes more complex and more integrated, its professional labour more differentiated and more subject to change, the cognitive demands on its professionals alter. No longer are the pools of knowledge and expertise acquired in initial education sufficient for the new order. What are now required are the abilities to put that knowledge and expertise to use in unfamiliar circumstances; and so we find demands for 'flexibility', 'communication skills' and 'teamwork'. Also required are the abilities to jettison that learning over the lifespan, to be prepared to take on new forms of experience and knowledge and to develop skills anew. In other words, the regeneration of capital requires not knowledge per se, but abilities to exploit and, if necessary, discard knowledge. We are in the throwaway society, cognitively speaking.

This ability to deploy knowledge purely as a resource with its disinclination to treat knowledge as 'given', this knowing about knowledge, is a double form of operationalism. It looks to individuals to be able to operate on their knowledge *and* to deploy those operational capacities in the world of work, and so to operate more effectively.

Accordingly, if there is a dominant ideology emerging in higher education, it is that of *operationalism*. Consequently, terms such as insight, understanding, reflection, wisdom and critique are neglected in favour of skill, competence, outcome, information, technique and flexibility.

This reading of our contemporary situation in higher education suggests a new one-dimensionality, that of operationalism; and we shall see that this view has substance. But our opening remarks about the interactions between higher education, knowledge and society caution against one-dimensional views (for things are more complicated than that), so a new one-dimensionality cannot be the full story. We cannot have a little bit of one-dimensionality. Instead, we need to be more discriminating and be willing to allow a more interactional picture.

Anticipating postmodernism

This pragmatic strategy has contemporary philosophical backing. We are moving into, so we are frequently told, an age of postmodernity. The postmodern society is a multidimensional society. No single world picture, unifying discourse or form of life is available. The legitimacy of the 'grand narrative' has been shot through (Lyotard, 1984, 1992). Given the abandonment of foundations of thought and life, all we have are constellations of ideas (Bernstein, 1991) or stories composed of different vocabularies (Rorty, 1989).

It follows that the postmodern society is characterized less by an enchantment with a single dominant form of reason than by contrasting forms of reason and experience, constituting so many language games with their own internal validity. Knowledge in the postmodern society – on this reading, at least – has been shorn of its value-laden component. Or, at least, there are only local values and no way of choosing between them (cf. MacIntyre, 1982). Society will simply, in a pragmatic spirit, develop, cull and exploit the knowledges its different interest groupings find useful (cf. Rorty, 1980, 1989).

These insights are reflected in the academy. Arguably, as recently as the 1960s, the academic community – even despite its growing 'fissiparous' character, as it 'professionalized' knowledge (Scott, 1984) – could feel that its disciplinary groupings were engaged in a common enterprise of safeguarding intellectual culture with a wider societal legitimacy and transmitting it to the young (cf. Roszack, 1969). Now, as an era of mass higher education develops with its manifold publics and kinds of consumer, and as the academic community splits apart into so many 'tribes and territories' (Becher, 1989), the university intensifies the fragmentation of cognitive capital present in society at large.

Some will say that the sense of there being a golden age of an academic community is misplaced (for example, Peter Scott, 1994). Certainly, for well over a hundred years, since the arrival of the term 'scientist', we have not had a common culture of intellectual discourse even in the university. Snow's idea of the 'Two Cultures' was a set of observations on a situation of relatively enduring character (Snow, 1964). The proliferation of intellectual codes and perspectives which we have witnessed since the Second World War is only a continuation of a process that has been under way for a long time.

However, the actual timing of this intellectual fragmentation is not much to the point. On either estimation (fragmentation before or after the turn of the century), the university turns out to have been a postmodern institution before its time. Indeed, the fragmentation of the wider society's discourse and culture is in part due to the centrifugal character of the intellectual forces at work within the academy, having a part to play in producing knowledge as well as reproducing it for its dissemination. Returning to our opening reflections, we have here an example of the way in which the structure of thought in the academy and in the wider society take in each other's washing.

In short, the university can be seen as a prototype of postmodernism: a type of postmodernism in the way it positively encourages cognitive differentiation; but merely a *proto*type rather than the real thing because, underneath the differentiation, the university has had claims to being founded on general principles of right reason. Still, the accommodation afforded to and the glorying of intellectual diversity and openness as defining characteristics of the university are anticipations of postmodernity.

Now you see it . . .

So there are two grand readings of our modern age, at odds with each other. Both have their imprint on the way in which we make sense of the society–knowledge relationship. One is of a proliferation of forms of knowledge and experience, with no way of arbitrating between them. The other is of a tendency of modern society to favour forms of knowledge of a particular – instrumental and operational – kind. Either of these views of thought within modern society can be read into our institutions of higher education. That is, programmes of study at degree level can be seen as tending either towards one-dimensionality *or* towards greater individuality and separateness.

The either/or formulation of this analysis requires clarification. The university (or the wider society) can hardly be at the same time a source of encouragement for cognitive proliferation *and* for one-dimensionality. Yet the position seems to be that both of these readings, at variance with each other, are plausible stories.

What is not entirely clear so far is whether these two viewpoints are mutually incompatible, in the sense of a logical incompatibility; or whether they are simply strange and uncomfortable bedfellows. If it is the latter awkwardness that we are faced with, it would be possible to hold both positions together, even if uneasily. If it is the former awkwardness, no such juggling is possible. The situation would be like the optical illusion in which, in one glance, the picture before us is that of a rabbit while, in the next glance, the picture appears as a duck. Both images are accurate readings, but they cannot be held at once.

Cognitive drift in higher education

It is the second view that will be held in this book: the two readings are compatible with each other and have to be held in view at once. Tendencies towards both one-dimensionality and cognitive proliferation are at work at the same time, in the wider society and in higher education.

That modern society is complex is a cliché. Part of the meaning of that assertion is that modern society is differentiated into separate spheres of social interaction, each with a definite (even if limited) degree of autonomy. This differentiation is not confined to the dominant institutional apparatus of the economic, legal and cultural spheres. More local groupings form themselves with their own interests. Forms of life, knowledges, discourses and perspectives arise, sometimes in opposition to each other, and in turn inform citizens' self-conceptions.

The central theme, within postmodernism, of indissoluble differences is resonant at a day-to-day level. We can easily accept that there is a multitude of forms of life in modern society. We know how, even within families, individuals having near-similar biographies and experiences can grow apart from each other and find little in the way of similar interests between them. The complexity of modern social and professional life is such that languages, forms of life and discourses exert a profound formative influence. Yet, in the midst of all this cognitive differentiation, we can still maintain that the societal forces being what they are, certain forms of action and thought tend generally to be favoured, while others are downplayed if not actually disparaged. Those encouragements and discouragements are finding their way into higher education.

Modern society is framed by definite dominant interests and ideologies. These include pragmatic interests in competing successfully in global economic trade, in being able to control the total (social, technological and human) environment successfully, and in producing a consensual allegiance across the manifold social groupings to the mission of the state itself. Higher education, as perhaps the key institution in the production and reproduction of knowledge and high level expertise for the modern society, cannot remain immune from such interests. Accordingly, these wider societal interests spill over into the definitions of knowledge sustained by the academy.

I have suggested that there is a super-dominant tendency in higher education which is reflective of these wider societal forces, termed here *operationalism*. A number of UK examples can readily be identified, and we shall examine some of them. The Enterprise in Higher Education initiative has been the most overt, being a state-sponsored scheme with considerable financial backing. Under its auspices, programmes of study have been refashioned so as to encourage entrepreneurial and 'enterprising' skills and aptitudes across the disciplines, including the humanities. The work of the Council for Industry and Higher Education, and the Higher Education for Capability initiative, although having different ideological positions, can also be seen as examples, for both are driven by a desire to enhance graduates' capacity to be able to operate effectively in and on the wider world. Correspondingly, the work (now beginning at higher education level) of the National Council for Vocational Qualifications, with its competency and outcome-based approaches to curriculum design, is further testimony to the drive to enhance the wider operational capacities of graduates as a result of their learning experiences.

Beyond these examples of large-scale initiatives are two other kinds of indicator. Firstly, in the UK at least with government encouragement, there has been an influx of funding from industry and commerce to enable institutions to act in new ways. Science parks, joint industry–university ventures, and the funding (or part-funding) of professorial posts in fields directly related to the interests of the funding corporation are obvious enough examples.

A second set of examples is less obvious. It lies in the shifting balance of studies pursued in the academy. A generation ago, the university was commonly viewed as an institution in which most important subjects were studied. It would have been difficult to imagine a university which did not support the study of philosophy in some way. Now, with the subject balance shifting in the direction of operationalism (as I have termed it), no such association between 'university' and 'philosophy' exists; and with justification, given that philosophy is a near-extinct species of disciplinary animal.

There is a conceptual point along with these empirical observations. In the wake of these changes, our sense of what counts as a 'university' continues to change. The recent changes in Australia and in the UK, in which polytechnics and like institutions have been retitled 'universities', are themselves indicative of this changing notion of 'university'. In both countries, the governments resisted for some time the demand by non-university institutions to be entitled to be called universities. And with good reason: governments feared that any such flexibility on their parts would lead to academic drift, with the claimants abandoning their distinctive role in higher education and adopting the character of the traditional universities. Part of the motivation behind the relaxation of policy suddenly exhibited by both governments presumably was a sense that, for whatever reason, that process of academic drift was not after all going to take place. Whether the governments were correct in that thinking and, if they were, whether the new state of affairs was due to the claimants being prepared to maintain their different role, or even (*sotto voce*) that the existing universities were at last showing signs of falling in with that alternative role, is immaterial. The point is that the change of policy is indicative of a readiness – indeed, a willingness – on the part of the state to extend the formal definition of 'university' beyond its previous connotation.

The substantive point, however, is to reiterate our thesis about operationalism; not to make specific claims about the precise forms that operationalism is taking but to reassert that a general lurch of this kind *is* taking place, and that that shift is happening under the direction, orchestration and active influence of the state. At the moment, this claim is offered simply as an assertion. The argument for it will constitute much of this book.

Correspondence or dialectic?

The academic corps has so immersed itself in its disciplinary interests that the problems of the wider society have been neglected. For Nicholas Maxwell, arguing trenchantly from a history and philosophy of science perspective, the inner epistemology of the academic community is unduly orientated to the cognitive problems of a discipline. This is a particularly narrow form of problem-solving. Consequently, the wisdom required to tackle the problems of the wider society is lacking in the university; its intellectual resources are focused inwards on problems of *its* making rather than those perceived beyond. For Weiner, due largely to the inheritance of a class society and nostalgia for matters rural, the issues of industrial and commercial life have been largely ignored by the universities.

Having a historical perspective, these analyses tend to live in the past. They underestimate the changes engineered recently by the state, some of which we have already touched on and will examine further. Higher education has begun to show a paradigm shift in reorientating its knowledge functions, its research projects, its curricula and its wider mission towards the wider society. 'Paradigm shift' is becoming an empty phrase, used all too readily to describe the first signs of any social change. It is justified here since there are indications of academe, in its most intimate recesses, thinking explicitly of the world beyond in framing and delivering a curriculum. Being a historian is no longer a sufficient *rites de passage*; higher education hears from society that an academic framing of knowledge is an inadequate preparation for the life ahead. Now, 'transferable skills' have to be imparted to students before they pass on to find their way in the labour market.

Yet to speak in such terms is to stay within images of separation between academe and the world of work (Weiner and Maxwell) or of correspondence between the two (old-fashioned Marxists), in which higher education as part of the superstructure simply responds to the demands of the economic base. What is missed in such diagnoses of the contemporary framing of knowledge is the possibility that higher education is both willing and able to act independently in interacting with its wider society, as well as taking on board and interpreting in its own way the messages it receives from society. In other words, to retain the vocabulary for the moment, there may be a process of dialectic at work, with each partner in the academe–society relationship informing and affecting the other. Or, more realistically, this may be a possibility, though not yet realized. That possibility, that

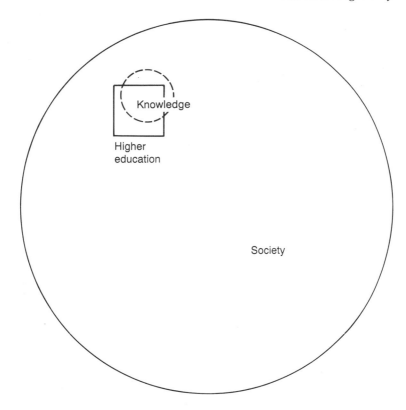

Figure 1.2 Higher education in society

higher education can act to widen society's rationality, will be pursued in this book.

From higher education in society to higher education of society

We are witnessing a fundamental change in the relationships between the three forces of higher education, knowledge and the wider society. Prior to the emergence of the knowledge-based society, the production and dissemination of knowledge was a small-scale affair and society could comfortably leave it to a limited number of institutions ('universities') which were granted privileges and autonomies and basically left to get on with things. The universities were on the fringes of society, performing not unimportant functions, but their functions were not of continuing and central interest to many in the land. In this set-up, the universities could control what counted as high-level knowledge and what went on within their portals. The three forces (knowledge, higher education and society) were arranged something like that shown in Figure 1.2.

Currently, all this is changing. Society–knowledge–higher education have come to form a nexus, an intertwined configuration of institutional forces. To talk of a nexus is, of course, to fudge the issue. It says nothing about the character or strength or direction of the relationships in question. Nor does it contain a sense of the dynamic at work; a nexus could be pointing to a stable set of relationships, which is far from the case here. 'Nexus' only serves to raise questions; it does not answer any.

Can we be more specific? Our observations so far yield four propositions:

1. An overlap of interests and commitments between society and higher education is developing and becoming more pronounced: higher education is becoming an institution of society and not simply an institution in society.
2. Knowledge (even high powered and formalized knowledge) is becoming a distinct force independently of higher education.
3. Society is forming its own definitions of knowing.
4. Higher education is being presented with those external definitions of knowledge and is falling in with the requirements being put its way. (The falling-in might sometimes be reluctant but it is happening with more equanimity than some would wish to believe.)

All these four developments are components of modernity and are new, new not just against the background of a thousand years of history of the university but new on any estimation. Roughly speaking, they are post-Second World War. However, those four propositions do not do very much more than suggest how the forces are distributed in relation to each other. They show what the institutional map looks like (something like that shown in Figure 1.3).

This depiction is unhelpfully static; it does not give us a sense of the balance of forces, of the flow of the dominant messages or of the give-and-take or even resistance between them. Here, it is tempting to retreat into bland statements about interrelationships, about autonomy of the separate forces, and about interactions in every direction. All that is true but we can say something more definite, even at this early stage in our explorations.

At one time, the relationships between knowledge, higher education and society *could* reasonably have been captured by the linear form we dismissed earlier, that is:

Higher education $\rightarrow$ knowledge $\rightarrow$ society.

Now, the relationship is being reversed. We are not there yet, but the direction of contemporary trends is towards a relationship of the form:

Society $\rightarrow$ knowledge $\rightarrow$ higher education.

Crudely speaking, society is coming to determine the forms of knowing that it wishes for itself. It is no longer content to leave their definition to the academics; or even, as we have noted, their production. Higher education,

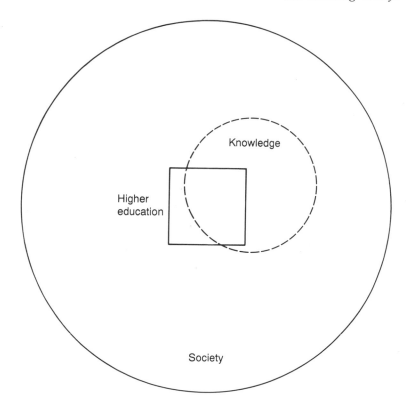

Figure 1.3 Higher education of society

furthermore, is having to respond to the epistemological agenda being put to it by the wider society.

This is a crude account on two levels, in fact and in logic. Firstly, to repeat, we are not there yet and may never reach such a situation. Indeed, there are reasons to be spelt out which suggest that it is not in the interests of society itself to attain such a position of epistemological domination. It will remain in the interests of society to continue to allow the university some autonomy in its knowledge functions, central as they are to modernity.

Secondly, it possesses a certain crudeness in simplifying to the point of near-contradiction. With the reflexivity built into modernity's forms of knowing (Giddens, 1991), no tight closure of the kind suggested by the linear depiction above can *ever* come about. This is a comment on the logical character of the forms of reason that have come to characterize modernity. Reason can reason about itself: there is always the possibility, therefore, of it breaking out of its own frameworks, however much those frameworks might be useful to the dominant forces in society.

This book, accordingly, is not to be construed simply as a critique of the shift of university in the direction of the wider society. The university is implicated in that shift itself; and in three senses. Firstly, it is often content to take on the agendas of modern society; 'issues' as identified by sectional interests beyond become the issues within. Secondly, having previously formed itself around its own sectional interests of the epistemic sub-communities, the academic world is hardly in a position to complain if the wider society – which is largely footing the academic bill – is intent on calling in the debt and is now requiring a more ready focus on immediate social and technological problems.

Thirdly, and ironically, higher education is underestimating society's capacity for absorbing the very forms of rationality for which higher education claims to have been in business. In a world of change, in the so-called post-Fordist world where 'flexibility' is the watchword, the wider world, despite itself, is coming to an appreciation of just those wider skills and capacities of human reason traditionally espoused in the university. If there is a correspondence at work, perhaps it is more a correspondence of society with higher education than of higher education with society. The only problem is that the university fails to practise what it preaches. The gulf between theories-in-use and espoused theories which the critical academics love to observe in others is to be found in glaringly sharp form in the academy. Having trapped itself into narrow definitions of knowledge, it is unable to provide the wider definitions of knowing and intellectual develop-ment which it supremely should have been in a position to supply and which are now required by society.

Conclusion

Society may have a limited sense of rationality but so does the academic community, albeit of a different kind. If higher education is to play a part in expanding the rationality of modern society, it cannot do it by complying uncritically with the agendas presented to it. But neither can it do so by holding onto its own form of rationality. Higher education cannot seriously entertain the prospect of promoting a self-critical, mutually self-informing society unless it takes on something of that form itself. Higher education cannot address the interdisciplinary problems of contemporary life unless it is thoroughly interdisciplinary itself. Higher education cannot expect society to examine critically its dominant forms of knowing, learning and interaction unless higher education is prepared to do so in and for itself. In short, a higher education for a rational society requires that higher education expand its own sense of rationality.

2

A Certain Way of Knowing?

Introduction

The introduction suggested that higher education, society and knowledge could be seen as three forces with some degree of autonomy but interacting with each other. The first chapter began to explore the relationships between all three forces but focused on that between society and knowledge.

The central issue was this: if the modern society has a fundamental interest in knowledge, can that interest be understood as one of increasing openness towards what counts as knowledge or is it more accurately depicted as one of closure? Is the learning society interested in learning only of particular kinds? The signs can be read in different ways. On the one hand, certain forms of knowledge are favoured by the state: the natural sciences, technologies, mathematics and computer sciences, and professional studies orientated to business management. On the other hand, the encouragement given to higher education to introduce 'transferable skills' reveals a sense on the part of the state that technical and scientific knowledge cannot be sufficient in the modern world. Instead, forms of capability and competence are required which enable individuals to transcend specific situations so as to operate effectively within and *on* them.

Closure *and* openness seem, therefore, to be the cognitive order of the day. We can now take that analysis further and, in doing so, shall shift the focus by taking up another dimension of our opening triangle of forces, namely the society–higher education axis. However, we cannot sensibly talk about one axis without acknowledging the other two and so our observations will contain allusions to issues of knowledge as well.

The society–higher education axis

Let us identify some key issues:

1. The character of the social formation provided by higher education: how far can the category of the labour market take us? Insofar as that

might suggest a responsive function on the part of higher education, might we also wish to counterpose a critical or at least a commentating function?

2. If society is a meaningful category, independent of the economic sphere, to what extent can higher education be understood as a process of social rather than economic formation? Can we make sense of higher education for life as distinct from higher education for work?

3. How does the wider society gain a purchase on the offerings of higher education? How is higher education breached? The disciplines differ over the extent and the ways in which they are permeable to the claims of society, but can we provide a general account of the differences between disciplines?

4. Are there general contours to the contemporary influences which the wider society is bringing to the higher education curriculum? Do categories such as vocational/liberal, pure/applied, relevant/non-relevant, or intrinsic/extrinsic do any conceptual work for us? Or do such terms have to be jettisoned as reflective of ideologies either internal or external to the academic life?

5. If the categories of openness and closure are of any help, to which pole in the society and higher education axis might either of the categories be applied? Is it that society is exerting a constraining effect on higher education in its inner life, or is it – *per contra* – that the closure lies within higher education, which is strangely resisting society's plea for a more open curriculum and for a wider student experience?

6. In the modern society, how do we understand the main function of higher education? Is it to provide technical cadres for the increasingly differentiated forms taken by intellectual labour? If so, is higher education supporting a fragmentation of cognition in society? In turn, is higher education reducing the rationality of society rather than extending it?

Correspondence or resistance?

The modern society is dependent on knowledge, on its transmission, understanding, application, storage, critical examination and development. Higher education is the only institution in society charged with all these functions. Other institutions play one or more of these functions; and these are not only formal educational institutions. Schools are involved in the transmission, but are not expected to inculcate the deep and independent understanding characteristic of a higher education. Research institutes, both small-scale and housed in large corporations, are found outside the academies. Even the 'quality' newspapers might be said to offer something of a critical function. And libraries and databases are proliferating, aided by the ubiquity of the computer. So higher education is not distinctive in virtue of any one of the six tasks just mentioned. Instead, its distinctiveness lies in its combining all those tasks together.

That combination of tasks imparts a particularity to each function. The transmission of knowledge, for example, can only be an injustice as a description of the set of activities it purports to describe. Precisely because the 'transmission' of knowledge takes place in a context of the critical examination, development and often the application of knowledge, it has an added edge which knowledge 'transmission' will tend to lack in other settings. Critical examination supplies a sense of possible otherness; knowledge development supplies a sense of debatableness; and application supplies a determination to test its soundness. All these practised together, and pursued in a culture of truth-seeking, impart demands on teachers in higher education. Their task cannot be one merely of knowledge transmission; or even in major part. Instead, their central – if unarticulated – task lies in drawing students into intuiting and taking on the higher order ends internal to the academic life. Those ends involve a sense of the non-givenness of truth claims and of their continuing contestability; of a willingness to form one's own views, or at least to proffer truth claims by being able to give them backing with one's own reasons and evidence; and a recognition that there is always more to be said and from other perspectives.

Only by developing an account along these lines can we make sense of a phrase like 'knowledge transmission' within higher education. Knowledge is not so much transmitted as painfully authenticated by each student.

Correspondingly, research is not as straightforward as it may seem. We do not have to assert a tight relationship between research and teaching to recognize their interactions, which are two-way. Certainly, researchers research, and research contracts are won, without any direct relationship with the teaching process. Also, research units are increasingly established, some with the ultimate end of winning profitable patents, again without any obvious spillover to the teaching enterprise. Yet, it remains the case that a significant proportion and perhaps still the majority of academic staff would claim to be involved in both teaching and research. Often, teaching activities will have some influence on the research enterprise, to put it no stronger than that. It might be in a direct way, particularly in the humanities and sometimes in the social sciences, where teaching commitments spark off ideas for research, if in the form of scholarly publications. In the sciences, it might take the form of the students themselves being drawn in (say, in third year projects) to assist bona fide research projects.

So higher education is a unique institution in modern society. Called upon by society to fulfil a variety of functions, it turns out to be more than the sum of its parts. Each aspect is coloured by the others. Loosely coupled it may be (Clark, 1983); but the functional parts *are* coupled together. In their coupling, there is formed a dynamic interaction between them. The conduct of one function affects the others, however unclearly we understand those interactions.

On one theory in the literature, educational institutions are part of the superstructure of society, determined by and reflecting the requirements of the economic base. To proffer such a theory as even the beginnings of an

account of higher education is to tempt the response, from the liberal and
Fabian quarters at least, that part of the function of higher education is to
provide an oppositional component of modern society. It is easy enough to
flag limitations in both accounts. The one does not admit to the real institutional autonomy higher education possesses, even now; the other is more
a normative view, an aspiration, rather than any dispassionate account of
the actual character of higher education in modern society, hedged about
as it is with societal demands. The main point, though, derives from taking
the society and higher education relationship seriously as a relationship.

No uni-dimensional theory is going to offer a satisfactory account of
the relationship between society and higher education. There are different
relationships between society and higher education across the disciplines.
Precisely because higher education is performing a range of economic and
cultural functions, there will be a number of different stories to tell about
its character and its connections with its host society. But there is a stronger
point to be made.

Given this internal complexity, of disciplines and functions in a dynamic
relationship both with each other and with society, legitimate stories can be
told about different disciplines and academic activities which are *in tension*
with each other. In the multiversity (Kerr, 1972), we have both correspondence and resistance.

If it makes sense to describe different parts of a single institution having
profoundly different relationships with the wider society, it also makes sense
for a differential to be identified in the realm of possible future relationships. To put it bluntly: some fields of activity in the university will wish to
exercise their autonomy and exhibit a degree of distance from the pervad-
ing culture whereas others will be happy to fall in with it. Blatant resistance
will be avoided; it leads to death. But underhand forms of resistance will be
developed in some quarters, sometimes so underhand that their own per-
petrators will be unaware of the force of their own actions.

All disciplines talk of developing the powers of critical reason, but those
in the social sciences, the humanities and the fine arts have a more inclu-
sive notion of what it is to be critical compared with their colleagues in the
technologies and natural sciences. The cognitive intent of different curricula towards the wider society differs. Some disciplines – being concerned
with social institutions, practices and values – bear directly on society in
their fields of attention. As such, they present opportunities for critiquing
society since their students will be encouraged to assess the gap between the
potential of their concepts and their reflection in society. To invite a student to unpick the concept of democracy is implicitly a critical practice
since the concept will come to be a standard against which the claims of
society (to be 'democratic') can be tested.

Three principal points emerge from this discussion. Firstly, given the
complexity and disjointedness of academic institutions, no simple story of
the relationship between society and higher education is going to be
adequate. Secondly, different activities and disciplines within academe have

different relationships with the wider society. Thirdly, those relationships are not static, but are doubly dynamic. Each has its impact on the other in the activities and disciplines; society and higher education are intertwined. This connection may be one – at opposite ends – of correspondence *or* resistance. Activities, values and systems may be developed with a sense that all is right with the world, and it is the job of higher education to give society what it desires; or they may be developed with a view to keeping society at arm's length and perhaps even with the intention of showing alternative possibilities (of thought and action) to society. All these differences may be apparent not just in the same university but even in the same department.

Uneasy bedfellows

Relationships can take various forms. Family relationships can be warm, strained or even antagonistic. Relationships can be genetic, that is, deep-seated; or social, having developed from a mutual purpose established over time. We might speak of A being related to B when they simply happen to possess similar features, without there being anything in the way of a real link between them. So talk of a higher education and society relationship is empty, unless we can begin to fill in its character.

Currently, we do not possess anything which amounts to a satisfactory theory of this relationship. We may wish to talk of higher education being 'accommodated' to the technostructure (Galbraith, 1969), or of it 'corresponding' to the economic apparatus (Bowles and Gintis, 1976), or of its different sectors 'matching' *and* 'monitoring' society (Brosan, 1971), or of its various elements being differentially 'permeable' to the external requirements (Brennan, 1985). All these, and other such descriptions, are suggestive metaphors, each carrying a greater or lesser value. But they are metaphors, offering at best some insight into complex processes.

Higher education has always had some form of relationship with its wider society, and that relationship is undergoing more change than ever before. Further, to reiterate, there are differing relationships across subjects and institutions. History at an élite university stands in a different relationship to society and the economy from history at a college of higher education. Further still, since higher education retains real pools of autonomy, the economic, social and epistemic relationships are two-way. Higher education remains something of an independent agent, exerting its influence in separate spheres; it does not just provide the economy with the cognitive capital being sought.

Single word descriptors are going to be inadequate, therefore, to capture the complexity of these interrelationships between higher education and society. The next step is obviously to say that a more subtle story is required. But there, we have to grind to a halt. No story is available which does justice to the complexities of the situation. There is a reason for this which goes beyond the familiar reflection that higher education will study everything else with seriousness before it gets round to examining itself.

Although the society–higher education relationship is changing, with the state taking a greater interest in academic operations and indeed increasingly impinging on them, the activity of higher education – as *higher education* – must retain some degree of openness. The key actors, staff and students, will have some measure of freedom to determine the patterns of their engagements with each other and their mutual responses. In practice, the students' room for manoeuvre is limited; but it is often more open than many students are prepared to admit. It is easier to get one's degree by reproducing the lecturer's offerings than to take the responsibility to engage oneself *with* those offerings. Also, in many professional areas, the lecturers' scope for curriculum innovation may be constrained. Nevertheless, there remains real openness at the heart of the relationship between teacher and taught. Oakeshott's key term of 'engagement' has point because both teacher and taught are more or less free to engage with each other, to say what they mean and to mean what they say (Fuller, 1989).

This openness is neither an oversight on the part of the state nor a matter of its generosity towards the academic community. To use a particular terminology, this state of affairs is *functional* for modern society. While other sectors of the education system may have their central freedoms reduced to vanishing point, higher education is likely to be left with real autonomy precisely in those central operations. At the very least, the state is ambiguous on this point. There is a tendency on the part of the state to approach ever closer the core of the activities constituting higher education. Having established systems of surveillance over institutional operations, it is now embarking on curriculum inspection *and* acting directly on its very shaping. Nevertheless, ultimately it is in the interest of the state to maintain a higher education enterprise with real autonomy. The interest in question is not a democratic one. The autonomy granted to higher education is not provided to preserve the open society. Popperians can still, however, supply a reason that does make sense for the state.

The reason is double-headed. On the one hand, the modern industrial society, faced with intense international competition and with challenges from new markets developing apace, has an inbuilt imperative to encourage and even sponsor change in those goods and services being placed in the market. On the other hand, there is the Popperian point: we cannot know in advance what we might imagine, or create intellectually, tomorrow (Popper, 1961). The two points are linked because change in goods and services is dependent on cognitive change, whether expressed in the form of technology, design, production or packaging. Much of this change will occur *in situ*; or in the world of work more generally, through in-company research, development or self-evaluation exercises. It remains the case, however, that higher education is the major institution in society organized for cognitive change and flexibility; and this is not only in the form of research but more strategically in the form of the intellectual capacities with which, it is hoped, graduates entering the labour market will be equipped.

Higher education stands in the dock of the employers' court for not doing sufficient on this front. Consequently, we hear pleas for even more flexibility in graduate employees (in addition to their possessing a range of so-called personal transferable skills). Nevertheless, it *is* one of the defining characteristics of a genuinely higher education that students come to a realization that, in the world of ideas, knowledge and frames of thinking, things could be other than they are. Higher education is supposed to encourage the toleration of ambiguity, of change, and of different ways of going on. These, prima facie at least, *are* requirements of the modern economy; and of the learning society (Chapter 1) that that economy is ushering in.

Undue angst

I have been suggesting two things. Firstly, that there is a necessary degree of openness in the character and form of higher education. 'Necessary' not in a formally logical sense but in the sense that it arises from the logic of the relationship between society and higher education. Yes, the state wishes to have influence – and increasingly so – over higher education; but it is also in the state's interest not to insist on complete control of what goes on in the lecture hall or seminar. Secondly, there are signs, prima facie, of some kind of congruence between the desiderata of the state and what higher education has taken itself to be in business for all along. Both seem to place a value on open-endedness, on continually challenging the given and on flexibility of thinking.

There is a further apparent similarity. The preparedness to share one's thinking with others, to open it for inspection and even challenge, to allow it to be taken up by others: thinking as a collective activity is present as a value both in higher education and in the corporate world.

The qualifiers 'seem', 'prima facie', 'apparent', 'some kind' are deliberate: the similarity in interest is more apparent than real. The same words – communication, problem-solving, creativity, flexibility – might be used by those in different camps; but do the words stand for similar concepts in both spheres of activity? There used to be a conceptual gap between the two. Once, communication in programmes of study meant students being able to form an intellectual argument in keeping with the implicit norms of their discipline. Now, they are being asked to develop presentational skills of the kind appropriate to business settings. So, any such a conceptual gap is closing. Yet, the question remains: how do we understand this closing of cognitive interests? Are important interests internal to the academic life being downplayed or is the academic world justifiably being asked to jettison values of a former age?

There is not one but two kinds of angst at work here within the academic world; they are not universally held, but are still evident in large segments of that world.

Firstly, there is a concern that we are witnessing a migration into the academic world of values and interests that have their home in quite different milieux. The concerns to get things done, to have people in work who have concrete effects on their situations, and to secure change for profitability, customer retention and even sheer survival: all these are interests that are spilling over into public services generally, and higher education (as a key potential provider of such human capacities) in particular.

These forms of concern have theoretical backing in the claim of Critical Theory that strategic reason is becoming the dominant form of reasoning in society and is driving out genuinely interactive and collaborative forms of reasoning *and* critical reasoning. Consequently, coming nearer home, the forms of reasoning and thinking that are becoming valued in higher education are forms of strategic reasoning.

For example, some talk enthusiastically of problem-solving or of problem-based learning or, with even more subtlety, of problem-focused learning (Margetson, 1994). All three, and problem-based learning in particular, can have an educational justification. Problem-based learning can point towards giving the learner real ownership of her learning and can foster independence of inquiry and of mental acts, since students can be encouraged to assemble their own evidence and formulate their own deductions and decisions. But all three terms, and especially problem-solving, can also stand for the incorporation into higher education of *decisionism*, another term from Critical Theory. Such teaching methods can be means, predominantly, of encouraging students to come to decisions as such, without having to justify their ethical or environmental (in the general sense) basis. Problem-solving appears to be value-neutral but, like all educational approaches, its instantiation as a practice is replete with values. Problem-solving is, whatever else it *may* be, a technique of the modern industrial society: a pragmatic response to pragmatic problems of the wider society.

The point of this excursus has not been to downvalue problem-solving as such, but to provide an example of the concern that the interests of the wider society are finding their way into the heart of the university's educational process. Some of those innovations may even wear educational labels and come dressed in educational justifications. This concern constitutes a certain kind of angst, an unease affecting the understanding that a significant proportion of academics have of themselves.

The other angst at issue is an even larger unease. It is the sense that the academic freedoms and institutional autonomy once enjoyed are diminishing. Here, it might be tempting to launch into an analysis of the differences between academic autonomy and academic freedoms. There are real conceptual differences worth drawing out, notably between the autonomy of institutions and the freedoms of academics within those institutions. However, that distinction does not carry us far, for we are then faced with the questions: what freedoms? What kind of autonomy? Addressing those questions seriously is just what we should avoid. The point at issue is one about senses, perceptions and surmises. A real angst is not to be dislodged by the facts and by nice distinctions. It reflects fundamental kinds of unease developed over time and which strike at the core of one's self-concepts.

To say that this angst is separable from its causes is not to downplay the attempt to understand better that portion of the world to which the angst is addressed. There is an important story to be told about the changing relationship between higher education and the state (Tapper and Salter, 1992; Jarvis, 1993). The modern state has its interests in control and surveillance and those tendencies become ever more apparent as – across the western world – state agencies are established to evaluate, monitor and inspect, and so impinge directly upon the not-so-secret garden of the curriculum. But what is of concern here is to understand the character of that angst.

In one sense, these mistrustful academics have got it right. Academic freedom and autonomy are diminishing. The more interesting point, however, can be put in the form of a question. Suppose it turned out that that angst was misplaced, that academics' basic freedoms and autonomy remain largely intact. Would the angst be immediately dissipated? The answer, surely, is: most unlikely.

As indicated, both of the angsts just identified have substance to them. The state is attempting both to shift the curriculum from 'process to product' (Scott, 1984) and to impinge on the academics' professional activities. The point, though, is less the object of the angst than the ideological anchoring. Being understandably concerned to protect historic social positioning and pools of professional autonomy, the academic class comes to over-focus on the sheer brute fact of the state's presence. The result is that the other side of the coin, the remaining autonomies and freedoms, is forgotten if not entirely neglected. The academic class takes pleasure in its own diminished freedoms. Therein lies an absolution of responsibility. The difficult choices of determining positions which recognize the reality of state intervention while doing justice to educational agendas are thereby avoided.

The argument deserves to be carried a little further. There are two large literatures which bear directly on the story here. On the one hand, there is a literature that essentially assumes that higher education should be more responsive to society, and is bent on working out ways in which society's claims can be softened so as to be made palatable to the academic world. On the other hand, there is a literature that takes it as read that the state's claims on education are ideological and hegemonic, and accordingly calls for forms of resistance. The problem is that the academic class rarely reads either literature – or if it does, remains pretty unconvinced – and so fails to act out either of the scripts written for it.

Certainly, no single story will suffice to describe the stance of academics to the claims of the wider society. The course leader in a programme of art and design at one of the new UK universities, many of whose students are looking to a career in the fashion houses of continental Europe, may well fall in with the responsive mode of operation; a course leader in another situation – environmental sciences, for example – might adopt a more oppositional approach in curriculum delivery. But to recognize these differences, cutting across subjects and institutions, is to accept a point often overlooked by the academic class. In being determined to maintain its historic freedoms, the scope for exploring and exhibiting the real freedoms that remain is all too easily neglected.

Professional responsibilities?

This perspective on the academic life offers a particular light on another aspect of the relationship between higher education and society, that of professionalism. Some recent accounts have suggested that we are witnessing a fundamental change in the character of the academic life; indeed, on one view, the academic corps has turned into a proletariat (Halsey, 1992).

There are two variants of the general argument. One considers that with the shift from an élite to a mass system, the academic class has seen its control over the forms of intellectual production in which it is engaged steadily reduced so that its work is not its own. We are seeing labour, not work; operations for another person, agency or body, not work entered into for its own good and owned by the actors concerned, in which they invest much of themselves, both their personal and social identities. Increasingly, academic labour is specified in advance and approved by a third party, with the scope for manoeuvre in day-to-day settings diminished.

The other variant is a form of: 'things aren't what they used to be'. Sheer numbers of students, new claimants to the title 'university', attention to teaching as a practice in its own right (and a corresponding downvaluing of research), a broader body of students, less time to devote to one's own projects, more inspection of one's activities, and a widening of tasks that academics are expected to perform: all these are testimony to the changing character of academic life and are among the causes of the unease felt in the system.

In either form – proletarianization or mere change – the unease raises the issue of professionalism in academe. Are academics professionals and, if so, what is the source of this status? One response is to deny that 'professional' is an appropriate description of the academic. Professionals are academically qualified people who secure remuneration for services rendered to clients. But the academic, until fairly recently, could count on *his* living being provided for by an external agency (whether the crown, the church or more recently the state). As such, considerations about the character and quality of the service on offer did not arise. The living was secure in any case. That such a situation is no longer available, that salaries have to be worried over and the claims of students in the mass higher education system have to be recognized, seems to be behind A.H. Halsey's recent lament about the *Decline of Donnish Dominion* (1992).

On the other hand, there are those who consider that the protected position of a monk-like group of scholars is not only past, but rightly so. That was an age of *absence* of professionalism; and that can constitute amateurism. An amateur may be someone who loves his work, but it can also connote a neglect of standards. Indeed, prior to the development of rival universities in nineteenth-century England, Oxbridge witnessed a remarkable decline in standards by any reckoning (Godley, 1908). On this view, it is only fitting that academics should be required to demonstrate their professionalism, to be explicit about the nature of their calling, and to be willing to be judged by others.

The problem is that no coherent idea of professionalism has been worked out to account for the academic life; and certainly not one that would command universal support (cf. Perkin, 1969). Professionals are supposed to have something to profess, to be in command of a body of knowledge denied to their clients. The professional–client relationship is essentially one of trust (cf. Giddens, 1991), in which the client expects the professional to exploit his or her knowledge in fulfilment of the client's best interests. But what knowledge is the academic, as a professional, supposed to be in command of in his or her interactions with the students? Is it a corpus of propositional knowledge? Is it higher order ways of going on, internal to a discipline? Is it an understanding of student learning? Is it an appreciation of theories of teaching? Is it an understanding of the principles of curriculum design? Or is it distinctive knowledge derived first hand from the academic's own researches?

In a paper sketching out the ideal components of professional life, R.S. Downie (1990) points to the right, indeed the responsibility, of professionals to speak out on matters in which they have a legitimate voice. Typically, for the law or medicine, this would justify professionals speaking out as appropriate about government policy on the legal, the penal or the judicial systems or, alternatively, on the health services available across society. By 'speaking out' we must mean here not necessarily taking up a particular position for or against government policy but, as professionals, informing the civil society so that it is better placed to make its judgements about government policy.

What would be the corresponding duty for academics? The academic's calling turns on knowledge as such (Squires, 1990). For individual academics, the knowledge in question is contained within definite fields within the total territory of legitimate knowlege. In this respect, there seems to be a similarity with other professional fields since they all have their own area of cognitive interest. But other professions are concerned with the pragmatic usefulness of their knowledge. The academic, in contrast, has to take an interest in the veracity, soundness and creativity invested *in* truth claims, whatever interest in their applications academics may also have as part of their calling.

This observation may seem to be a plea for the separation of the academics' knowledge interests from the wider society. The argument does not need to go like that but can turn, instead, towards a new kind of society–academe relationship.

One feature of the learning society is an interest in knowledge. The learning society wants to keep its cognitive options open and has an in-built need to access untainted knowledge, relatively free from ideological distortion. Academics, both having a professional interest in knowledge and being required to be relatively immune to cognitive corruption, have a professional duty to place their knowledge at the disposal of the wider society (which, after all, is now responsible for securing their livings). This argument is not to be dismissed but it relies on the contingent character of the wider society – as it happens to be at present. Fortunately, a stronger argument is available.

Nicholas Maxwell touches on it in arguing that the academic enterprise has lost its way, being dominated by a knowledge-for-its-own-sake epistemology, and should be orientated to maximize what is of value in the world. There are problems with this line of argument, namely that it is normative in character and leaves open the question: who is to determine what is of value in the world? But it reminds us that the wider world has interests that academic knowledge might be able to meet.

Jurgen Habermas has argued that the human use of language posits an interest in reason as such. He has also argued that reason takes different forms, each form having a different deep-seated human interest, and that different knowledge forms reflect and address those interests. The Habermassian analysis, therefore, is doubly powerful. Firstly, the academic exploration of knowledge and its transmission can be seen as an institutionalized embodiment of a general human interest in seeking what is true. Secondly, we can say that the different forms of knowledge to be found in the academy *between them* address different kinds of human interest. Science has a legitimate interest in controlling the general environment; hermeneutic fields have an interest in human communication; aesthetic fields have an interest in human expression; and critical fields have an interest in human emancipation.

There are a number of charges that can – and have been – levelled at this transcendental argument. Nevertheless, we have here a suggestive and a powerful argument. The academic interest in knowledge is particularly legitimate because it expresses a *general* human interest in knowledge. That being so, academics as professionals have a professional obligation to put their knowledge at the disposal of society.

This obligation could have the narrow interpretation of developing knowledge and understanding, and abilities to exploit that knowledge and understanding, in one's students. Or it could point to the possible sharing of one's knowledge with the wider society in a more generous way. In the nineteenth century, Faraday and others in academe took it as part of their calling that they had a responsibility to inform the citizens of society of their research findings (Heyck, 1982). In this way, the civil society was better informed and was able to understand itself in new ways.

We have lost that civil role which academics naturally assumed at one time. Consequently, it has become easier for certain forms of reason to become dominant in modern society. This, too, has been part of the analytical insights of Critical Theory: the neglect of the ethical sphere, of communication in general, and the rise of instrumental reason and the impoverishment of civil society (Test, 1992). Society is more rational; but it is a rationality of a limited kind.

Conclusion

This chapter has explored aspects of the society–higher education relationship and has distinguished three strands.

Firstly, there are the *actual* empirical relationships. These set limits to what can be done. In the modern world, higher education has become more closely incorporated into the state's operations, because higher education is strategically implicated in the state's projects and motivations. Traditional autonomies and freedoms enjoyed by higher education have been diminished. Some of these changes have come about deliberately; some have happened as an unintended outcome of the emergence of a mass higher education system. Possibilities for response have to be worked out against this societal background.

Secondly, there are the *perceived* relationships. Irrespective of the actual empirical relationships, the key actors in the system, the academics, entertain views of the changing relationship with the wider society. These views vary across the system relative to discipline and institutional location. Some observe their new relationship with society with anxiety; some see in it new opportunities for curriculum design and professional operations. The moonlight academic economy has never been stronger. For our story, both optimists and pessimists have much in common. The attitudes of both groups centre around their own perceived interests and limit their capacity to respond rationally to the circumstances of our age.

Thirdly, there are the *possible* relationships. The modern state will exert its claims on higher education, both operationally and – even more significantly – in its inner form of life. What counts as knowledge and education *will* be changed, if the state has an unchallenged time of it. In some ways, those changes will be beneficial: internal definitions of knowledge and education may be widened. But in other ways, those changes may lead to a narrowing of human consciousness. Understanding is replaced by competence; insight is replaced by effectiveness; and rigour of interactive argument is replaced by communication skills.

In these circumstances, two questions arise. Firstly, is the academic class going to be able to form a *disinterested* appraisal of the situation facing it? 'Disinterestedness' points to putting aside interests that are protective of self-serving interests. It does not mean acting without interests. There may be necessary interests, which are constitutive of the academic life, contained within the demands of rational discourse. The life of reason contains an emancipatory prospect, of making connections between an open discourse sustained by academic life and the distorted character of the communicative structure of modern society. A radical reappraisal of the potential connections between higher education and society opens the possibility not just of responding to society's definitions of reason, knowledge and skill but also of offering alternative forms of worthwhile understanding.

The second question is this: is the academic class going to be able to realize the potential of its intellectual space to develop an idea of academic professionalism, which includes a responsibility to form bridges with and to open the discourse and self-understanding of society? Exploring the potential for a renewed academic ethic (Shils, 1984) of this kind will occupy much of our attention in the chapters that follow.

3

We *are* all Clerks now

The knowledge game

The third side of the higher education, knowledge and society triangle, the higher education–knowledge axis, has now to be addressed. As a way into tackling that relationship, I shall examine a claim repeated over the past thirty years by Ernest Gellner and recently reiterated in polemical fashion by Douglas Hague. Gellner's point of interest here is that we are all clerks now. In the literate society, there is nothing particular about having a command of texts. It follows that institutions of learning have lost their association with a particular clerkly stratum of society. In this situation, simply being educated is no longer a mark of achievement. Everyone is educated. In itself, having attended a university cannot confer any distinction. Specific capabilities have to be acquired for any worth to be attributed to the educative process.

An associated point is that, in the modern society, the systematization of knowledge is not confined to educational institutions. The clerks do not possess a monopoly of knowledge. This point has been seized upon, somewhat mischievously, by Douglas Hague (1991). If educational institutions do not possess a monopoly of knowledge functions, do we need them at all? Perhaps we should have a market situation in which all traders in knowledge offer their wares competitively and openly. Universities are not doing anything special. Their activities are not self-justifying. Very well: do away with their protective position. Let them compete with allcomers in the knowledge industry. Knowledge is simply a commodity to be transferred at a price that the customers are willing to pay.

This, then, is the background to our present discussion. Higher education is in the knowledge game, but the learning society in general is in the knowledge game, too. What, if anything, is or might be distinctive about the knowledge services that higher education offers?

There are clerks and there are clerks

Among his many intellectual fortes, Gellner is an anthropologist. From his anthropological perspective, a key feature of modern society is that it is a supremely literate society. Not only in comparison with primitive society but even with its predecessor societies of comparatively recent vintage, modern society is characteristically literate in the sense that one cannot function without being literate. This is an extremely recent and, even now, far from universal property of societies. On this perspective, the singular and special nature of education vanishes. Everyone is – or is expected to be – a clerk. The former association of education with a small group, stratum or élite disappears, to be replaced by a universalizing function. Once it was the task of education to ensure that a small proportion of society was able to perform sacred, bookish or administrative roles. Now, it is the function of education to ensure that everyone has much if not all of those capacities. Education is literally common: less a right, it is a duty for everyone in society to undergo.

But Gellner overpresses his case; and for two reasons. Firstly, Gellner refutes himself: we are not all Gellners. There are clerks and there are (one or two) Gellners.

Secondly, in the highly modern society, there are different orders of clerks. There are clerks who essentially reproduce and perhaps slightly repackage the information they receive. There are clerks who generate *that* information. There are yet other clerks who originate the ideas which generate the information . . . and it is the task of a layered and stratified education system to produce those separate orders of clerks. By definition, a 'higher education' is in business to produce the higher order of clerks.

Within the higher order, too, there are differences. There are those who have technical functions, those who have administrative functions, those who have aesthetic functions, those who have reproducing functions (they are teachers of computing skills, the modern-style form of literacy), and so on. So clerkly differentiation is part of modern society. All this is reflected in the university. Becher's (1989) account of contemporary *Academic Tribes and Territories* is a story of internal differentiation within the inner sanctum of the fully paid-up clerks. But the disciplinary differentiation of the academic world reflects the differentiation in the wider culture of modern society.

This should not be surprising. Since modern society has spawned knowledge-forming capacities outside the universities and has, in effect, become a university writ large, it is inevitable that the university should take on much of society's own definitions of knowledge and learning. What counts as knowledge is not fixed by the university but consists of social concepts, which undergo continuing reformulation in response to social as much as to technological change. In becoming more integrated with the cognitive orderings of society, the university is bound to reflect society's new definitions of what it is to know and to learn.

Arguably, the definitions of knowledge and learning embodied in the academy *have* been unduly limited, and their scope has been too little open to any widening. The university, left to itself, has been unwilling to engage in fundamental rethinking about its own core concepts. The inertia which many say characterizes the university affects its central assumptions. For example, that real knowledge has been felt to be both propositional in form and communicable in writing has held quite extraordinary power over the organization of the curriculum and its pedagogy. These two beliefs – the legacy of an era when the university was a genuinely clerkly business – have become embedded as ideologies in the inner life of the academy even if (as in medicine and in science) they have long been abandoned in practice.

Changes are now afoot and, to repeat, are not to be caught by any one-dimensional description. The inertia and resistance in the academy to adopting new ideas of knowing are testimony to its continuing autonomy. In turn, it has used that autonomy on occasion to respond to the situation confronting it with educational interpretations. Notions of personal meaning, active appropriation by the student and deep understanding: these notions are embedded in emerging practices even if not articulated and do justice to important strains in liberal education.

Knowledge as information

And yet . . . The admitted complexities of the interchanges at work should not prevent us from understanding the main currents. Earlier, we noted Douglas Hague's polemical essay. One plank of his argument, that about the loss of academe's monopoly over knowledge functions, rests on the point that modernity is dependent on information and that much of that information is available outside the university. Since information, whether in the minds of consultants or in the electronic workings of computers, is readily available, those seeking knowledge – whether as initial students or for professional development – no longer have to turn to the university. However, there is a slide in his argument in identifying knowledge with information.

This is no accidental slip. Consider this quotation:

> In its main activity – preparing students studying for first degrees – the university provides three things: *information*, integration, and inter-action.
>   The *information* role is obvious. Students obtain information from lectures, articles, books, etc., and . . . *most* students obtain *most* of the information which their university education gives them from lectures.
>   (Hague, 1991: 43, RB's emphases)

The key term here is 'information'. Another related term, which appears throughout the booklet, is a description of one function of the universities as 'knowledge banks' (1991: 59, 64, 69), 'open to all who want to learn'

(p. 9). This is, explicitly, a banker's epistemology (cf. Freire, 1972a and ch. 9 below). Knowledge is 'deposited' (p. 64), held secure, but released for a price. The student as 'customer' (p. 75) would be able to purchase the required slice of knowledge, much as purchasing a slice of ham in the grocery.

Missing from this conception of learning and the acquisition of knowledge is a sense of a genuine transaction, in which not only the student is changed but also the acquired knowledge is transformed in the mind of the student. What we have here is a nice example of the overweening interest in information characteristic of modern society described recently by Mary Midgley (1989) in *Wisdom, Information and Wonder*. That information cannot amount to wisdom is clear enough. But Midgley points out that information cannot amount to knowledge either. For 'information' read sense data: sense data constitute knowledge only with the active intervention of a conceptual schema being brought to bear on them; and such schemas are not found in sense data. Without insight, interpretation and understanding, information is blind.

Here, we have another instance of the ambiguity of 'the learning society'. The modern society has become saturated by information – much of it computer generated – not accidentally, but because certain of its key activities are information dependent. In a fast-changing world, those who have only the world picture of yesterday, or even of the last hour, are left behind; or think they will be. At the same time, many operations simply call for extraordinary amounts of information and of different forms. A project like the building of the channel tunnel demands vast collections of data, compiled by different groups and teams working in a range of specialties. Much of that information does not simply lie around waiting to be swept up or even to be discovered. With, for example, computer modelling and computer-aided design, information can now be generated *ab initio*; and in literally infinite quantities.

In this situation, it is easy for learning to be construed simply as the addition of data to the already accumulated stock. The learning society is a society that generates more and more information. Consequently, we hear phrases like 'the information society' and 'the knowledge society'. We do not hear of 'the understanding society' or 'the wise society'. Nor is this a matter of awkward terminology. It is of the essence of modern society with its interest in data and information. Data and information, too, we may note, can be stored, sold and bought in the market economy. They become commodities. Understanding and wisdom cannot so easily be traded. In a higher education system driven towards the market, universities come readily, if unwittingly, to adopt such an emasculated epistemology. Hague's universities as 'knowledge banks' and information providers are concomitant with this mode of thinking. 'The learning university' (Duke, 1992) is not an idea to be embraced uncritically, after all. Its definitions of knowledge reflect a new sense of what counts as learning but it is, at the same time, a narrow conception.

Students as products

Despite some reluctance, universities are becoming more responsive to, and becoming part of, the learning society in the narrow sense just noted. The new vocabulary of 'competence', 'learning outcomes', 'credit accumulation', 'learning profiles' and references to students as 'products': all these are not just symptomatic of internal changes to the higher education curriculum but also indicative of a reshaping of knowing in response to the contemporary demands. In a society where immediate mastery, action to effect, and information count, what is regarded as knowing undergoes change within the academy. We lose the idea of 'engagement' with a tradition, insisted on by Oakeshott, and substitute for it a given corpus of information to be divided into modules and assimilated by the student. The only question to be asked is how the student performs in relation to the given corpus.

It is worth dwelling briefly on the idea of students as products, a notion to be found widely in government statements, the pronouncements of captains of industry and even the occasional vice-chancellor.

The idea of student as product implies some kind of transformation from the moment of entry, as does 'education'. But the idea of product also carries with it connotations of meeting some pre-specified end, of uniformity of outcome, and of a process in which things are done to students. In this conception, students are literally the product of happenings they encounter. But this cannot be a genuine higher education. That implies some active response on the part of the student, to include both an indwelling (Polanyi, 1962) and a dynamic interchange so that the student's thoughts and actions are his or her own. To allow this, however, is to assert that the educator's aims can only be a general indication of intentions; they cannot be construed as a set of techniques that will act on the student to produce guaranteed outcomes. Nor will the outcomes be uniform, for each student's response will be different. And nor are things simply done to students since their active involvement is inescapable: their propositions and actions have to be theirs.

What, therefore, is happening behind talk of students as products? It is precisely that uniformity and predictability are *required*. Employers wish to be able to specify in advance the nature of the resources they will work with, including their graduate labour force. Indeed, more so, since graduates once employed are an expensive component of the resources at their command. Mistakes are costly. The employers want to be sure that those acquisitions are going to turn out to be non-injurious to their sense of the organization's well-being. Consequently, it is the capacities pre-identified by the labour market that are governing the reshaping of a curriculum for a mass higher education system.

One implication of this way of thinking for higher education is that the process is immaterial provided that the necessary competences – knowledges and skills – are acquired. But in a genuine higher education, the process is not an add-on but is integral to the development being sought. We cannot promote first-hand thinking, deep understanding, independence of thought, collaboration of intellectual effort and responsibility for one's words and expressed thinking unless all that is built into the curriculum. Again, a curriculum construed in this way is less a pre-packaged assembly of information and methodology to which the student is subject than a relatively loose framework in which students can develop and ultimately take off on their own. A higher education is an open-ended process, not a delivery of pre-specified products.

A new liberalism?

Just as there might be elements of closure in those societal ideologies that find their expression in higher education, so there might be elements of openness.

We see signs, albeit fragmentary, that the forms of production being called forth in the modern society are offering new elements of openness. Two obvious signs are firstly, the sense in some major companies (even if confined to high tech and service industries) that a relatively flat organizational hierarchy is required, with the working units having considerable autonomy (Handy, 1985; Drucker, 1992); although not the degree of autonomy that the vocabulary of employee empowerment might imply. Secondly, the labour market is loudly voicing a claim that higher education should produce graduates who are 'flexible', able to cope with and respond to change and the complexities of commercial life.

Demands of this kind are having their impact on the curriculum in two ways. Firstly, the process of learning is placing more responsibility on the student. 'Open learning' is an ambiguous term but, in whatever variant, the student is offered choices, whether over content, method, pacing, location, or even aims and assessment methods. There is a correspondence here with the extramural demand for flexibility since the open curriculum (as we should rather term it) can open a range of possibilities of thought and action on the part of the student. The repertoire of the student's responses will often be wider than in the conventional curriculum. A genuinely problem-focused curriculum (Margetson, 1991, 1994), for example, can pose the student with problems that call for the student to exploit imaginatively all the institutional resources available.

Secondly, efforts to produce graduate 'flexibility' can be detected in the content of the curriculum in the move to develop in students 'personal transferable skills' (Bradshaw, 1985). Every term in this phrase warrants critical scrutiny but that would divert us. The key notion is that of transferability; and three issues are worth noting. Firstly, there are questions to be raised about the reality of 'transferability'. While research and development work has been conducted (Sheffield, Wolverhampton), the introduction of initiatives carrying this label is being effected on the basis of assumption and hope. Secondly, its adherents betray an easy readiness to accept on trust the appropriateness of such an initiative for higher education. Hardly at all, if ever, is the case for personal transferable skills – even if they could be shown to exist – argued through as a curriculum strategy for higher education. Thirdly, those human capacities that are picked out are intended to improve economic competitiveness; other possible general human capabilities and virtues which might promote different kinds of human society – friendship, altruism, ethical concern, carefulness, generosity and a myriad others – are entirely neglected.

These two strands of 'flexibility' come together in such portmanteau terms as 'metacompetence' and 'metacognition' (Fleming, 1992; Baird, 1988). These terms, often coined by educational researchers, act as a bridge between process and content, between open learning and non-specific skills. The hope and the claim is that the student can transcend the here and now, and develop a repertoire of higher order capacities which enables her to interrogate and marshal her particular knowledges and skills. For this, there has to be an open textured curriculum, which will enable the student to feel her way into such autonomous states of mind, reflection and action.

'Flexibility', then, turns out to be a code underlying much of contemporary thinking about the curriculum. It points to new definitions of right knowing, which appear to echo traditional ideas of autonomy and breadth; indeed, of liberal education itself. But it also, as with other notions already encountered in this chapter, imports interests into the curriculum from the wider society. The relationship between higher education and knowledge is dynamic, constantly shifting; but the modern movements have to be primarily understood as a response to the claims on higher education from the host society. Higher education accepts fairly readily that extramural agenda, especially if it can convince itself that the new agenda is only a recasting of its traditional agenda.

The curriculum: an epistemological project

The central point just made is that the higher education and knowledge relationship is changing in ways not so much of *its* making, but more of the state's making. Some will urge caution against such a claim, suggesting that the examples identified are testimony less to changing ideas of knowledge in higher education than of the form in which it is made available in the student experience. Credit transfer, open learning, transferable skills and the like are matters of packaging, not of substance. This is a story about medium, not about message.

This objection has already been countered implicitly but it is worth doing so explicitly. The framing of the curriculum necessarily contains an epistemology. A curriculum is more than its knowledge components; much more. Interpreted broadly and correctly, 'curriculum' embraces the students' engagement with the offerings put before them. But a curriculum is, in any case, a statement of what counts as knowledge in several senses. It represents a prior identification of worthwhile knowledge, albeit in particular epistemic fields. The ordering and presentation of those knowledge elements in a curriculum reflect a sense on the part of the educator as to what counts as a genuine act of knowing. Further, the pedagogical relationship that the educator determines for his or her curriculum itself acts as an epistemic framework. The medium *is* the message.

It may be said that these points hold for the whole of education; so they do. But higher education is distinctive across most of the western world because individual lecturers have continually to make these decisions for themselves. Academic freedom retains much of its de facto reality. Academics are literally knowledge-mongers: they decide which knowledge components to put before their students and in what kind of display, the method by which those students can reach out and acquire those components and, thereby, the knowing experience that accompanies that acquisition. Lecturers are epistemologists, whether they realize it or not.

That decisions have to be made by the educator about the order, conceptual density and conceptual level of the curriculum components is obvious enough. And decisions about these elements reflect views as to what counts as the form of knowing in a particular field. But questions have also to be answered about more experiential elements of the curriculum. To what extent is the knowledge field offered as given, and how far is the student encouraged to develop his or her own position? To what degree is the student encouraged to view the field as a dynamic process of human negotiation, story-telling, power struggle and fierce dispute? Are students enabled to see and feel the field as a way of going on, as a continuing process, with existential commitment and momentum, or is it paraded as a relatively static corpus? Is knowing – of any kind, even philosophy – understood as a form of knowing how, of knowing how to engage in and to conduct meaningful, albeit limited, transactions with others, or is it presented simply as a series of propositions and theoretical entities? And is knowing realized – both intellectually and in the curriculum – as a collaborative endeavour, or is it felt to be an individualistic enterprise?

All these questions amount to decision points which educators in higher education have continually to confront. A curriculum, accordingly, has to be a classification of knowledge. A curriculum is an epistemological project.

Changing frames of knowledge

Our epistemologies do not just lie about. They inform society but they reflect the society of which they are a part. The higher education curriculum is a witness to just this interchange. Especially so at present: we are in the midst, I have been contending, of a paradigm shift. The term 'paradigm shift' is often overplayed, so it is employed with some caution here. But we are entering a climacteric in which the long-held sense (since

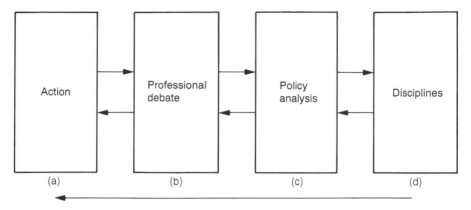

Figure 3.1   The shifting curriculum

the late nineteenth century, at least) of propositional discipline-based knowledge can no longer capture the high ground of the curriculum.

Terms such as 'experiential learning', 'transferable skills', 'problem-solving', 'group work' and 'work-based learning': these do not just point to new teaching methods but are illustrative of the changing definitions of knowledge that are taking place. Put very crudely, we see legitimate knowledge at least being broadened to embrace 'knowing-how' as well as 'knowing-that'. The story being mapped out here is more assertive, however. My claim is that, left to themselves, the dominant social forces at work are such that the curriculum would in time become saturated with forms of knowing-how. To return to Chapter 1, the curriculum could end up as a major site of *operationalism*.

Knowing how to do things as well as knowing that such is such is the core of this epistemic change; and this change is affecting our sense of what the academy is for. Enabling students not just to know things but also to do things: this is the new order. The key question to pose of the graduate about to enter the labour market is not so much: what does he or she know? Still less: what does he or she understand? But rather: what can he or she do?

The framework illustrated in Figure 3.1 indicates something of the shifting pattern of the curriculum. Box (a) is that of professional action, including both unreflective and immediately reflective action.

Box (b) is that of public commentary on action, both of professional groupings and the more public debate, in which action is situated in the context of contemporary 'issues'.

Box (c) is that of analyses of action, whether as modern texts or conferences (whether of an 'academic' character or, increasingly, a mix of academics and others, including independent analysts, research institutes and civil service officials). These analyses are prescriptive in tone, if not in fact.

Box (d) is that of academic disciplines, which may be drawn on in order to give shape, substance and depth to the analyses of box (c).

Both boxes (c) and (d) offer a form of evaluation of action, but it is through recourse to the perspectives and analytical frameworks of box (d) that fundamental critique becomes possible. Box (c) is closer to the action and its propositions tend to be coalescences of ideas and themes. Box (d) especially strikes against a sense of 'givenness' and, instead, sponsors a sense of 'things could be otherwise' and a more disinterested appreciation of the object of an inquiry. Precisely because the cognitive insights of box (d) are most distant from the action, and because box (d) furnishes the conceptual apparatus for the task, it is there that the most searching critical illumination of those objects becomes possible.

The contemporary curriculum, we might hypothesize, is seeing pressures to shift its weight to the left of the diagram, that is from (d) to (c) to (b) to (a). All elements, of course, can be found together in a typical curriculum; although to make even that apparently innocuous assertion is to claim more than would have had made sense just a few years ago. However, the stronger claim presses upon us: the balance between the four elements is progressively moving from right to left.

Two qualifications: firstly, the extent to which such a framework has application will vary across subjects, courses, levels of study and institutions. The UK binary system was always an over-simple classification of curriculum possibilities. The reality was, and is even more, a many-textured criss-crossing of patterns in contrasting modalities: the ubiquitous computer *in* the curriculum could also be put to good use in attempting to produce multi-dimensional models *of* the curriculum.

Secondly, I am not positing a simple shift from thought to action. What I am suggesting is that the relationship between thought and action is changing, with action elements becoming more explicit and more significant parts of the curriculum, even if only in the form of hypothetical case studies of simulations. Also, and just as significant, insofar as knowledge and thought are valued, it is in the formulation of 'solutions' to pre-identified 'problems'. So the epistemology of the curriculum is undergoing a double change. Our conception of what counts as knowing widens to embrace action, whether of a first person or of a third person variety.

In both senses, knowing acquires an operational character, in which the historical mission of the university to sustain and pass on the virtues of universal knowledge is surrendered. Knowledge to tackle the here-and-now problems, as identified by the wider society, becomes the knowledge function of the modern university. The university, and the programmes of study it offers, takes on the role of handmaiden to the modern society.

We can summarize the argument so far with the aid of the following table:

knowing-that	knowing-how
written communication	oral communication
personal	interpersonal
internal	external

localized capacities	transferability
intellectual	physical
thought	action
problem-making	problem-solving
knowledge as process	knowledge as product
understanding	information
value-laden	'value-free'
discipline-based	issue-based
concept-based	task-based
pure	applied
proposition-based learning	experiential learning
individualized learning	group-based learning
holistic	unitized
disinterested	pragmatic
intrinsic orientation	instrumental orientation

In effect, our argument has been that higher education can be construed as moving from the left-hand column to the right-hand column.

In offering this list of distinctions, the earlier qualifications are worth repeating. I am not arguing that there are wholesale tendencies of those kinds taking place. In any empirical investigation of these currents, we would inevitably find differences across dimensions, subjects, institutions, sectors and countries. Nor am I taking up a clear value position to the effect that the concepts and epistemologies of the left-hand column should be retained at all costs. Indeed, I have suggested that the academic world, left largely to its own devices, has for too long operated with a narrow and usually unreflected set of knowledge policies. The question is, when taken collectively, whether these possible tendencies point to a major realignment of the knowledge functions of higher education in contemporary society. The response has to be 'yes'. If much of the story implied by the above table has even face validity, then we are at a turning point in the long history of the western university.

The closing of the western mind

Allan Bloom's magnum opus *The Closing of the American Mind* (1987) recently enjoyed a *scandale du succès* on both sides of the Atlantic. Inveighing against all things *moderne* – relativism, student culture, multiculturalism, political correctness and a general anti-intellectualism – Bloom sought stable ground in the Great Books approach to curriculum design. The book's title indicates the closure Bloom saw in the intellectual culture of modernity. The universities were pilloried for their connivance in the shallowness that passed for genuine first-hand thought.

At best, Bloom was one-third correct. The universities *are* in danger of contributing to an intellectual malaise, and are culpable. That bit Bloom got right. But the primary cause lies not within the university, as it loses its way over its own redefinitions of its intellectual mission. The primary cause lies outside, as the wider society seeks to impose its claims on the university, now seen as offering the economic salvation of the western economy; and only then, as a secondary cause, within the university through the university's acquiescence in the role being cast for it.

Nor is the solution to this problem to be found in the reassertion of a former canon of absolute epistemic value. If relativism is to be combated, it will not be through a redefinition of objective knowledge. After all, we are faced with a more strident form of relativism in the shape of postmodernism. If relativism was the philosopher's debunking of objectivity, postmodernism is the debunking of objectivity by intellectual culture in general. The new debunking is no neutral and cold appraisal; no mere intellectualism. Postmodernism revels in the debunking; the ensuing fragmentation of intellectual life is positively proclaimed. The Great Books approach is repudiated and is now off limits.

For one thousand years, the university of the west has served the particular function of widening the concepts by which the wider society understood itself. Certainly, breakthroughs occurred outside the university; and (for example, in eighteenth-century Oxbridge) the university fell at time almost into desuetude. No matter: the university was the one social institution that had a particular knowledge function of examining critically contemporary concepts in scholarship and teaching. In that examination, as stated, the range of available concepts widened. Nicer discriminations led to the formation of new concepts. But something else was happening too. That something else is connected with the university's critical function. The notion of the university as a critical institution contains an equivocation which turns on the ambiguity of what it is to be critical (Minogue, 1973). Polemical tracts, intellectual culture and newspapers can, at times, be said to exert a critical function. The existence of such institutions constitutes a civil society, a realm of social interchange independent of the state (cf. Test, 1992). The critical function of the university, however, is fundamentally different; and potentially even more radical.

By examining seriously and disinterestedly the concepts available to society, the university opens and sustains a gap between the civil society and those concepts being examined. The searching examination of beliefs and ideas (whether of the natural world, the social world or the world of values and experiences) produces a conceptual space between those ideas as ordinarily grasped and understood in that inquiry. This inquisitorial activity is essentially a critical inquiry. The university shows the wider society that its understandings are limited and could be other than they are.

Conclusion

We should now return to Gellner and Hague. Gellner's point, it will be recalled, is that we are all clerks now. In contemporary society, there is no fundamental difference between the cognitive powers of those within and those outside the university. This point Hague seized on: for him, knowledge is produced equally well outside the university and perhaps even better than inside it.

The really unsettling thing is that they may both be right. The modern university is so in danger of reflecting society's own understandings and actions back to itself, of falling in with society's agenda, that the former critical space between the university's readings of concepts and society's readings is on the point of disappearing. We may be in danger of all becoming clerks in the sense of all of us – in the university and outside – working within contemporary cognitive frameworks. We are all clerks in the Victorian sense rather than the mediaeval sense. No longer does the university do anything special, cognitively speaking. Instead, it assists society in addressing society's problems in society's own terms, providing the understandings and skills which society defines in advance. Pedestrian, routine, non-challenging, supportive, predictable, orderly, disciplined: it is precisely these attributes that society thinks it needs and now demands of the university.

Gellner was commenting anthropologically. His point has that kind of force: a reminder of the general character of cognition in modern society. It can be read as a commentary on the ubiquity of formalized reason in modernity. But that reading opens up the way for the university to capitalize on its new importance and, indeed, on its centrality as a key site of reason, reason now being required across society rather than being confined to specific realms. Reason contains within it a critical potential and, therefore, can be deployed by the university legitimately to widen the form of reasoning in society. Hague's application of Gellner's thesis, on the other hand, would deprive the university of any critical knowledge functions. All the university could aspire to is a matching of extramural epistemic productions.

This, then, is the issue in front of the western university: does it simply fall in with society's definitions of knowledge, problems and skill (even if, as we have seen, some of those definitions represent valid challenges to the epistemic understandings of the university) or does the university seek to maintain the intellectual space to develop its *own* advances in understanding, conceptual grasp and reflection? Given its location in the social structure of modern society, the university has to be a responsive institution; but can it also retain its role as a critical institution?

Part 2

The New Vocabulary

4

'Skills' and 'Vocationalism'

Continuity and discontinuity

It is now obligatory for any government report on higher education to use the term 'skills': the economy needs skills and it is the function of higher education to supply them. Some will say that there is nothing new in this. It was part of the function of the mediaeval university to provide the callings of church, bureaucracy and medicine with the skills they required. On this view, the current demand for transferable skills is a reminder to higher education of its wider societal mission, a mission that it lost as the knowledge functions of the university were hijacked internally by the academic class of the late nineteenth and first half of the twentieth century. Although a modern term, 'vocationalism' resonates with the long-established and evocative idea of 'vocation'. Skills and vocationalism, far from being imposters from a new and external agenda, speak directly to the traditional idea of a university. They remind it of its origins and so rescue it from an unfortunate amnesia.

This, then, is the claim to be examined in this chapter: the ideas of skills and vocationalism are not new and represent no fundamental challenge to the historic conception of the university; rather, they are entirely in keeping with its traditional mission. We can term this the argument for continuity. Instead, I shall argue for discontinuity, namely that the contemporary demand for universities to concern themselves with the production of skills among their students is a form of radical discontinuity with the past.

Further, the clamour for a skills-focused curriculum is representative of a power-laden discourse. It is ideological and contains a thinly veiled threat. It is ideological in attempting to shift the university in a direction that reflects particular societal interests and it is threatening in that its assimilation into higher education will reduce the scope available to the university to fulfil the emancipatory potential in the idea of higher education. The *contemporary* language of skills has to be recognized for what it masks. There is a conceptual and societal archaeology at work in which the embedded interests have to be dug out and exposed; otherwise, they will continue to influence and diminish our practices in the university in ways that we can hardly comprehend.

On being skilful

Skills are not to be downvalued. To perform something, to write something, to say something, to argue something, to carry out an experiment and to cause something to happen *with skill* is normally to achieve something worthwhile. The idea of skill, therefore, is both descriptive and evaluative. The descriptive element itself contains evaluations. It indicates that the activity in question has come up to the standard appropriate to that activity. To describe an activity as having been performed with skill is both to categorize the activity and to place a high mark on it.

There are four criteria for the application of the term 'skill':

1. A situation of some complexity.
2. A performance that addresses the situation, is deliberate and is not just a matter of chance.
3. An assessment that the performance has met the demands of the situation.
4. A sense that the performance was commendable.

This analysis indicates two areas of openness in the term 'skill'. The first criterion, 'a situation of some complexity', leaves open the form of complexity. Complexity in human action can be present in many forms. Aesthetic performance, musical performance, spoken communication, interpersonal action, writing and physical actions: all these and literally an infinite range of other possibilities are domains of human action where skill is to be found. Precisely because the term 'skill' is nonspecific about its substantive content and the situations for its applicability, the term can be used in a wide variety of circumstances. This simple point is crucial for the argument that follows.

We can make two sets of discriminations. Firstly, actions can be distinguished in terms of the balance between formal knowledge and physical activity. At the polar ends of this axis we have, for instance, the pure mathematician and the grand prix racing motorist. In between, but towards the respective ends just indicated, would lie the medical surgeon and the opera singer.

Secondly, actions can be classified according to the extent that two-way communication is essential in the performance. At the polar ends of this axis would lie the psychoanalyst and the clay-pigeon shooter. In between, and towards those respective ends, would lie the physiotherapist and the currency dealer in the dealing room. However, a further distinction has to be made in the form of the communication. The central question is: Is the communication one of interaction in the cause of an end that stands outside the participants (as with the currency dealer) or is the communication integral to the development of at least one of the participants (as with the physiotherapist, whose conversation with the patient is aimed in part at assisting the healing process)?

The term 'skill' has *no* substantive content: it acquires substance in definite circumstances. We cannot teach 'skills' as such: we *have* to specify the skills we have in mind (What skill is 'required'? What skill do we have in mind?). Further, the form of acquisition of the skill will affect the character of the skill being developed. Also, while used as a noun, 'skill' is always quasi-adjectival. The term is a commentary on the attributes of a performance in a particular situation. Each of these aspects – the identification, the form of acquisition and the judgement – are inherently controversial. A higher education cannot pretend that they are given.

Turning to our second criterion of a skill, 'a performance that addresses the situation', this leaves open what might count as 'addressing the situation'. Situations do not present themselves in any absolute way. They have to be interpreted as such-and-such a situation. The situation has to be defined; indeed, it has to be constructed.

This is a matter of import for situations in both the natural world and in the human world. Do we understand our technologies purely in terms of their operating efficiency and productivity, or do we take their situation to include the wider natural, societal and human environment? Does the development, in higher education, of the skills associated with operating those technologies incorporate a sensitivity to such wider dimensions?

Where human being is involved, which means all educational situations, how are individuals perceived? Are they perceived as objects, obstacles or additional factors in the pursuit of efficiency or economy, or are they perceived as subjects with an intrinsic otherness of their own to be understood in its own terms? To pick up a Habermassian distinction, is the form of reasoning being deployed essentially strategic or communicative? Does it take persons into account only strategically in achieving some external end or does it begin sensitively from their own centres of consciousness? In higher education, in developing teaching skills, are we attempting to do so in order to maintain our institutional throughput in a 'situation' of worsening unit costs, or are we prepared to try to understand the hopes, anxieties and learning problems of our students as individuals? Adopting the latter definition of the situation and attempting to address *that* situation may, of course, produce actions and educational processes which run counter to those that flow from a more strategic definition of the situation.

The points just made can be summarized in this way. Skills are infinite in variety with some, for example, calling for a high degree of cognitive insight while others do not. However, 'the situation' in which skills are determined is open to interpretation so the range of skills that can be brought to bear in 'a situation' is itself open.

So much for the first two of the four criteria of skill identified. Two other criteria were offered: there has to be an assessment that the performance has met the demands of the situation; and there has to be a consensus that the performance was commendable in some way. A point made in relation to the first two criteria also applies here. Both the latter criteria call for judgements *outside* the exercise of the skill (that the performance has been adequate to the situation and that the performance was commendable).

An important preliminary conclusion can, therefore, be drawn. The very application of skills calls for *prior* judgements both as to the boundaries and nature of the situation and over the range and character of the skills appropriate to the situation, however defined.

If higher education is in part the acquisition of skills, we must conclude that a *higher* education must develop that double capacity: the ability to frame a situation in a range of possible ways and the capacity to identify the appropriate skills to bring to bear on the situation as defined. This interim point is significant. Alone, it indicates that *a higher education cannot be skills based*. In a genuinely higher education, skills will, at most, form part of the repertoire of capacities to be developed and which graduates will, with discrimination and care, deploy or not according to their reading of a situation.

Higher education, accordingly, is a meta-education, in which students develop the emancipatory capacities to call upon a range of skills in the context of *their* reading of a situation.

Ten theses

Skills, then, are complex, more so than is normally allowed for in talk about skills in higher education. We need, however, to muddy the waters still further. I offer the following ten theses, some of which are implied in our discussion so far and others not.

Thesis one

All skills contain some blend of action and reflection. However, for a skill to be legitimately developed in higher education, it should be associated with a high degree of cognitive content. (This could include performing arts, for example, where the claim would be that the cognitive content is part of the performance. But the claim would have to be substantiated.)

Thesis two

Too easily, we slip into linguistic formulations such as: 'the application of skills (to situations)' or 'the need for skills (in the economy)'. In formulations such as these, one has skills which are brought to bear on given situations. There is a situation and there are skills. This is a form of technicist thinking: it overlooks the fact that the skills in use define and change the situation; they are not independent of it (Schon, 1987).

Thesis three

Talk of skills often takes the form that 'we can use our judgement in apply-ing our skills'. Indeed, it might be thought that this is a defining character-istic of professional life, that the professional has a responsibility for judging how his or her skills are to be used, assessing their possible effects, and choosing between the wide repertoire of skills at his or her disposal. The demands of professional life lie very much, it may seem, in determining how to bring one's skills to bear on an unpredictable situation.

The problem with this way of looking at things is that it separates the skill from the judgement; the action from the reflection. This is another mistake underlying much of contemporary thinking in social policy, including higher education. It is misleading to think of the surgeon in the operating theatre as being engaged in two sets of activities: the use of advanced complex pro-fessional skills and the application of cognitions, insights and judgements. The judgement of the surgeon in the operating theatre is significantly embedded in his or her skill. There are not two sets of activities, but one. Enlightened action is an intricate complex of skill and judgement (cf. Schon, 1987; Eraut, 1992).

This was Gilbert Ryle's argument in *The Concept of Mind* (1949). Ryle's thesis, however, was too bold. Collapsing body and mind together left him devoid of any account of reflection and consciousness as such. This con-ceptual move, if taken on board by higher education, would reduce it to a form of training, albeit a sophisticated training of reflection-in-action; and that is Donald Schon's position.

Alongside a sense that action contains reflection, we need to retain a sense that reflection can be conducted in and by itself. Reflection com-prises a complex of activities, albeit cognitive activities, which respond to the demands imposed by the related form(s) of reason. The surgeon should be able to reflect on the action separately from it, to give an account of the problems encountered and the reasons behind the strategies adopted, and – even more challenging and counterfactual – to develop new strategies that frame and make possible new situations. In other words, to Schon's idea of reflection-in-action, we need to add the idea of action-in-reflection.

Thesis four

Judgement is integral to the performance but it is also *prior* to the demon-stration of skills.

Thesis five

Judgement is also consequent upon action, attesting that the action has been skilful.

Thesis six

Not far from the idea of skill is the idea of reproducibility. Given this situation, x will apply these skills; and, *being skilful*, we can count on x to be able to apply these skills in similar situations in the future. Part of x's skill lies, indeed, in being able to reproduce the skills when called upon to do so; it isn't just accident that she produces these performances. However, the corollary of reproducibility is that skills have to contain elements of routine.

Accordingly, the call for higher education to devote itself more seriously to the production of skills is a demand for predictable behaviours in its graduates. When it is said of graduates that they are skilful or have highly developed skills or have useful skills, we are entitled to ask: 'But are they merely skilful?'

Thesis seven

Picking up a theme from Foucault, we can say that 'skills' is a power-laden term. That is, it reflects certain kinds of dominant interest in modern society. The call for a skills-led curriculum issues from an interest structure which is intent on shifting the definitions of what counts as higher education. This is not a value-judgement but is a matter of fact. A determination to shift the definitions of higher education and to combat an aristocratic-rural ideology still underlying the current idea of the university (Weiner, 1981), overlain by an ideology of the pure intellectual (cf. Becher, 1989), constitutes this power struggle. The term 'skills' becomes a symbol of this site of contestation.

Thesis eight

The application of skills is not value-neutral. On the contrary, it is inherently value-laden. Values are embedded in the choice of the boundaries of the situation in which the skills are deployed and they are contained in the decision to adopt one set of skills rather than another.

Thesis nine

Since skills can range from those that are relatively undemanding to those that are highly demanding, we can take it that a higher education should be characterized by a determination to foster skills that are especially demanding. The logic must be that, even if skills are to be primarily based in the world of work, to justify their presence in higher education they must contain complex cognitive components.

Thesis ten

Since the central business of higher education is to do with knowledge and understanding, there is a particular responsibility on higher education to foster skills that are knowledge-based and promote understanding. This leaves open what is to count as knowledge, a category that is changing rapidly. It also leaves open 'Whose understanding?' Understanding might refer to the student's understanding or to the wider understanding of society, which it is the responsibility of those who receive a higher education to develop.

The collective point made by these ten theses is simple; and it should not be shirked. To say of someone that he or she is skilful is to damn with faint praise. It is to imply that he or she is merely skilful, no matter how complex the skills in question.

A higher education designed around skills is no higher education. It is the substitution of technique for insight; of strategic reason for communicative reason; and of behaviour for wisdom.

Who's on whose side?

The modern university curriculum can be understood in terms of two superimposed axes. One axis is formed by curricula characterized by whether they derive from the internal agendas of the academic community or the external agendas of groupings in the wider society. The other axis is formed at one pole by curricula that are specific to definite epistemic interests (typically, discrete disciplines) and at the other pole by general aims transcending discipline-specific interests. This grid, illustrated in Figure 4.1, can be read as a commentary on skills.

This analysis indicates again that skills are not all of a piece but that they can be understood in terms of the interests from which they derive. Some skills derive from interests internal to the academic world, while others are prompted by interests external to academe. The skills characteristic of the mathematician, the geographer, the historian, the sociologist and the physicist are internal to the practices of those disciplines. The disciplines constitute social practices, with their characteristic methodologies and bases for argument and verification, for conducting their discourse and for assessing their truth claims. The disciplines form (to use Oakeshott's term) conversations with internal norms of what is seen as right behaviour (Fuller, 1989). Where philosophers such as Oakeshott and Peters are mistaken is in underestimating the extent to which those norms are contested, not only across the generations but even at any point in time (cf. Bloor, 1991). Disciplines are not the harmonious enterprises sometimes assumed but are, rather, the territories of warring factions, often leaving a bloody mess in their internecine struggles (cf. Gellner, 1974). Nevertheless, the point remains: these

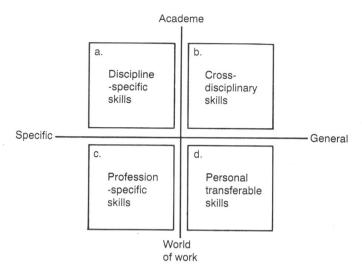

Figure 4.1   Poles apart: skills in higher education

epistemic communities have norms and values internal to their activities which all novitiates from first-year undergraduates onwards are expected to assimilate.

It will be said that the examples cited are selective. What of engineering, medicine, nursing, architecture, librarianship, accountancy and so on? Are the norms of soundness characteristic of disciplines such as these not drawn, in part, from practices conducted outside the university? Indeed, it could be said that epistemic practices of this kind are constituted primarily in the professional practices that bear their name. The presence of these forms of thought in academe is parasitic, it can legitimately be claimed, upon their existence as major social institutions in the wider society. Those institutions exist independently of, and predated, their presence in the university. The internal/external distinction does not stand up to scrutiny (so the argument might run). Many skills fostered by the university have their point in and often derive from their institutionalization in the wider society.

At one level, Figure 4.1 allows for just this spread of influences on the curriculum. The diagram indicates that there are different influences on the curriculum, distinguishing – along one of its axes – between internal and external influences. These latter curricula, accordingly, are located in box (c); the earlier programmes are situated in box (a). That response, however, does not seriously deal with the point just made, that the conversations of some academic groupings stand in the external world at least as much as in the internal world.

There are two moves open. Firstly, the diagram is intended to have analytical or heuristic value. This is a rather weak response. It implicitly accepts that the charge has force, that some academic conversations are situated in the external world. On this view, some skills on offer in the academic world are extramural skills more than they are skills of academe itself. The horizontal boundary is the fundamental break: it reflects the division between a higher education that is in society and a higher education that is of society. Curricula of the second kind – that is, below the line – are creatures of society as much as they are of higher education. This argument says that the internal/external division is real, but that it lies within academe.

The second move also says that the internal/external distinction is real but that the division comes between academe in toto and the wider society. It echoes Minogue's argument (1973) that the discourse of academe and the discourse of the world – even if they appear to be about the 'same' state of affairs – are ultimately different. The practice of medicine and the academic discourse called 'medicine' may be about disease and the treatment of patients, but the two discourses are different. The practical discourse is about wrestling pragmatically with all the medical, interpersonal and ethical issues presented by individual patients to busy practitioners lacking most of the desirable resources; the academic discourse is about forming truth claims, hypotheses and theories, and presenting evidence for critical scrutiny by one's peers. In Minogue's terminology, rather than being in the presence of a 'monistic' world of extramural practices and academic discourses, we are in the presence of a dualism of discourses (cf. Goodlad, 1992; Walsh, 1993). The truth criteria of the one, it is being suggested, are not the truth criteria of the other. The busy practitioner has to make decisions on limited evidence with insufficient resources: she cannot wait for the next research evaluation to report on the new drug she is contemplating prescribing. She just has to make a professional judgement. Accordingly, so it is said, the skills of the practice and of the academic discourse remain fundamentally separate.

There is something in this argument; but not as much as Minogue thinks. One qualification is to remember that the problems of academe are often exacerbated by the practical concerns and interests of the wider society. A second is to observe that the imagery, metaphors and ideas often attracting support in the academic community have been born outside and taken up by academe (Barnes, 1974). A third is to accept the argument that the academic discourse is ideologically saturated across many if not most disciplines, in the sense of fulfilling agendas of the external world. A fourth is to buy the strong programme of the sociology of science, which asserts that the rationality of academic discourse is no different from that of propositions found in the external world (Bloor, 1991).

All these somewhat technical qualifications are worth taking seriously. They are to be found in the literature and should give us pause for thought before arguing for a sharp break between the discourses within and outside academe. But a much more straightforward argument is available to the sceptic of dualism.

The claim that the discourses within and outside the academy are radically distinct implies that the practices associated with those discourses are also distinct. The claim holds onto the hope or pretence that higher education is separate from society. But no such boundary exists in the modern society. Higher education is inexplicable today apart from the interests of society and state in it. Those interests spill over into the operations and values of academe. The boundaries can and have been breached. Indeed, in many places, those within academe have themselves opened the main gates to allow in those external forces; and those forces have become internal ones. The forms of skill, knowledge and capacity required by the external world are willingly supplied by academe.

It appears, then, that there is no marked difference between the discourse of academe and that of the external world. There is continuity both in time and in geography (within and beyond the academy). The university has always been in the business of skills and of supplying the skills required by the host society. The new demands on the university are at most a strengthening of influences long felt. The argument for continuity seems to have it.

However, the argument for discontinuity is not defeated yet.

On transferability and generality

Figure 4.1 distinguishes two forms of generality: forms of general education that spring from the values of the academic community and those that reflect a keenness to impart general capacities which will carry graduates forward as on the labour market. This distinction, between internal and external forms of transferability, is often neglected (although not always; for example, Bridges, 1993; Griffin, 1994).

'Transferability' *could* refer to the higher order academic skills of analysis, argument, evidence gathering, written communication and making connections in cognitive domains; the term could be a way of suggesting that there are academic skills which transcend disciplinary contexts. Transferability could, therefore, imply the existence of metadisciplinary skills.

However, the term has come to refer to the second form of transferability. Almost invariably, it is used to pick out capacities that are thought to be evident in different kinds of work context. Through the acquisition of such personal transferable skills, graduates will develop the flexibility to cope with changes in the world markets, national economy and labour market.

Both sets of views are dependent on the presumption that transferable skills – albeit their own brand – exist. However, the literature, especially that of the philosophy of education, has generated a near-consensus in expressing doubt over whether transferable skills – in the second, labour market, form at least – exist. If doubt can exist over transferability in the second form, so too can it and ought it to be expressed over the first form. In both cases, the doubt is whether skills, at any serious level, can be independent of the context, the forms of life, the traditions and the expectations in which they are embedded. Analysing a text, for example, is quite a different form of activity for surveyors, cooks, ballet dancers, historians, social workers and physicists. Indeed, what counts as text in those different domains is itself problematic.

That doubt over transferability can be side-stepped here. What is pertinent is not the philosophical questions (What is meant by generality and transferability? Do they exist?) but the sociological questions: are the concepts of generality and transferability helpful in understanding the development of the higher education curriculum? Were such ideas present in the minds of the reformers? If so, how can we understand such intentions? What social and cognitive barriers were generality and transferability intended to overcome? What were the social interests behind these movements?

We do not have to wrestle with all of those questions to make progress. There are two points to be made. Firstly, intentions in themselves are real. Insofar as individuals, groupings and agencies are pressing curricular agendas of this kind, that in itself is important as a social fact. And those intentions have influence, notwithstanding the caveats of the philosophers. As Griffin laments in reflecting on this matter (1994), no-one seems to take any notice of simple philosophical points, even where, almost uniquely, there is a consensus on the matter among philosophers.

Secondly, as just indicated, we can detect significant differences of intention among those who have attempted major reforms of the higher education curriculum. The USA has seen a long debate over the character of general education (that is, non-specificity within the curriculum), with Harvard and Stanford as well as Chicago attempting to provide, through a course of general education, forms of intellectual development that reflect a sense of what it is to be educated. Lately, that debate has become heated *within* academe as the espoused canon of western thought has been attacked (e.g., Gless and Herrnstein Smith, 1992). This counter-argument has insisted that the canon that was intended to impart universal values was a selective slice of *western* thought; a case of the specific masquerading as universal.

Correspondingly, in the UK, the debate about establishing the universities of the 1960s was largely driven by the academics. Some of them, especially James (York) and Briggs (Sussex), glimpsed an opportunity to rewrite the map of knowledge. Contrast those efforts to impart a general education from within the academic community with more recent attempts to inject transferability from the perspective of the world of work. The pleas from employers for better communication skills on the part of graduates is not to be taken as a demand that essays should be written with greater stylistic flourish, or that graduates should be more effective in communicating their critiques of social and political policy, or even that graduate managers should be sensitive listeners to shareholders' views and communicate those to the management with a view to changing radically corporate policy.

What is at stake is not a philosophical argument about the reality of transferability or generality but a contest of different agencies and interest groups with quite separate agendas. To see the debate as a question of conceptual points is to miss its real nature as a sociopolitical battle in determining the character of the higher education curriculum.

A typical aspect of embattlement is that the parties to the dispute do not see each other as others might see them. Rather, they see in each other what they wish to see. They miss opportunities for rapprochement; or fail to take seriously those that do arise. A key question that we have to address, therefore, is this: are the forms of transferability that are characteristically internal to academe and those that are external to academe at all coextensive? Do they overlap? Is the work of educators in higher education, as educators, at all relevant to the agendas of senior managers in the world of work? Are the demands of the labour market for transferable skills related to the intentions of those who would urge academics in their disciplinary specialisms to think of their wider educational role? While there might be differences, might there also be *some* similarities of purpose between what might be termed the internal and the external agendas? Ultimately, is there a transferability *across* forms of internal transferability and forms of external transferability? We shall come back to these questions.

Skilful amoebas

In the grid we looked at earlier, the polarities are complementary, not opposites. A curriculum can have elements drawn from both ends of an axis; a programme can be designed around disciplinary frameworks and contain educational processes intended to promote students' general skills for the labour market. Virtually every curriculum will extend beyond one box and spread across the grid in a specific formation. The experience of a student on the resulting course will be some particular amalgam of the elements of the grid.

The examples of a curriculum in a particular subject will differ. In a mass higher education system, history degree programmes will vary according to the status of the institution and the department in question. In a system that is also more market sensitive, the precise character of the curriculum – and its spread across the grid – will be subject to the interpretation of possibilities by the course team, to its perceptions of the market and the market position that the course team sees for itself (all of which will be reflected in its recruitment and access strategy).

An individual programme of studies is far from static. Its position on the curriculum grid changes over time; and differs as the market position and mission of the university change. Amoeba-like, the curriculum alters its formation, shifting the balance of the elements involved. At one moment, a curriculum may be weighted in terms of the discipline-specific skills. At another time (for example, under the influence of the Council for National Academic Awards), general educational capacities (box b) might have been given conscious attention. At yet another moment, transferable skills with an exchange value on the labour market (box d) could be addressed. A curriculum is, therefore, the current outcome of a negotiation of interests reflective of definite constituencies. The extent to which a curriculum inhabits any quarter of the grid can be seen as a telling commentary on the weight of influence of the different interests (discipline; education; profession; labour market) impinging on its formation at any moment in a particular institution.

Despite the differences between courses in the 'same' subject, and despite those relative differences changing across time, two trends can be identified. Firstly, there is a shift in the weighting of curriculum elements from the left-hand to the right-hand side of Figure 4.1, from the subject-specific to the general. Secondly, there is a shift from the upper to the lower, from the world of discipline-based thought and reflection to the world of action and work.

The modern curriculum is seeing a dominant movement from the top left-hand quarter to the bottom right-hand quarter; from curricula driven by discipline-specific concerns to curricula influenced increasingly by an interest in promoting transferable skills with a value in the labour market. This is not to say that any curriculum will be found to inhabit that quarter entirely; it will not.

These changes *can* be read as a sign of continuity with the university's past. But that reading fails to do justice to the marked changes now taking place in the curriculum with the shifting changes in the society–higher education relationship. The key change is profound and deserves reiteration: the university is moving from being an institution *in* society to one that is fairly fully incorporated into the apparatuses *of* society.

Since the university is part of society, the outside has become the inside. Talk of internal and external, of inside and outside, attempts to perpetuate a view of the university as apart from society. That language is nostalgic and interest-laden (wanting to put the clock back) and should be discarded. It pretends to a mythical essence of the university. There is no such thing. The university is an institution in a dynamic relationship with society and its functions change over time as that relationship changes.

Still, the internal/external distinction is worth holding onto in analysing the modern higher education curriculum. Yes, what was on the outside is now on the inside – the boundary keeps moving – but motives remain that are characteristic separately of the academic world and of the outside world. It is the contemporary *displacement* of internal interests by external interests that constitutes the discontinuity in question.

Conclusion: vocation and vocationalism

A sign of this discontinuity comes through in the ideas of vocation and vocationalism raised at the start of this chapter. The idea of vocation has virtually dropped out of the contemporary debate on higher education and has given way to vocationalism. To say of x that he has a vocation or of y that her vocation is so and so is not just to describe x or y as having a calling; it is also to say, in effect, that the calling is an honourable one. 'Vocation' is explicitly value-laden. That term, too, has longevity.

'Vocational', by contrast, appears to be value-free. Prima facie, it is descriptive. Against the background of an expanded system of higher education, it points to the explicit links that are developing between curricula and the external world. Not only engineering, business studies and pharmacy (and similar subjects with an explicitly vocational orientation); computer science, economics, chemistry and even history and archaeology are also becoming vocational in orientation.

To talk of x having a vocation is to say something about x's existential being. It implies commitment, and not just to personal whim but to an external set of demands and standards inherent in the career being followed. Vocationalism is silent on the matter. It is unconcerned with feelings and attitudes. It is concerned more with behaviour, with accomplishments and outcomes.

Vocationalism is not as value-free as it would pretend. It is an ideology representing the interests of corporatism, of economy and of profit. Vocationalism asserts the desirability of a fit between higher education and the world of work and of graduates being enterprising in it. Consequently, vocationalism drives up the value of the world of work as such.

Accompanying 'vocational' is the idea that graduates should be adaptable to the changing demands of the world of work. The graduate who understands the inner message of his vocational programme will be prepared to move from one career to another, to take on new behaviours, values and attitudes as the new position requires. The spirit of vocationalism stands for temporariness, and a shallowness of commitment. Permanent allegiance to a set of values, or even to an organization, is too costly. What is required is adaptability, a willingness to embrace new values at a moment's notice and to get on one's bike, attitudinally speaking.

The idea of vocation, by contrast, implies a durability of commitment. To have a calling requires a preparedness to commit oneself to one's profession and its demands, irrespective of whatever personal difficulties may befall one. To have a vocation means to surrender self for the worthwhileness, complexity and standards of the calling. The spirit of vocation stands for permanence and a deep commitment.

Disciplines can be considered as vocations. They can exert a lifelong claim on individuals' attention; they call for skills of a high order; they contain their own standards, to which academics have to give their allegiance; and they call for devotion, in the real sense of the word. However, this sense of disciplines as exerting a calling is fading. Having a vocation is inappropriate to the modern age. The substitution of 'vocation' by 'vocational' is a radical form of discontinuity.

5

'Competence' and 'Outcomes'

Redefining knowledge

The terms that we are exploring in this section – concerning the relationships between knowledge, higher education and society – are part of the new vocabulary of higher education. Some terms may have links with earlier traditions (vocationalism with vocation; skills with powers and capacities), but they also stand for newish sensitivities and interests to which higher education is called upon to respond. Vocabularies, after all, do not fall upon us. They are organic, springing from and reflecting collective agendas, even if unarticulated. Strikingly, however, the new vocationalism is frequently articulated; there is nothing coy about it.

The cause of the new vocabulary has two strands. Firstly, it is explicable in terms of the state's steering needs and motivation. Here, we can usefully draw on Jurgen Habermas' *Legitimation Crisis* (1976). Habermas argues that the modern state is faced with a series of structural problems of systems steerage, each arising to displace the one before it. The problems arise successively in different spheres of society. To begin with, the state finds the task of solving the periodic economic crises of late capitalism intractable. The failure to solve the economic crisis leads to a motivational crisis in society (economic expectations having been generated and now being thwarted), and to the state backing off from its economic mission and sponsoring market mechanisms while turning also to handling the motivational crisis. This last challenge obliges it to take an interest in the life-world of individuals so as to resolve the new legitimation crisis.

This analysis we can see reflected in the UK, as the state has developed its agenda in relation to higher education. An interest in the 1950s and 1960s in manpower planning (through higher education) was supplanted by budget-capping (1970s), then by an insistence on commercial models of management and of performance review (1980s), and (late 1980s onwards) by an intervention in the character of the education itself on offer (through state-sponsored curriculum initiatives). The state's modus operandi has developed from a distant interest in economic value, through concerns over the efficient management of the system to the character of the life-world promoted by the process of higher education. Each move on the part of the state has brought a deeper involvement in the inner life of academic institutions, such that now the state is intervening in the character *both* of the student experience and of the teacher–student transactions.

The second causal story behind the new vocabulary lies in the demands on society itself. 'The learning society' is a phrase testifying to the demands in question. The modern society cannot risk standing still. The world moves on; and the nation state must move with it. The competition that is characteristic of international trade is one feature of the changing world. Others are the increasing use of computers in their various forms, widening the scope and forms of communication; the growing number of countries that see themselves in this arena; the incipient use of science and technology in domains of life; and the growing complexity of modern society, with proliferating centres and institutions all exerting their own influences.

'The learning society' is an ambiguous term. It is descriptive, pointing to these complexities and underlining the centrality of change; it is analytical, suggesting the possibility that modern society – despite unparalleled complexity – may be in command of itself, forming a sense of itself, continuing to learn about itself and (with adequate feedback mechanisms) steering itself along its chosen path; it is normative, urging the need for learning to have a high profile at both the individual and the societal level; and it is ontological, making a statement about the fundamental nature of modern society and pointing to the centrality of rationality. On each interpretation of the learning society – descriptive, analytical, normative and ontological – education emerges as the key institution in modern society, but education conceived in terms broader than curricula framed by the academic community for young people.

Two kinds of change underscore the new definitions of education. One is institutional: education is now to be a lifelong process, available widely throughout society and offered by public and private institutions and agencies. The other change is substantive, to do with our very conception of what counts as knowledge.

Of all sectors of education, knowledge is most central to higher education and in two senses. Firstly, the kinds of meaning that we call 'knowledge' are elaborate, built around clusters of issues, problems, concepts, strategies and forms of communication (all of which we term disciplines). Secondly, contained within the specific forms of knowledge that inhabit higher education are metadisciplinary forms of understanding and command of the world. These higher order and generic forms of understanding constitute right reason as developed and sustained by the western universities for one thousand years.

These metadisciplinary forms of cognition include (following Habermas): (i) a determination to arrive at propositions with a truth value; (ii) a tentative offering of those propositions to others (that is, embodied in a public language); (iii) a structuring of those propositions according to the conventions of the disciplinary context; (iv) a commitment, even if only temporary, to those propositions on the part of the proposer; (v) a willingness to expose those offerings to critique; and (vi) a preparedness to listen to that critique and engage with it, modifying one's position where necessary. This form of discourse is orientated to some kind of progress, depends on written language and is highly structured according to interpersonal rules which have both a generic character and characteristics particular to the field in question.

The new vocabulary in higher education is a sign that the modern society is reaching for other definitions of knowledge and reasoning. Notions of skill, vocationalism, transferability, competence, outcomes, experiential learning, capability and enterprise, when taken together, are indications that traditional definitions of knowledge are felt to be inadequate for meeting the systems-wide problems faced by contemporary society. Whereas those traditional definitions of knowledge have emphasized language, especially through writing, an open process of communication, and formal and discipline-bound conventions, the new terminology urges higher education to allow the term 'knowledge' to embrace knowledge-through-action, particular outcomes of a learning transaction, and transdisciplinary forms of skill.

This new vocabulary is no linguistic window-dressing. It represents an epistemological assault on the very character of what counts as reason in the university. Nor is this assault necessarily regrettable. The definitions of knowledge by which the university has operated have been unduly closed. But openness to wider definitions is not, in itself, to be welcomed. The key test of appropriateness must be: does this new definition of knowledge widen our sense of rationality or is the new definition of knowledge likely to amount to a form of epistemological closure?

The problem of competence

We can extend this general line of attack by exploring the ideas of competence and outcomes. Competence and outcomes are two terms being adumbrated (in the UK) by the National Council for Vocational Qualifications (NCVQ). Introduced as part of an overarching rationale for systematizing 16–19 education and training, that framework of concepts is now being extended to higher education.

As with skills, we talk naturally of individuals being competent, and with some sense of praiseworthiness; and of events and actions having outcomes. There can be no objection *in principle* to the application of the terms (competence and outcomes) to educational processes. However, characterizing educational processes primarily in these terms, and deploying these terms as criteria by which educational processes are to be designed and evaluated, are matters of concern.

To say of an individual that he is competent is to assert that his actions are coming up to a standard. The standards might even be demanding. Being adjudged to be performing at competence level 5 (in the terminology of the NCVQ) is to meet more demanding standards than those of competence level 1. Level 1 requires:

Competence in the performance of work activities which are in the main routine and predictable or provide a broad foundation, primarily as a basis for progression.

Level 4, in contrast, consists of:

Competence in the performance of complex, technical, specialised and professional work activities, including those involving design, planning and problem solving, with a significant degree of personal accountability. In many areas competence in supervision and management will be a requirement at this level.

(Jessup, 1991: 23)

It is intended that, when defined, level 5 will be applicable to programmes of study in higher education; so competence at the level of higher education will be even more demanding. The higher the level of competence, the more demanding the standards being expected.

Two obvious challenges to this competency approach arise – and can *apparently* be quickly countered by the competence lobby.

Firstly, it will be pointed out by many that higher education is not just (or at all) a matter of developing competences for particular occupations. Even programmes designed to definite professions (pharmacy, teacher education, librarianship, social work, engineering) have broader aims than just the development of particular competences. The response of the competence lobby is: very well, but the onus on educators is still to state the competences which they *are* attempting to develop. Gilbert Jessup is quite definite on the matter: 'Outcome statements can be created for all learning which is considered important or that people want' (1991: 130). After all, 'If you cannot say what you require, how can you develop it and how do you know when you have achieved it?' (p. 134).

A second possible charge is that the notion of competence is concerned with predictable behaviours in predictable situations. The response from those favouring the competency approach to learning is to embrace that very point:

Performance criteria should refer to successful outcomes of performance ... Procedures can vary with circumstances, context or organization. We want learners to recognize that the purpose of an activity is to achieve a successful result ... When unexpected circumstances occur the procedures are often not appropriate or sufficient and the performer must improvise to achieve success. Coping with the unexpected is a crucial part of the concept of competence we are trying to foster.

(Jessup, 1991: 33)

Jessup wants to dampen any suggestion that a competency approach unduly limits the range of possible outcomes. For example, 'If an objective of a programme of learning was to develop creative writing or designs, these objectives could also be formulated as outcome statements' (1991: 130). Competences, therefore, can allow for the ability to cope with unpredictability and even allow for creativity. This seems to be an approach to curriculum design which higher education can embrace after all.

Before enthusiasm overwhelms us, a number of counter-objections to this approach to assessment must be lodged.

The approach begins unashamedly from the concerns of interest groups in the world of work. Lead bodies are charged with identifying the occupational standards from which are derived the necessary competences. In the professions to which programmes in higher education are orientated, it is likely that the professional bodies and perhaps even the practitioners will have a considerable influence, if not the sole part, in determining the required competences. This may seem uncontroversial: if we are trying to train competent professionals, then we should surely enlist the help of those currently practising in the profession.

One difficulty lies in promoting a necessary component – competences as identified by practising professionals – as the sole criterion of worthwhileness. Even if professional competence is itself the driving goal, questions arise over its identification by the professionals. Firstly, are the practitioners, particularly in a profession like, say, social work or the law where interaction with clients and other agencies is paramount, the only authorities on best practice? What counts as good practice in social work, the law, medicine and so on are contested goods: the public generally – as potential claimants of the service – and other groups have legitimate voices to be heard in framing the worthwhile competences. The identification of the occupational standards is not something that can be settled, and competences read off, in any absolute fashion. That debate must go on. Any attempt, therefore, to draw up a list of competences is bound to be partial and debatable. To any such list of competences we are entitled to respond: whose competences are these?

A second difficulty follows. We live in a changing society. Today's competences are not tomorrow's. Competent professionals will be able not simply to cope with change but actively to shape change. They will be able to form a view of their own profession and its changing relationship with society, and society's evolving demands on and expectations of the profession. These are not simply 'competences' but the abilities to carry on a conversation about competences, to evaluate them, to embrace new ones and discard old ones; in short, to point the profession in new directions.

To respond that these capabilities can be embraced by the competence perspective is too easy. Nor is it adequate to respond that there are, after all, different levels of competence and that these higher order competencies can be embraced by the higher competency levels.

What is in question here is the belief that *any* competence can be identified to carry us forward into a changing world. Profound societal, international and ecological change – when taken on board seriously – denies validity to the very notion of competence, if by that term is taken to be any set of behaviours, activities or responses that will tomorrow carry the value that they have today.

There is a third, more technical, difficulty with the NCVQ approach to assessment and curriculum. At its centre is a belief that competences can be stated independently of the learning process. The question is: does x have the competences in question? How competences are acquired is irrelevant for the NCVQ. This leaves open as a virtue, it claims, all kinds of learning possibilities for learning providers, trainers and learners themselves. Indeed, it allows for the possibility that individuals may have acquired the competences in their working lives or may determine to acquire the competences themselves. The key issue for the NCVQ is whether the stipulated competences can be assessed. But this belief – that competences can be identified and sought without implications for the learning process – is naive or mischievous.

In helping to promote the philosophy of education in the 1960s, one of Richard Peters' early themes was that of educational aims. In *Ethics and Education* (1966), Peters pointed out that an educational aim is not extrinsic to the process of education but is integral to it. On Peters' analysis, it would even be inappropriate to say that the aims are a reflection of the process. Rather, the aims are a specification of the process. If we want to stimulate students' firsthandedness, for them to become autonomous and able to offer views of their own, that has to be built into the process of learning. If we want students to make fine discriminations, to evaluate carefully and to think critically about all they encounter, all that has to be part of the curriculum. A statement of competences is a statement about the kind of curriculum we want. We cannot pretend that a specification of competences has no curricular implications: on the contrary, it has inescapable curricular implications.

Putting knowledge in its place

An even more serious set of problems with competence is not far away. It has two parts, epistemological and ontological. Statements from the NCVQ stable frequently use the phrase 'skills, knowledge and understanding' in depicting the general character of competences. However, the primary focus is on skills. Knowledge is allowed into the model only insofar as it is necessary and can be demonstrated. Understanding, a far more elusive matter, is given no serious attention at all.

The NCVQ starts from the belief that competences are best or ultimately demonstrated in work situations, but it grants that high level knowledge may need to be assessed in something like conventional assessment settings. Assessing knowledge in this way is a matter of last resort, when work or quasi-work settings (such as simulations) inadequately provide the range of possible situations that might be encountered. However, the knowledge required has to be specifiable in advance and amenable to multiple-choice questionnaires. The *judgement* of assessors will be avoided as far as possible.

The concept of knowledge represents a major challenge to the notion of competence. How, in a professional field in which knowledge is changing, is it possible to specify in advance the knowledge that is needed for professional competence? Who, again, will determine the contents of that knowledge? Either the knowledge that will do for today will do for tomorrow, in which case we are in the presence of narrow professional*ism*, characterized by a tight control – perhaps by a professional body – over what counts as standards and legitimate cognitive responses to situations; or we are in the presence of an open profession, responsive to change, characterized by a debate within and beyond the profession, in which case the knowledge that will do for today will not do for tomorrow. In either case – tight control or openness of response – the application of competence to knowledge acquisition is suspect.

Whatever happened to understanding?

Few of the writers in the NCVQ lobby have anything much to say about understanding; and this is understandable. Ideas of competences, outcomes, performance and activities sit uneasily with understanding. It is tempting to say that understanding is not observable, while the former are characteristics of human accomplishment. That is too easy a distinction and not entirely accurate. Understanding can show itself, and that is what we look for in higher education among students. We look for signs of deep understanding. Understanding may show itself, indeed, in a performance of some kind. But we *can* understand something without showing the external world that we understand.

Even if demonstration is necessary for some purpose – such as satisfying examiners, employers or professional bodies – the point remains that understanding can be present without it being demonstrated. In contrast, competences have to be revealed in some way: they take their meaning from some kind of public demonstration.

The attempt to reduce understanding to observable performance has four ontological deficiencies. Firstly, there is the problem identified by Peter Winch over thirty years ago (1963) in his book on *The Idea of a Social Science*, in which he produced a powerful demolition of a causal account of human action. We cannot know what individuals as social actors are up to by observing them, even if they act in statistically regular ways. Ultimately, we shall only fully understand their actions by taking account of their definitions of their situations, of their intentions, of their conceptual frameworks and of their forms of life. Full understanding requires that we understand the individual's understandings. Real work or real competence cannot be read off from activities from the outside. It cannot be seriously assessed by observing it. For that, we have to take into account the actor's understandings. It is not that the understandings lie behind the action. It is the much stronger claim that the actor's understandings are constitutive of the action.

Secondly, in the NCVQ approach, we are being offered a particular and debatable view of human *being*. It is a view in which the relationships between thought and action, between practice and reflection, are not so much crude and ill worked out as virtually absent. It is a view of human being as being operational, as performing, as working as such. A sense of persons as thinking, thoughtful, discriminating individuals is absent from the model. The neglect of the concept of understanding is symptomatic of this lacuna.

A third ontological void in the NCVQ's concepts of competence and outcomes is any worked out sense of the relationship of persons to their work. In this philosophy, the distinction between labour and work which comes from Marxism and has been articulated by more modern writers, such as Arendt, Habermas and R.J. Bernstein, is absent. We might say, indeed, that labour is precisely a set of competences, of performances according to an external standard. Work, on the contrary, is endowed with personal meaning, the standards being set or at least lived-in by the individual. For work, ideas of ownership, authenticity (cf. Taylor, 1991), care, craft and identification are relevant; as are, for labour, ideas of alienation, estrangement and commodification (since the products of labour stand externally to the labour itself).

Mere performance

The final ontological challenge to be levelled against the NCVQ approach is that it has no serious account to offer of the relationship between thought and action. Being so concerned with action and behaviour as such, the ways in which – in professional life, at least – action is saturated with thought, understanding and reflection is entirely neglected.

Donald Schon has argued persuasively against a technicist conception of professional education, in which theory is applied to practice. Instead, he suggests, in our educational practices, we should recognize that professional practice is a matter of reflection-in-action and knowledge-in-use. Picking up Gilbert Ryle's phrasing, for Schon there is no ghost in the machine: human being is not thinking being plus acting being. The two are necessarily intertwined.

However, Schon goes too far in running action and reflection together. In wanting, rightly, to counter the academicism of those who would prize theory before action, and wanting to point up the complexity of action as such, he downplays the role that pure reflection can play in evaluating and critiquing action. But to say this, contra Schon, is to underline still further the paucity of the NCVQ conception of action. Not only is action saturated with theory, with tacit principles, with understanding and practical wisdom, all of which are inseparable from and are constitutive of action; we can always bring yet *further* perspectives, frameworks and paradigms to bear on action to illuminate it and to critique it. It may be said, of course, that the NCVQ model can cope with all this. The higher levels of competence will look to individuals coping with unpredictability and acting in enlightened ways. But this is no answer at all. Or if it is, then it scuppers the NCVQ model.

In complex discriminating action, there lies a pool of independent reflection which provides the power to critique taken-for-granted competences. Keeping step-by-step with competence are knowledge and understanding. Deep knowledge and understanding have to be built in from the start, integral to and significantly constitutive of the competence. They are not mere add-ons. Some knowing and understanding will be tacit, not easily amenable to examination. In addition, any adequate account of human being – especially in those fields of human endeavour linked to higher education – has to find space for insight, understanding and imagination *not* obviously prompted by a professional situation. Emancipatory human action is driven not by a determination to perform against an external standard, but by internal standards which are all the time subject to internal evaluation and self-critique and produce, in turn, a continuing process of self-learning and self-renewal.

Summarizing this ontological critique, we can say that – in the NCVQ philosophy – there is a conceptual thinness in its conception of the character of human being. What we are being given is an impoverished view of human action in which individuals are caused to perform against external standards. This is a conception of human being in which power is denied to individuals: no longer are they to be seen as authors of their own actions and even thinking. It is a conception that sees human beings as mere performers rather than reflective actors. It is a conception that neglects the power of self-generated critique, critique that may strike at the heart of the given standards of competence. This is not so much a philosophy of technicized reason as of technicized performance. It is a philosophy devoid of enlightened and critical (and self-critical) reason.

Outcomes and life

Suppose we suggest, heretically, that higher education is for life. Negatively, we would be saying that higher education should not be construed or designed *primarily* with careers and the demands of the world of work in mind. More positively, we could mean a number of things. We might mean, as John White has argued (1982), that higher education should enable individuals to frame a coherent set of life projects for themselves. Higher education would become a combined intellectual and ethical affair, giving individuals the wherewithal to conceive a morally defensible set of projects for themselves and the capabilities to pursue them.

We might, however, wish to go further. We might sense that the world is not simply out there, waiting for us to imprint our purposes on it (as Richard Peters once remarked), but is imposing its meanings and orderings on us. In the light of the analyses of Critical Theory, we might consider that, in the modern society, those meanings are skewed in the direction of instrumental reason. In its various forms – bureaucratic, purposive, strategic and technocratic – instrumental reason so seeps into social institutions and human affairs generally that it becomes the dominant mode of reason. In the terminology of Jurgen Habermas, instrumental reason colonizes the life-world, which would otherwise be the domain of open, interpersonal reason. Instead of engaging with each other and with the world in mutual interaction, we end up by always having an eye to the main chance and by getting out of our transactions with each other and with the world whatever we can get away with.

A higher education for life would not rule out instrumental reason, for that is part of life. But it would give due space to interpersonal, critical, aesthetic and other forms of reason that are not necessarily in the main-stream of modern society.

In a higher education for life, the concept of outcomes would have little if any place. In genuinely open, interactive, forms of reason and engagement, there are no outcomes. Only continuing processes, with intermediate stopping points before the discussion is resumed. The notion of an outcome is characteristic of instrumental reason, of getting things done or of saying things for a purpose.

In life, it may be said, we want to get things done. We may want to stop further ecological degradation, or redistribute resources more equitably on this planet, or reduce the global birthrate or improve the quality of our health and other public services. Outcomes and instrumental reason have their place: this much I have just agreed. So this does not constitute an objection; only a reminder of my plea for different forms of reason to find a proportionate place in the higher education curriculum.

But a stronger thesis is available to us. The questions arise: Why might we wish to protect the natural environment? or Why might we wish to produce a minimal standard of life for those on this planet? These questions can only be answered, to borrow a phrase from Charles Taylor's recent book, through recourse to 'horizons of significance'. We wish to do those things because of the rightness that we attach to them. But rightness is a term that has its basis in principles of human behaviour which are arguable. Our instrumental purposes – however laudable they may be, and some may be – only gain their validity through their anchoring in a discursive way of life, in continuing processes of open discussion and reflection. Our purposes of instrumental reason are not given but, if they are to be rationally based, must derive from the continuing processes of reasoned discourse. Outcomes of instrumental reason are not given either: they are always susceptible to debate, evaluation and criticism.

We can conclude that outcomes, which are being suggested by the NCVQ as a generalizable substitute for competences, can provide no firm basis for curricula in higher education. This holds, perhaps, for all forms of education. But it holds above all for higher education; there, all our cognitive options are potentially contestable.

On transferability, again

There are those who observe that we live in a world of change and face continuing new challenges, whether from international trade or as a result of the technological development and dynamic built into modern society. The result of living in a world of change is that those changes cannot be foreseen. We cannot live in the future. Accordingly, we need to develop the capacities to respond intelligently to change. This line of thinking then proceeds to turn to education, for education will supply the kinds of flexible responsive capacities that are required.

I have drawn upon Critical Theory, particularly the work of Jurgen Habermas, to make a distinction between instrumental and non-instrumental forms of reason. Instrumental reason is the dominant form of reason in modern society and, consequently, our educational institutions are liable to be skewed in that way. However, it could be argued that the 'transferable skills' movement represents a counter to that analysis.

Part of the thinking behind transferable skills is to develop skills that are not tied to specific foreseeable situations but which enable individuals to cope successfully with the unexpected and the unforeseen. Communication skills, mutuality (listening to others and taking their point of view seriously), working in teams, general analytical skills and so on are what the modern economy requires and are what higher education has been in business for all along. Commentators of that persuasion might add two further points. Firstly, these skills are not outcomes in any narrow sense but are process skills calling for attention to the character of the educational process. Secondly, these skills cannot be seriously construed as instrumental. On the contrary, they are examples of interpersonal and critical (and even aesthetic) reason. On this view, the higher education curriculum of the modern society has to be multifaceted. There is no gap, no divorce, between the curriculum required by the modern economy and a curriculum designed with non-instrumental ends (the good life) in mind.

This line of thinking runs together several arguments and begs many questions. For instance, it runs together the claim that, as well as having transferable value in the world of work, transferable skills are generally useful *both* in academe, the world of organized intellectual work, and in the life-world. There is no reason why we should buy this argument. It may be that the kinds of communication skill and analytical skill required by most disciplines (for they vary between the disciplines) are excessively narrow and of limited value in the openness and interpersonalness of the life-world.

Questions are also begged in the view that the transferable skills required for a successful economy are the same metacognitive skills sought by a genuine higher education. We *may* use terms like communication skills, analytical skills and so forth to describe what we are up to in programmes of study in universities; and they may be terms that are in use to describe skills felt now to be appropriate in the world of work. But are they, in fact, the same terms?

Are the communication skills that are felt to be desirable in the world of work the same communication skills that are to be encouraged from an educational point of view? Is the communication of the world of work really one of the mutual reciprocity that we may feel is characteristic of an intellectual discourse at its best? Is even listening the same in the two milieux? Or does listening in the world of work all too often take the form of allowing employees to have 'their say', only for the hierarchies of work to assert themselves in the following decision-making?

Strategic reason rather than real interpersonal reason is likely always to assert itself, not for any reasons of malevolence or shortsightedness but because that is the inbuilt cognitive structure of the modern world of work. Yet there is no necessity about such trends. It just may be that new forms of reasoning are being opened up in the world of work which allow real rather than superficial reciprocity. That will require different forms of organization giving real autonomy to individuals and units; and perhaps something of this form of organization is beginning to appear. If so, higher education will have a part in encouraging the formation of those human capacities. And in that case, we are in the realm of an interventionist role for higher education, a role far removed from the reproduction of competences currently identified in the world of work.

The new professionalism

We are beginning to see signs of professional education narrowing to sets of practical skills – indeed, to competences – and behavioural operations, with clients reduced to being recipients of those skills rather than joint authors of the professional services that they require (cf. Phillips, 1987). In law, social work and education, for instance, we see indications of a shift in this direction, albeit of a particular character in each instance. The skills or competences of the professional are supposedly identified and a curriculum is reorientated around those competences.

Far from being a more comprehensive form of professional education, this is a reduced form. Professional education, especially for those professions in which interaction with clients is constitutive of the professional practice, cannot be a summation of skills. The general point was argued in the last chapter: skills cannot be a sufficient way of describing genuinely open-ended transactions of the kind that should characterize a professional–client relationship. Skills are competences which are applied to situations.

To conceive of professionalism in this way is quite inappropriate. Clients should be conceived of as subjects of their own affairs, not as objects on which skills are wrought.

The work of Foucault is a substantiation of the connection between professional power, knowledge and control. On that reading, competences turn out to be the manipulation of clients not just in the internal interests of the profession but in the service of the state, as a form of social control or amelioration. What is required, on this view of professionalism, is *less* competence and more critical reflection (Grundy, 1987). Professionalism – even the professionalism of scientists (Feyerabend, 1975) – can become an ideology, a set of dogmas. A genuine higher education for the professions will not be content with reflecting the professionally defined competences but will insert alternative modes of reasoning, action and reflection into the curriculum. An adequate professional education cannot rest content with the contemporary definitions of professionalism but must seek to inform the dominant professional ethic. The hope must be that it is possible to integrate vocational and educational aims into a liberal vocationalism (Brennan and Silver, 1988). If it is to be more than a slogan, liberal voca-tionalism must amount to a curriculum aimed at both self-enlightenment and societal enlightenment. However, the counter-forces are considerable. Such a conception of professional education is not obviously in the immedi-ate interests of the profession or the wider society.

Conclusion

Competences and outcomes cannot provide guidelines for a higher educa-tion curriculum. It is the business of higher education to develop critical capacities, which must include the evaluation and possible repudiation of contemporary competences. Even the idea of metacompetences – higher order competences that enable one to call upon a repertoire of competences – does not take us much further forward, attractive though it might be (Fleming, 1991). For whether meta or not, competences will remain behavi-ours and capacities to act as desired and defined by others. They reduce the authenticity of human action (cf. Taylor, 1991). The idea of a competence that allows for unpredictability is ultimately incoherent. In the domain of competence, *some* degree of predictability there has to be; and the NCVQ is quite clear about this. The difficulty that this produces for the NCVQ is to specify the range of allowable behaviours at the higher levels of com-petence. This difficulty is a product of the NCVQ's own making in wanting to construe right action in terms of prespecified behaviours and skills rather than the actor's own understandings and reasonings.

Outcomes, too, have to be challenged as an approach to learning in higher education. To conceive the development of mind as an outcome, which is what the idea amounts to, is a hopelessly limited way of construing higher education. As with competences, outcomes represent a form of closure. They predetermine the required characteristics students should end up with. Both terms are part of a language of prejudging, imposition and inevitable narrowness. They spring from a particular form of reason – instrumental reason – and seek to extend its domination in the wider society into higher education, so further marginalizing other forms of interaction and reason.

The emerging postmodern society is reaching out for new definitions of reason, interaction and responsiveness (cf. Giddens, 1991). Transferability, flexibility, reflection and higher orders of cognition (metacompetences and metacognition) are signs of this new searching. It may be that some of this is promotable within academe without distorting or narrowing its claims to openness of discourse. The worlds of corporate life and of the university may live together after all; and all of that may be helpful in maintaining the life-world. But even if all is for the best in all possible worlds, if it turns out that the interests of the modern corporate world and of academe can live with each other and with the requirements of the life-world, those interests will not be captured in a language of competences and outcomes. Following Rorty (1989), we can say that we will need an entirely new vocabulary. And, following Rorty still further, we can say that designing and carrying off a curriculum will be less like falling in with a blueprint of predetermined competences and outcomes and more like the characters of a novel holding a conversation and making it up creatively as they go along.

6

'Capability' and 'Enterprise'

Being and nothingness

All societies have to present an answer to the problem of being. Or, to put it slightly differently, societies embody an ontology. They are obliged to furnish a sense of the ideal kind of person appropriate to the society. Societies change; so the ideal changes. The pre-literate agrarianism of mediaeval society produced, we might surmise, a role-model of serfdom: the true serfs knew their place, identified with matters of the land, accepted 'fate' and did not ask too many questions. Serfs could recognize each other as serfs, not just through their economic position (or lack of it) but through their mutual understandings of the serf *Weltanschauung*.

Picking out the essential modern person poses difficulty. Modern society is characterized by competing images to a degree that mediaeval society was not. The knowledge society gives way to the technological society which in turn gives way to the learning society. Man as knower, man as fabricator of artefacts intended for the infrastructure of society, man as continuing self-critic willing to jettison yesterday's ideas for those of today and even 'tomorrow': these are characteristic of the contemporary images that confront us.

In modern society, education is thought to have a large part to play in forming the necessary types of consciousness. Latterly, higher education has been incorporated into this mind-formation business, since many of the modern images turn around knowledge and learning; although not just any form of knowledge and learning. The modern society has a sense of impending disaster, which can only be kept at bay by enlisting the university in advancing strange forms of knowing and understanding among a large segment of its population. *These* forms of knowing have little to do with substance; quite the reverse. Indeed, what is stressed as an emblem of modernity is the very provisionality of what is 'learnt'. Modern man is characterized by his willingness to abandon cherished ideas, beliefs and practices. To repeat, we are in a throwaway society not only with consumables but cognitively speaking as well.

Until recently, higher education was a fringe activity and it hardly mattered what images of personkind it promoted. Now, higher education is big business with a number of 'stakeholders', in which many pass through or see themselves as having an immediate interest. Consequently, higher education is being pressed into service as a carrier and a supplier of new images of modern man; and of society's hopes. Its ideological function rivals its substantive function. It is not just a case of what do we want our graduates to know and to do, but how do we want our graduates to see themselves? What kind of relationship to society and its dominant institutions of work and the economy do we want our graduates to consider themselves as having? Is it to be a matter of taking what comes their way? Or are they to see themselves as change agents, contributing to the deconstruction and reconstruction of society itself? In the new order, nothing is to be taken for granted; everything can be questioned. There are no resting places. Cognitive and conceptual change are seen as good in themselves, for stasis means atrophy. Graduates especially are expected to be in the vanguard of change.

What is at issue here is that higher education is being enlisted to form metacognitive capacities in its students. We are familiar enough with assertions of the kind that half of what a graduate has learnt will be out of date within five years, and the majority of the rest of it within another five. Whether there is backing for the assertion is beside the point. But the knowing being called for has nothing to do with the mastery of individual units of information. Employers want expertise, but the expertise they are crucially after is not the expertise of propositional knowledge. It is forms of knowing how, to do with the ferreting out of the latest findings, being able to connect up those findings with the practical problems faced by the organization in a competitive environment, and being able to share those understandings with others in the company (many of whom will lack a deep understanding of the relevant specific fields of inquiry).

These are large enough sets of expectations but they require yet others if they are to be brought off successfully. Having a clear understanding of the structure of a knowledge field, of its special character, and of its points of contact and divergence from other fields relevant to the problems at hand: there are epistemological capacities of this kind. But to these capacities having a cognitive purity, there are others to be added of a more messy and operational variety. To be really attractive to the modern organization built on change, the would-be graduate employee has to be able to show an interest in making links between the world of pure understanding and the world of action (Birch, 1988).

Bridging these two worlds is a crucial capacity: a metacapacity. 'Meta' because its possession enables the graduate to see both worlds at the same time and to see ways of deploying the two sets of capacities that they point to. Action without insight, we might say, is blind. On the other hand, insight, without being tested through implementation, is helpless. So far as the modern society is concerned, it is a form of nothingness.

In the general run of things

We arrive, then, back at an issue that continues to break the surface of our discussions. The issue is one of generality: are the general accomplishments sought by the world of work (to which higher education is to be responsive) similar to the general accomplishments that higher education has claimed to be in business to promote all along?

The modern society looks to higher education to supply higher order capacities likely to offer a degree of value-added to the economy. The higher order in question here is a logical one rather than a matter of status. Employers want graduates who can skilfully deploy their knowledge as a resource in the service of the organization's problems and to meet its challenges. Since the problems and the challenges change, and since we do not know what they will be tomorrow, the abilities to use, manipulate, apply, communicate, evaluate against mixed criteria (cost-efficiency, quality, impact, applicability with the given human resources), create, innovate and – in the end – discard on grounds of timeliness rather than epistemic validity are all much more important than the possession of any sets of items of propositional knowledge.

It is counterproductive from the viewpoint of producing graduates for the economy to overpack a curriculum with propositional knowledge (as groups of professors in physics and engineering in the UK have recognized). Modernity requires skills of metacognition – knowing what to do with knowing – rather than a command over bundles of facts. It is not even that much interested in the graduate's ability to manipulate those facts in a straightforward academic sense, of feeling at home and making progress in a field of knowledge. It is the abilities of being able to call upon that knowledge in a discriminating way, in the service of the organization's goals, that are sought.

Higher education has, however, always claimed to be doing something remarkably similar. When pressed, academics with the responsibility of teaching will often emerge with claims to be promoting students' analytical or critical thinking skills or wanting their students to develop independent minds. Behind such terminology lies a sense that the sheer acquisition of facts is an illegitimate way of conceiving of higher education. It is not Whitehead's observation (1934) that is at issue here, that 'A merely well-informed man is the most useless bore on God's earth', but the logical point that the massing of units of information is not a higher order mental act constitutive of *higher* education. For that, mental acts have to take place which give individuals power to deploy and manipulate such items of information.

The mental acts marked out by such terms as analysis, synthesis, evaluation, criticism and even imagination are higher order acts in the sense that these mental powers enable individuals to take up a stance in relation to discrete units of information, to discriminate between them, to classify them, to see relationships between them and to set them in a larger context. They bestow independence of mind precisely because the acts to which they point are open-ended and unpredictable. If a student is engaging in a process of analysis, we cannot be certain in advance what distinctions or observations she will emerge with. Learning that x is y cannot be constitutive of higher education. It becomes higher education when the student is starting to ask: In what sense do we understand x as y? or, Is x really y? Perhaps x might even be thought to be z.

Higher education is in the business, then, of developing general capacities of the mind, capacities that enable students to engage in an open-ended way with new items of information, new ideas or new kinds of experience. In this sense, academics have always been trying to bring off transferable intellectual skills; 'transferable' in the sense that the higher order skills provide students with a means of going on when faced with something new. An organic compound, a historical period, a literary text, a philosophical argument or a professional practice: any of these encountered anew can be met with a range of strategies. The challenge can be met; the student – armed with the general intellectual capacities – can respond meaningfully. She is not bereft.

This sounds very much like the kind of skill that employers are looking for in the modern world. The possibility arises that the modern demands of the world of work and the traditional demands of academe are, after all, not perhaps two worlds; or, at least, not entirely so. Both worlds value human capacities of a general kind, which enable individuals to transcend the here and now and to take a larger view of things (cf. Newman, 1976), and to be able to take up a constructive or meaningful position in the face of all of that.

Taking up a recent paper of Basil Bernstein (1992), what is at issue here is the construction of a 'pedagogic identity'. Through their experiences *as* students, the recipients of higher education are, wittingly or not, engaged in a process of identity formation. In the midst of the kinds of changing relationship between higher education, society and knowledge that we have been charting, it is inevitable that the pedagogic identities produced by higher education will change. The pedagogic identities characteristic of British higher education in the immediate post-war period, in the 1960s, in the 1980s, and as we move into the new millennium are – we might hypothesize – distinctive. Crudely, the pedagogic identity of the immediate post-war period was of an initiation into a general academic culture; that of the 1960s, into separate epistemic traditions of the disciplines; and that of the 1980s, into market-specific sets of capacities; while the pedagogic identity of the turn of the century will be a *common* set of market-related 'flexible' capacities. From generality to specificity and back to generality: this seems to have been the pattern of pedagogical identities.

Higher education, therefore, is being enjoined to shift its curricula in the direction of pedagogies intended to develop common properties in its graduates. Society seeks, accordingly, to cut through and to cut across disciplinary boundaries and loyalties.

This sounds as if higher education is being encouraged to return to that former age that we posited a moment ago when we could speak of 'the academic community' without embarrassment; when there was a definite sense of a common cause across the knowledge fields. That, at any rate, was surely implied in Robbins' evocative talk of a 'common culture'. At that moment, the undergraduate curriculum was inspired by a sense of general properties (both of pedagogy and of mind) above and beyond the loyalties and distinctive epistemic transmissions of the disciplines. The formation of the new universities in the 1960s, with a programme of redrawing the map of knowledge to overcome the rampant specialization (Becher, 1994), was testimony to the fact that, if there had been a common academic culture of this kind, it was already breaking down.

At the same time, too, the Council for National Academic Awards (CNAA) was born, and an immediate policy it framed was that of identifying and sustaining a set of general intellectual capacities. The CNAA's attempts to maintain that policy was never far from its deliberations and activities over the next twenty-five years (Silver, 1991). Every few years, the relevant policy document was recast, usually to prune it and make it less onerous, in the wake of the relentless tide of disciplinary assertiveness. But what is fascinating from the point of view of our story is the very last formulation, on CNAA's deathbed. Far from repenting the faith (the belief in general capacities), it was proclaimed with even more vigour *but* this time in the form of transferable skills for the labour market. *Plus ça change . . .* Generality is dead; long live generality.

The question returns, however: is this new form of generality the same as the older variety? Or are we witnessing a call to embrace a new cultural and social order in our higher education pedagogies? We can best make progress by examining two further contemporary attempts to shift the curriculum in the direction of generality.

Learning, not teaching

'Enterprise' and 'capability' are two more terms that have recently entered the language of British higher education. Both represent national initiatives intended to change the internal culture of the academic community. Each seeks, in a different way, to encourage curriculum development but that is only a limited aspect of their agendas. Their main target is to stimulate a realignment of the general consciousness among the academic community of what higher education is. What changes are we trying to bring about in our students? That question and new answers to it are behind these initiatives.

These initiatives are, therefore, highly ambitious even if the operational practice has differed markedly. As a government-backed scheme, the Enterprise Initiative has had several millions of pounds at its disposal. By contrast, the Higher Education for Capability initiative was funded by an independent organization, the Royal Society for Arts, and was much less well endowed. Nevertheless, both were conceived and driven forward as national initiatives, intended to bring about altered forms of higher education across the whole system.

As with any national initiative orientated towards a system with considerable autonomy in its operating units (Becher and Kogan, 1992), both have seen a degree of fluidity in the way their central idea – respectively, enterprise and capability – has been taken up. Secondly, those running each initiative looked to enlist the support and active involvement of institutions in the hope of getting their ideas taken up across institutions as a whole. A change in the internal culture of institutions was sought. But their most important point of similarity is to be found at an even more stratospheric level.

What is to count as higher education? Each programme had a different answer. But it was in their raising this question implicitly, and even, at times, explicitly that these two initiatives offered their most signal point of overlap. Simply in forcing the question, *both* initiatives represented a particular affront to higher education.

The first affront was not that these two initiatives directly challenged the existing consensus. It was, rather, the discomfort felt when one was obliged to make clear to oneself, in the first place, assumptions about one's central practices and approach which up to now had never been clarified. The frisson of discomfort which both initiatives produced was particularly acute because, in its self-defining rhetoric, the academic community had long prided itself on its 'elaborated' thinking, making things explicit and working things through. The discomfort was as much a reflection of the consequent embarrassment of an empty cupboard, cognitively speaking, as it was a direct assault on an articulated position.

Having said that, it was still the case that the discomfort did have a rational basis. *Both* challenged much of the belief structure embedded in the practices of British higher education. The challenge was different in the two cases, but it was real. Crudely, the challenge was to academics as educators rather than as scholars or researchers; and was dual-pronged. Firstly, the challenge was that academics should think of themselves as educators and should think *through* what they were in business for in that capacity. That was heady stuff, for while the UK academic community had grown used to the expression 'higher education' over the previous forty years, the term 'education' had been significant for its near absence on campus (or in the quadrangle).

Secondly, and more fundamentally, both initiatives sought to overturn the lecturer–student relationship. Henceforth, it was the student and his or her development which was to take centre stage. Learning had been an adjunct to teaching; now, the relationship was inverted.

In the new regime, base and superstructure were recast. Higher education had been conceived fundamentally as a process of teaching, of an authorized individual standing (often literally) in a definite pedagogical setting. The main task was that of stimulating the students, capturing their attention and ensuring that they were active recipients of the messages they encountered. Issues of understanding, active engagement, personal inter-pretation, and individual ownership of ideas by the student formed the pedagogical superstructure on the teaching base. But, with the two national initiatives, that relationship was overturned.

Henceforth, it *was* the student's own development that was the starting point. The issue now was whether, and in what ways, teaching might con-tribute to the desired development of mind. Teaching was now to be a kind of technology, with an instrumental value only insofar as it shored up the central aim of furthering the envisaged student development. If teaching – ordinarily conceived – could not contribute to that end, then it was to be jettisoned. Higher education, as a process of student formation, was not dependent on teaching. Teaching wasn't a necessary part of higher education.

The Enterprise in Higher Education Initiative

Enterprise is necessary to running a business and working in industry and commerce but the term embraces a wide spectrum of human endeavour and is needed in a variety of situations and contexts. Enterprise makes for both effective performance in employment and personal fulfilment in a changing world.

The Training Agency's Enterprise in Higher Education Initiative is part of the broader enterprise movement. It has been introduced to encourage the development of enterprise amongst those seeking higher education qualifications.

(Training Agency, 1989)

The spirit of enterprise, it seems, can be all things to all men and women. Running a business, working in industry and commerce, personal fulfilment, effective performance, coping with a changing world: these are, indeed, a variety of situations and contexts. Is this a plausible position? Can a pro-gramme be designed and brought off which delivers all these possibilities? But there is a more profound issue at stake.

Is there – or might there be – a logical incompatibility between personal fulfilment and the development of qualities needed for survival in the world of work? That is never raised as a problematic matter in the sponsoring literature, or in the official commentaries (National Foundation for Educa-tional Research (NFER), Tavistock). Yet further questions loom into view: if the aims turn out to be logically incompatible, is that a matter of bad luck, negligence or mendaciousness? In seeming to allow for objectives of both personal fulfilment and business effectiveness, is there at work a hidden drive to define personal fulfilment in terms of business effectiveness?

Simply putting down the questions has point because we are offered no proper exposition of 'enterprise' in the Training Agency literature, an exposition that would enable us to rule in or rule out possible interpretations. Some will say that the implied plea – that we *should* be given some more detailed explication of 'enterprise' – misses the point. One value of the Enterprise in Higher Education (EHE) Initiative, so it might be claimed, is precisely that the meaning of 'enterprise' has been left open and has been taken up in different ways by the universities involved. Whether by design or by 'enterprising' manoeuvring by institutions, no one idea has taken root in the participating institutions. Interpretations of enterprise have been a moveable feast.

We can counter this claim in more than one way. Firstly, we can ask whether any interpretations of 'enterprise' would have been ruled out of court by the initiative. However, going in this direction demands a prior sense of the dominant interpretations or the limits of the interpretations available. So umpiring 'in and out' senses of enterprise is not a course immediately open to us. Preliminary work is required.

Secondly, picking up a term of R.J. Bernstein (1991), we can enquire into the 'constellation' of ideas and concepts related to the one before us. Here, we need to go a little beyond Bernstein's conception of mapping the complex of associated ideas to recognize that ideas are linked to social practices and institutions. And in a public service like higher education, linked to agendas of the state as its primary sponsor, the social practices are not likely to be a random collection but will probably cluster in particular forms of life.

We have already begun to see something of a pattern in the earlier quotation on p. 89. The reference to personal fulfilment is embedded in two sentences which include the terms 'business', 'working in industry', 'commerce', 'effective performance', 'employment' and 'changing world'. A little further on, we find the following sentence:

> The need for graduates who are in tune with the enterprise culture, who are aware of the needs of industry and commerce, who know how to learn and have had some experience of the world of work has been highlighted in several major reports.
>
> (Training Agency, 1989)

The key terms are clear enough: 'enterprise culture', 'needs of industry and commerce', 'know how to learn' and 'experience of the world of work'. Again, we see a relatively neutral idea – (graduates) 'who know how to learn' – but linked to a larger constellation of ideas turning around the world of work, defined as industry and commerce. We see, therefore, that the cluster of ideas that is defining the sense of enterprise in question here *is* located in a certain domain. The occasional phrase or idea might suggest that there is no one dominant sense of enterprise. But that there is a dominant location to this particular constellation is clear enough.

I said that ideas are linked to social practices. What are the social practices intimated here? The document is explicit:

The cornerstone of the initiative apart from enterprise itself is partnership. EHE [Enterprise in Higher Education] makes possible a substantial and productive role for employers and practitioners so that they can become more involved in the work of the institutions, particularly in curriculum design, delivery and assessment.

To assure the funders that this cornerstone is firmly in place, it has been a condition of each grant that successful institutions should demonstrate 'the commitment of the whole institution and the commitment of a number and range of employers to participate in the programme' . . . 'and to have devised . . . a plan for employer partnership and involvement in the design, implementation and resourcing of the programme with predictions and costings of employer input'. Given practices of this kind, the requirement that institutions demonstrate 'a substantial commitment to enterprise education' has been, we can surmise, not a completely open invitation to hopeful institutions in their interpretation of 'enterprise'.

Having, then, a sense that the particular constellation of ideas and social practices in question has a definite location, we can turn back to our other possible assessment strategy, that of asking if any interpretation of 'enterprise' would have been ruled out of court for funding purposes. Like 'competence', 'enterprise' can have a relatively straightforward sense in ordinary language; and, like competence, and skills too, a sense which is praiseworthy. We say quite naturally of x, in drawing attention to a recent accomplishment of hers, that she has been enterprising. By that, we might have in mind that she formed an idea for practical implementation, used initiative in putting it into action, surmounted obstacles that came her way, and won through to the goal she had set herself. The goal in question might have been small-scale and of personal significance only, and have virtually no financial implications. Some will say that, in its actual development, the Enterprise Initiative allowed for such a low-key interpretation; or that, as a matter of fact, some participating institutions did subvert the proclaimed intentions by substituting relatively value-free interpretations of this kind.

Pointing to a wide range of interpretations of 'enterprise' does not represent any kind of qualification on the original intentions behind the scheme. Right from the start, it was part of the official doctrine that 'institutions requesting funding were expected to demonstrate . . . a broad understanding of what enterprise in higher education would mean' (Training Agency, 1989: 6). Indeed, a subsequent document begins with the recognition that 'There are perhaps as many definitions of enterprise as there are people defining the word!'. But following passages attempt to bring a little clarity. The next sentence reads:

However, there is a great deal of common ground, and most people would agree that the enterprising person is resourceful, adaptable, creative, innovative and dynamic. He or she may also be entrepreneurial.

A little later, the document attempts further elucidation:

Definitions [of enterprise] may focus on:
- *Entrepreneurship*: the qualities and skills which enable people to succeed in business enterprises;
- *Personal effectiveness*: the qualities and skills possessed by the resourceful individual;
- *Transferable skills*: the generic capabilities which allow people to succeed in a wide range of different tasks and jobs.

The document also considered that:

Problems arose when institutions' staff were uncertain about – or even disagreed on – the model of enterprise being aimed for. It seems clear that agreeing a positive definition of enterprise is much more than an abstract academic exercise – it is a vital first step in ensuring the success of the Programme.

(Training Agency, 1990: 5)

We can see the line of thinking in these quotations. It starts from the acknowledgement that enterprise is susceptible to different interpretations. Even so, a particular acceptable range of interpretations is set down *and* each institution is expected to come to a consensus on its interpretation of enterprise within the stated range deemed valid. The acceptable range is marked out by the terminology of success in business, resourcefulness and success in tasks and jobs. Resourcefulness is an open-ended term but its connecting terminology suggests that the kinds of resourcefulness being sought are those that will lead to success in tasks, jobs and business.

The definitions of 'enterprise' being driven forward in this initiative are, then, bounded within a particular range of interpretations. Nor are institutions to debate the matter: they should come to a definite view within the permitted range. That we might want to call a student 'enterprising' who had managed to find a copy of a book in a tutor's bibliography in her local library rather than depending simply on the university's library is not the kind of sense of enterprise being promoted here. Some interpretations are ruled in; and others are ruled out.

There is another point to be made, which is reflected in the penultimate quotation. A major plank of the Enterprise Initiative is that it is trying to foster across institutions the acquisition of transferable skills. Some rejoice in this aim, since it forces participating institutions to identify general sets of skills that they wish to foster across all their programmes of study (Wright, 1990). In turn, institutions are obliged to conduct an internal debate about their educational mission. But the debate cannot be an open debate: the above quotation makes that clear. The transferable skills to be adopted under the banner of this programme are those that 'allow people to succeed in a wide range of different tasks and jobs'. Not just skills; not just skills that enable individuals to engage in a wide range of tasks and jobs; but skills that have demonstrable and successful effects: these are the desiderata of curriculum design.

We can now draw some initial conclusions from this sketch of the Enterprise Initiative. This book, it will be recalled, is an examination of the relationships between knowledge, higher education and society. My argument is that these relationships are changing. Putting it crudely (and despite the qualification at the beginning of Chapter 1), we are seeing a move from a situation of:

Higher education → knowledge → society

to a situation of:

Society → knowledge → higher education.

In the former situation – call it epistemic supremacy – definitions of knowledge were formed by the academic 'tribes and territories', and these reciprocally served to define the nature of higher education (as an initiation into the conversations of the academics); and that form of higher education was assumed to have a benefit for society, even if diffuse. Now we are moving to a situation in which the wider society is defining for higher education the forms of knowledge and being it deems valuable; and these in turn are serving to frame the character of higher education.

We have seen the signs of this latter movement in the Enterprise Initiative (and in the competence and outcomes movement). The state identifies the forms of knowing and development it sees as worthwhile and these messages are communicated to the higher education community, participating institutions being expected to find ways of bringing about curriculum change across all programmes of study. In this situation, academics become state servants, fulfilling the state's agenda. Transferable skills are a means of disenfranchising discipline-based academics of their expertise. The curriculum is framed and owned by the state. Higher education becomes part of the ideological state apparatus (Althusser, 1969b). The student's pedagogical identity is predetermined to fulfil instrumental ends of economic and state survival.

Higher Education for Capability

Higher Education for Capability has a different pedigree from the Enterprise Initiative. Sponsored by the Royal Society for the encouragement of Arts, Manufactures and Commerce, the ideas behind the scheme were first created by a mixed group of individuals, including educationalists but also others (Stephenson and Weil, 1992). In 1979, an initial 'manifesto' (as it was termed) lamented the presence of 'a serious imbalance in Britain today . . . described by the two words "education and training" '. It went on:

this imbalance is harmful to individuals, to industry and to society. A well balanced education should . . . include the exercise of creative skills, the competence to undertake and complete tasks and the ability to cope with everyday life; and also doing all these things in co-operation with others.

There exists in its own right a culture which is concerned with doing, making and organizing and the creative arts. This culture emphasizes the day-to-day management of affairs, the formulation and solution of problems and the design, manufacture and marketing of goods and services.

Educators should spend more time preparing people in this way for a life outside the education system. The country would benefit significantly in economic terms from what is here described as Education for Capability.

(Stephenson and Weil, 1992: xiii)

In this opening salvo, we find several themes echoing those that we have already encountered in the Enterprise Initiative. They include a sense that education is insufficiently responsive to the requirements of the wider society, particularly the economic sphere; a desire to shift the pedagogic journey to one of skill development; a belief that students are suffering some kind of deficit in their learning experience; and a focus on doing interpreted as achieving in the context of manufacturing industry.

Subsequently, in 1988, the Higher Education for Capability project was born, and the earlier general manifesto was given more substance. As with the Enterprise Initiative, we see no single definition: indeed, 'Capability does not lend itself to detailed definition.' However, as with Enterprise, we can identify a constellation of ideas. These include:

- [Giving students] confidence in their ability to (1) take effective and appropriate action; (2) explain what they are about; (3) live and work effectively with others and (4) continue to learn from their experiences.
- Taking effective and appropriate action within unfamiliar and changing circumstances [which] involves judgements, values, the self-confidence to take risks and a commitment to learn from the experience.
- [Giving] students confidence and ability to take responsibility for their own continuing personal and professional development.
- [Preparing] students to be personally effective within the circumstances of their lives and work.

(Stephenson and Weil, 1992: 1, 2)

All this points to a particular kind of pedagogy, the key idea of which is that students should 'have experience of being responsible and accountable for their own learning, within a rigorous and interactive environment'.

The pedagogic identity that Capability seeks to form is even more of a total identity compared with Enterprise. Whereas Enterprise looked to create a particular set of skills, capacities and attitudes (of an enterprising character), Capability seeks to invade wider spheres of the mind. 'Self-confidence to take risks and a commitment to learn from the experience' could equally have been drawn from an Enterprise manifesto, but recognizing values and taking responsibility for one's own learning are characteristically components of the Capability perspective. We are given a glimpse of autonomous persons, effective in the world of work (as with Enterprise), but here work is part of life and not entirely constitutive of it. In their 'lives and work', individuals will be forming their own value judgements, presumably about what they consider to be *proper* courses of action, within a framework of personal responsibility. The notion of personal responsibility points – as the quotation indicates – to a notion of personal accountability. It was a notion absent in the Enterprise Initiative: there, the criterion of success was all important.

Values, personal responsibility, collective endeavour and the life-world: these are vital elements of the Capability thinking that are absent from the Enterprise Initiative. The Capability person is a citizen of the world; the Enterprise person is more intent on seizing his main chance in the economy. But despite these differences, the two movements can be read as having much in common.

Conclusion: the total curriculum

Erving Goffman talked of the total institution, in which the identities of the inmates were entirely formed and sustained by the institution. Enterprise and Capability are attempts to reform the higher education curriculum into a total identity formation. We can enumerate some of the components of this claim. Both schemes:

1. are national in scope;
2. are intended to work across institutions as a whole;
3. gain a purchase at the curriculum level by being embedded in the mainstream of existing programmes of study;
4. attempt to dissolve boundaries between the world of higher education and the wider world;
5. look to unite mind and body, knowing and action;
6. assume a criterion of *successful* or *effective* action; of persons conceiving of possible effects of their actions and bringing them about;
7. believe that attitudes towards the external world are important aspects of student formation;
8. are intended to develop risk-taking as a personal capacity;
9. are intended to develop coping behaviours in a changing world;
10. broaden the definitions of right learning and knowing. The definitions of the knowing and learning required are now to be drawn from the wider world and imported into higher education.

Within each approach, therefore, higher education is to take responsibility for the total – or near total – formation of the student's development. The implicit charge contained in both schemes, that of the lack of responsiveness of higher education to the wider world, can be read as an unwillingness of higher education to cross the boundaries in selecting criteria and aims to determine the identity to be achieved by the students. With each programme, it is not so much a matter of society inserting itself into higher education, as of higher education being annexed to the wider society and of the student's formation becoming a function of others' agendas.

This can only be a matter for regret if we can show that criteria, definitions and aims characteristically internal to higher education both are being neglected and are worthwhile. Just this I shall argue in the next section of the book.

Part 3
The Lost Vocabulary

7

Understanding

Introduction

'Understanding' is a difficult term for contemporary advocates of a competence approach to education. It is either tacked on the end of the triple-
term phrase 'knowledge, skills and understanding' and then given *no* separate
treatment in what follows; *or* its problematic nature is admitted, but it is
then suggested that knowledge and understanding amount to the same
thing so no separate treatment is required in any case (Wolf, 1990). I shall
adopt the opposite tack and make the claim that, for higher education,
understanding is a central and *irreducible* concept.

More than mere knowledge

Understanding is a description of a mental state. The application of the
term requires a person of whom we might typically say 'she understands the
idea that so and so' or 'her understanding is weak'. What is being described
is the person's inner grasp of what is at issue. Understanding, accordingly,
is a description of a state of consciousness. In attributing understanding to
someone, we are doing more than we would in saying that he is able to
discriminate colours or even respond appropriately to a request to add two
and five. A mental state fulfilling certain demanding kinds of criteria is
being identified by the term 'understanding'. Further, our employing the
term is more than to offer a description, for the term is ineradicably evaluative in character. To say of x that she understands is to give high marks;
it is to say that her state of consciousness being described is a worthwhile
state of mind to be in.

That latter point, about the praiseworthiness of understanding, may be a
temporary matter. Up to now, in western culture, the cognitive state marked
out by the term 'understanding' has been felt to be deserving of praise.
Now we are seeing signs that understanding is less likely to count as a

virtuous state of mind. With public documents appearing which advocate state-sponsored initiatives in education and training and which either omit the term 'understanding' or suggest that its meaning can simply fall under other concepts, we are heading for a major shift in our understanding of understanding. Some will think that not much should be read into an omission of this kind. But this is not a case of absence making the heart grow fonder; or even of our retaining the idea but expressing it in different ways. What is before us is a pedagogical amnesia, a forgetting of one of the central concepts of the idea of the university.

We saw the beginnings of this claim in the earlier chapter on competence and will now pick up that story again. I want first to draw on a paper by R.F. Elliott, which appeared twenty years ago. (It remains, I believe, the most astute analysis of the concept of understanding available to us.) I quote one paragraph from the paper:

> There are a number of criteria for a person's having a fully developed understanding of a complex topic, e.g. Wittgenstein's philosophy. First, for an understanding to be perfect it must be a true or correct or valid understanding rather than a misunderstanding. Secondly, it must be a profound understanding – one which goes deep to fundamental principles, presuppositions and motivations. Thirdly, it must be comprehensive, not ignoring anything of significance. Fourthly, it must be synoptic, getting a view of the thing as a whole. Ideally, it will also relate this whole to ever broader backgrounds. Fifthly, it must be sensitive to hidden significances, delicate shifts of emphasis and nuances of expression. Sixthly, it must be critical: a person does not fully understand Wittgenstein's philosophy if he is blind to its errors, weaknesses and omissions, and to the possibility of alternative descriptions or explanations. Seventhly, it must be steady, not insecure or intermittent. Eighthly, it must be fertile or creative: a person does not really understand Wittgenstein's philosophy if he cannot begin to apply its principles to any topic unexamined by Wittgenstein. Appropriate evaluative response may be a further, ninth, criterion, since we might be reluctant to allow that anyone fully understood Wittgenstein's philosophy if he did not have even a grudging admiration for Wittgenstein's achievement. An understanding which is true, comprehensive, profound, synoptic, sensitive, fertile, critical, firm and justly appreciative would be a fully developed or excellent one. The characteristics named in this list are more or less separate virtues or excellences of understanding. In particular cases some may be present to a much higher degree than others.
>
> (Elliott, 1975: 47–8)

This account of understanding is helpful in a number of ways. Firstly, it shows that understanding is itself a complex. There are many strands to understanding; and the filling out of those strands will begin to fill out what we take higher education to be.

Secondly, we have here a long paragraph about understanding, making several discriminations in the concept, but which uses the term knowledge not once. On this account alone, therefore, the attempt of the competency lobby to reduce understanding to knowledge has to be suspect.

However, the concept of truth *is* invoked: to have an understanding of something is to have a sense of it which has validity. This point suggests another difference between competence and understanding: the criterion of competence is effectiveness whereas one criterion of understanding is truth. There may be implicit truth claims in actions that accompany claims to competence, but the underlying interest in competence is practical in character, not epistemological. What counts *essentially* is whether the competence has the desired outcome: 'Does it work?' is the key question; not 'Is it true?'

Thirdly, it is clear from Elliott's account that of the development of understanding – of anything really worth understanding – there need be no end. Understanding can always be deepened, widened, clarified further, refined, improved or set in different contexts. Understanding can always be changed. We can go on attaining deeper levels of understanding, seeing into a topic with ever greater insight; and we can go on broadening the way in which we see the topic, against a widening range of analytical perspectives. This continuing refinement of understanding is a contrast to the view that one either possesses a competence or one does not.

Fourthly, understanding, being a property of the human mind, has a double character. We can understand theories, ideas, actions, events, other human beings and our own bodies. But we can also take a view of our own understanding: we can evaluate it, criticize it, value it, and want to go on improving it. We can understand our own understanding. This is not a nice philosophical point. It is central to higher education. Whether we formalize the idea in self-assessment practices or whether we leave it more informal by encouraging students and helping them to be self-critical, developing this capacity of understanding their own understanding is at the heart of many academics' sense of their professional responsibilities towards their students.

Fifthly, deep understanding can be present without it being apparent to an external observer. If – as educators – we wish to be assured that a student has a clear understanding of a concept, we may invite her to engage in an action of some kind to reveal the extent or depth of that understanding. But understanding can be present without it being demonstrated. We cannot say the same for competence, since part of its essential meaning is an ability to perform in public settings.

Lastly, understanding is an active state of mind. To understand something is to take up a stance towards it. That being so, the stance is *bound* to be partly personal in character. Elliott mentions, as his sixth criterion, the attribute of being critical of the object in question. That is an essential condition of true understanding; but we need to distinguish being critical of an object and taking up a stance towards it.

To understand something is to see it as something; and since there can be no absolute perception, to see it as something is to see it in a certain way. A deep understanding exists where a person has a particularly clear perception. Although this cannot be a sufficient condition, a perception that supplies understanding has to be sharp and well-focused. To have such a perception is to bring an object into view, and to hold that view 'steady' (to use another of Elliott's terms). Understanding is necessarily an active state of mind.

One person's clear perception offering understanding will not be the same as someone else's. Here, we alight on another difference between understanding and competence. Whereas understanding is, in part, unique to each individual, we can talk reasonably enough of different people having similar competences. Indeed, that is one of the features of competence: to call forth reliable and bounded performances from different people. Competence is indifferent to persons. What difference is to understanding, sameness is to competence.

Freedom and necessity

To understand something is to act freely. To form a clear and insightful sense of a complex matter is to place one's own stamp on that insight. And placing one's own stamp on a perception, having one's own perception, is to perceive freely.

One cannot understand simply by taking over someone else's idea. One might entertain another's ideas or insights; one might play with them; or one might subscribe to them (and become 'a follower' of an intellectual celebrity). An understanding might be a pale reflection of the understandings of those in whose footsteps one follows. In such a case, virtually no mark will be left behind of one's intellectual strivings for one's own footprints will fit comfortably within the larger footprints of the earlier pathbreaker. The only mark left behind will be a slightly heavier imprint of the predecessor. Yet, whether producing a distinctive imprint or not, *if* real understanding has taken place, then we are witnessing an act of freedom.

There are two senses of freedom at work. Firstly, there is a *personal* aspect to cognitive freedom. Whether shallow or deep, elementary or profound, understanding requires a personal ownership of the insights in question. It makes no sense to say that that student understands this difficult theory when her hold on the theory amounts only to being able to repeat formulations of the theory already encountered. The student has to take into herself what she has seen and perform a mental act on it if understanding is to occur. In Piagetian language, assimilation has to be accompanied by accommodation. More colloquially, understanding requires that the student invests something of herself (as Richard Peters put it). One price of investment is risk. And one necessity of investment is that the student gives freely of herself. An act of freedom is entailed.

To understand something, at any level, is to make a claim. It is to say: this is my perception. It is not necessarily to assert distinctiveness or originality; it is to assert creativity and particularity.

I said a moment ago that this first sense of freedom is personal. I did not say that it is psychological. The difference is important.

Elliott pointed to a validity criterion. The concept of understanding is connected with the concept of truth, though the two concepts are not identical. We would be misusing the term if we were to say that that student has a firm understanding of his topic but unfortunately his work on it is covered in errors.

In the work of writers in diverse camps, truth has recently come to be seen as a process rather than an outcome. Truth is less the result of a pursuit (a correspondence with reality or a coherence with other established truths) than the pursuit itself. The pursuit is not, so the story runs, conducted by individuals. The old image of the idiosyncratic professor either lost in his own thoughts or burying himself in the laboratory was misleading. What is characteristic of a form of life orientated towards truth is that it is necessarily conversational. Truths are truth *claims*, at best the latest view attracting support from others already in the know. There can be no private truth. That there are views to which we can attach the title 'truth' – if only for now – indicates the presence of some degree of consensus on the topic. No consensus: no truth.

There is a paradox here. Understanding is linked to truth. Truth is intersubjective. Yet understanding is an assertion of freedom. It is to say: this is where I stand. Understanding is both an expression of independence *and* is necessarily linked to others' viewpoints. One cannot have an understanding which no-one understands; that is, takes it seriously as a possible understanding. The creative moment in authentic understanding is necessarily accompanied by ties to a wider network of viewpoints. Understanding is both freedom and necessity.

How might the paradox be unravelled? One tempting solution must be rejected. It may be the case that one's own understanding is sharpened, is brought into focus, by the comments of others. We are familiar enough with the experience in which colleagues help us in coming anew to our drafts, and often enable us to see something which was near at hand but which never quite came into the centre of our vision. This is an important part of the conversational character of intellectual life and links the personal with the intersubjective, but it is a largely psychological point which does not reach the heart of the issue before us.

The link between independence of mind and the necessity of intersubjectivity is logical. Understanding is an understanding of something. That something will be an entity in the world. But our access to it is through the ideas, theories, accounts and stories that already exist about it: the first task is to grapple with those understandings that are available. In the process, those understandings undergo a transformation in our own minds. The clearer *our* understanding, the more we develop a viewpoint of our own and the less it is reliant on another's viewpoint, even if there is a close resemblance. Having been taken up into our own schemas, and having become part of a network of ideas in our own mind, it will be psychologically free of others' understandings. But it will retain its ontological anchoring in those ideas; and it will be perceived as a valid understanding by others in terms of that anchoring. They in turn, in order to value it as an understanding, will need to be able to take it up and to relate it to their own schemas.

There is a dialectic at work. One's understanding is an understanding of others' understandings; and one's understanding counts as an understanding in virtue of its finding a resonance in others' understandings. However, there is a potential for slippage. One can gain an understanding by listening to and participating in the conversations of others. But one's understanding can be granted the status of understanding by yet another set of others. The first lot of others may dismiss what one has got to say while the second lot of others may feel that it is casting an entirely new light on things; *their* things, that is.

To express the dialectic another way, one's intellectual freedom is won on the back of others and one cannot ever entirely be free from others; *some* others, at least. To have an understanding is to assert one's independence of view but it is also to pass muster with others. Just as (so we learnt from Wittgenstein) there can be no private language, so there can be no entirely independent understandings.

Mind the gap

The second sense of freedom that characterizes understanding is epistemological, being connected with the status of an understanding. Specifically, understanding carries within it an essentially critical moment.

To form an understanding of something is to form *an* understanding of it. An understanding can never be absolute or totally comprehensive. It is always possible to add to the understanding.

It follows that there is bound to be a gap between the understanding and that which is being understood. We can never fully grasp the object of our understanding. A pessimist might call this the bad news. The good news is that since an understanding is a particular understanding, it has its own distinctiveness. Every student's understanding of even elementary matters will be distinctive.

We have already recollected that understanding can always be deepened or widened. Understanding can move from a superficial or partial level to a profound level. The metaphor of level is instructive, because it implies that one can rise above one's initial understanding. On gaining a higher level of understanding, one can take a view of one's hesitating early attempts to understand. Understanding contains the possibility of meta-understanding, that of understanding or evaluating one's own past understandings.

Understanding, therefore, can become a matter of self-critique. Students can engage in a process of self-assessment; and often, when they do, they are their own severest critics.

There is, though, another sense in which understanding is connected to critique and most of the ingredients for this next claim are to hand. Understanding, we have seen, is necessarily *an* understanding; there is an epistemological gap between understanding and its object; an understanding is bound to be distinctive; and understanding can, strata-like, exist at high levels connected with but building on others' understandings. If we put these points together, we can see another sense of critique. Precisely because an understanding is particular, is one perspective on a topic and is separate from the object being understood, understanding is inherently critical of its object.

Expressing an understanding is tantamount to saying: see the topic in this way, not in that or the other way. It is evaluative, immediately, of those other possible understandings. But it is evaluative of its object as well. An understanding says: this object is this kind of entity, not some other kind. Possible interpretations are ruled in while others are ruled out. An understanding is a classification of its object. It is an implicit evaluation.

Higher education likes to deny this point. Value freedom is its watchword. Analysis and interpretation, yes; evaluation, no. Part of the difficulty is the defensiveness of higher education towards anything smacking of values. The trouble is that higher education operates with too limited a sense of the range of evaluations. Remarking that a strawberry has a sweet taste is not to make an ethical evaluation. It is, though, to do more than simply describe the strawberry. It is implicitly to form an evaluation of it. The understanding is both interpretative and evaluative. This simple example has analogies in any discipline studied in higher education. The students' interpretations will carry within them implicit evaluations. The acts of judging, classifying, ordering and analysis are implicitly evaluative.

In human-orientated disciplines, understanding is critical in yet another sense. Understanding in the social sciences or the humanities does more than say: see things in this way. If the practice in question has an infinite number of readings, as it will have, the practice illuminated by an understanding takes on a sense that things could be other than they are. Its practitioners, sensing that infinite variability of interpretation, will also begin to have a sense that their practices could be other than they are. So, in the human disciplines, developing understanding is inherently a subversive activity.

Against these reflections, the near absence of the concept of understanding in so many government documents on higher education takes on an ideological tinge. Its omission is not just a sign of temporary amnesia. The amnesia is structural and explicable. The operationalism of competence is what is required, not the critical edge that understanding would bring.

Levels of engagement

To understand a difficult idea, in any discipline, the student has to yield to the concreteness of the idea. The idea exists outside the student, and the student has to get on the inside of the idea. In anything more than super-ficial understanding, the student will eventually find herself on the inside of the idea, able to see it this way and that way. There has, therefore, to be a lived quality to understanding; it has to have an existential character. Richard Peters (1966) talked of a change in cognitive perspective. That is a necessary ingredient of developing an understanding, but it does not tell the full story. If understanding involves a changed outlook on the world, even if just on the topic or idea in question, it will also involve a new relation between the student and her world. However cerebral and abstract the understanding will appear, there is a lived component to real understanding. Understanding invades the life-world. Through his intellectual work, Stephen Hawking *lives* in a different world from most others; he does not just think in a different way. His hold on life is different, owing to his understanding of the cosmos.

Since, in higher education, we cannot predict exactly what changes in understanding will result from the students' learning experiences, we can-not entirely anticipate what existential changes will occur. But changes there will be, or should be. An educator's work has been done when the student says at the end of a course, or even during it, that 'This course has changed me' or 'I see things quite differently now'. The student is not saying just that her thinking has changed or that her behaviour has changed, but that she has changed. The concept of competence cannot accommodate this kind of existential quality of understanding. But that is a problem for the advocates of competence, not for the educator.

Understanding, we have been saying, is necessarily *personal understanding*. No-one else can reach the student's understanding for her. But the idea of personal understanding has point, too, in another way.

Michael Polanyi (1962) developed the idea of 'personal knowledge' as the basis of an attack on the scientistic notion that real knowledge is public and objective in character. For Polanyi, especially among those who are deeply on the inside of a form of life (such as academics), there is a large element of 'indwelling'. The individual so lives a form of life, and is so immersed in it, that much of what is known – known deeply and utterly – is *tacit* and unformulated. As Polanyi saw it, it is precisely through the deep-seated but largely unnoticed sub-strata of such personal knowledge that individuals are able to build up their knowledge of newly encountered entities. On the basis of our previous experiences and now-taken-as-given knowledge so derived, we can focus our attention on what is in front of us: we 'attend from' what we already know (and can therefore take that as given) and address the present object of our attentions.

Polanyi's contribution here has been to point out that understanding has different layers. Our understanding of situations is both acute and vivid *and* dim and shadowy. We see someone we have not seen for some time and immediately recognize the person. Our understanding of 'x' as 'x' is present and lively. But our understanding of the crowded train in which we recognize our friend is much less present to our senses, being entirely familiar and redundant to the object of our attention. We do not notice many of the features of the train carriage or its other occupants, although they are real enough. For such levels of engagement, we are better off using the term 'personal understanding' rather than Polanyi's 'personal knowledge'.

This discussion has several implications. In higher education, we are attempting both to add further layers of understanding and to prize open layers of understanding laid down in a person's mind perhaps some time ago. The metaphors of depth and height come to mind in the context of higher education precisely because understanding has this multi-layered character.

This discussion also sheds further light on the notion of competence. For any one competence, as we noticed, assessment is a matter of whether the competence exists; of whether or not the specified standards have been satisfied. Understanding, at least of anything of complexity, cannot be like this. The multi-layered character of understanding means that we can always ask a student: 'Tell me more; where does that thought take you? What more can you say about that? How further might you explain this matter? Can you supply anything further by way of analysis or interpretation?'

The rejoinder may come that this is all very similar to competence. Our expectations of a person's competence in a situation can be higher or lower; and, after all, the NCVQ has sorted competence into five levels of complexity. However, this rejoinder misses the point: a person's understanding of any issue or situation or entity or idea is itself a complex and *at any one time* exists at different levels and in a range of mental structures. The NCVQ approach to competence is clear: competence is all or nothing. Either one can hit the nail on the head or one can't. Either one can meet the pre-identified standards or one can't. Understanding, however, is quite a different kind of concept. At any time, a student's understanding of an issue is expressible in an infinite variety of ways, many of which will surprise the student herself. The student will have multiple engagements and be more *and* less engaged in them all at once.

Understanding and discovery

Unlike competency, in the approach to curriculum design in which the idea of understanding takes centre stage, the educational process is all-important. Some of the reasoning behind this claim has already become clear. Understanding is transactional in character, depending in part on the warrant of others; it has a validity component, so it has to be tested to see if it is a true understanding; and it can be built up over time, so it becomes both deeper and higher, enabling individuals to take a view of their own understanding. But there is another sense in which the process of developing understanding is important.

In advancing a student's understanding, the educator's role in higher education is twofold. The first requirement is to help the student to appreciate that there are alternative ways of understanding an issue or of approaching a complex task (in mathematics, say). This role has the educator as subversive. The main purpose is to lessen the hold that any one form of understanding has on the student. To put it another way, it is to develop the stages of relativistic thinking and then commitment that, for Perry (1970, 1988), constitute the higher stages of intellectual development among students. The student comes to realize that there are always counter-claims that can be brought against any one position, but is still able to transcend that stage and go on to take up a reasoned position of her own. The educator's task is to promote an understanding that is held, perhaps with some passion, but against a deeper understanding that this *is* a particular position that might have to be yielded sometime; as Goodlad (1976) put it, to develop a state of 'authoritative uncertainty'. One's understanding might change tomorrow. (To say one's competence might change tomorrow would be a near absurdity.)

This is not a content-based form of understanding but a dispositional form of understanding. The challenge to the educator lies in bringing about this dispositional change; and, for that, careful attention must be paid to the educational process. A dispositional change calls for lengthy processes gently encouraging the intended forms of intellectual development. Here is another fundamental difference between a competency-based programme and one intended to bring about deep changes in understanding. Competence eschews any concern with processes; for understanding, the process is paramount.

We have seen that understanding is not an all-or-nothing affair. Simultaneously, understanding of anything complex has gradations, limitations, particular strengths, murky patches, and perhaps daring insights. This is possible because of the multilayered and multidirectional character of understanding. But we can challenge the all-or-nothing description in a more profound way.

We have already seen that understanding has a dialogical character. For understanding to count *as* understanding, it has to be tested on others and to gain at least someone's assent somewhere. We have also noticed that, very often, we are not always fully aware that we possess certain understandings. As Polanyi (1966: 8) put it, 'One can know more than one can tell.' If we bring these two points together and add them to the educator's tasks we have just alluded to, another task begins to form. It is that one of the educator's tasks in higher education is to help students become aware of understandings that they possess but of which they are unaware.

The notion of experiential learning has quickly taken a place in the higher education lexicon over recent years. It is something of a weasel term, being unclear, susceptible to different meanings, and attractive to groups with markedly contrasting agendas. It is also incoherent since *all* learning has to derive from some kind of experience: it is either stating the obvious or trying to demarcate certain kinds of experience as especially worthwhile. Even so, the idea of experiential learning does contain the important truth that we learn things and come to know things without always being aware that we have learnt and that we know. That is why much time is spent, where experiential learning is prized, in getting individuals to reflect on their experience so as to identify and bring into full consciousness what it is that they have learnt.

If that is a legitimate technique for those who have had 'prior experiences' upon which to reflect, then it also serves as a prompt for our efforts as educators in general. For students will have had some relevant experiences to the topic in question and, therefore, some kind of understanding: it may be rudimentary and may even contain some degree of error, but it is likely to be more than the student senses she understands. So another role of the educator must lie in helping the students to search their understandings and to bring out what already lies there. The educator is not, in the first place, adding anything, but is inviting the student to search her understandings to bring to the surface an understanding buried at a deep level.

Through reflection or dialogue (for instance, structured group discussion among students), students come to see that they understand more than they realize. Their understanding can grow without any particular unit of knowledge being put their way. This, again, is possible through the multi-layered and dialogical character of understanding. The educator's challenge is to enable as much of the student's understanding that is in the mind, but in an inchoate state, to form coherently and to be fully transparent to the student. The student's confidence grows because she realizes that she understood something worthwhile all along.

Coming to an understanding is, in large part, a matter of discovery; of discovering what one already, although tacitly, understands. Coming to an understanding is less a matter of appropriating external offerings and experiences than it is a case of *self-discovery*. Coming to an understanding is an expression of one's own agency.

Understanding is not a zero-sum entity. It is neither limited in quantity, being passed from educator to student; nor is it limited in the mind of the student. To a large extent, more than we commonly acknowledge at any rate, the student can educate herself. The process of higher education consists as much in making explicit to oneself and putting into some kind of order one's own inner hidden understandings as it does in taking on new understandings. Nor are the two forms of development separate. All the time on a programme of study, students will be acquiring new understandings – through their reading, their interactions with other students, their lectures, their laboratory sessions and their training placements – all of which will be leaving an unacknowledged deep deposit of 'understandings'. Space needs to be found in a programme to enable these unformed and

weak awarenesses to be discovered and to be turned into explicit understandings, over which the student has control.

Conclusion: Understanding and enlightenment

Understanding, I have been urging, is active, is an engagement, is a form
of agency, and is a form of self-expression. It is an expression of individuality; and it strikes against the conventionalism of competence, insofar as
competency is a fulfilment of standards determined in advance.

Since understanding is personal and has to be owned by the individual,
we cannot predict in advance any particular understanding a student may
frame for herself. It will be distinctive, come what may. No other understanding on earth will be identical. It may be so unusual that we may grant
the designation 'original' to it. The undergraduate may end up producing
a paper in the literature. Her understanding may overtake that of her
lecturers.

Given this openness in the idea, an education orientated to producing
real understanding is subversive. Indeed, the educator has to be prepared
to be educated; and many bear testimony to this education in the acknowledgement 'to my students' in the front of their books.

But this potential points to another subversive force at work. To have an
institution in society of this kind, in which the developmental outcomes
must contain large elements of uncertainty and may turn out to challenge
conventional understandings, is subversive at the societal level. Whether
such outcomes are regular, or frequent, is immaterial. The point is that the
university is an institution for fostering unpredictable outcomes. Provided
that this kind of university can be maintained, society will contain an element of openness in one of its dominant institutions. The students' emer-
gent understandings just may help to exert a rational scrutiny of society's
self-understandings.

There are, then, in the concept of understanding, two levels of enlightenment at work. In coming to an understanding, the student is necessarily
enlightened. The ocular metaphor is potent. Recalling Plato's cave, the
student comes into the light, as it were. She comes to see things with a clear
apperception. More than clarity of vision is at stake, however. A true
understanding is attained partly through being tested in dialogue with and
by gaining the assent of others. Understanding is backed, therefore, by
reason. Enlightenment is based on reason grasped by the individual for
herself.

But alongside this personal sense of enlightenment, there is the societal
sense. In earlier chapters, we remarked on the idea of the learning society.
One of the components of a learning society is a society in which understanding is growing. The university, as a social institution organized for the
advancement of understanding (that is, students' personal understanding),
helps directly to widen and deepen society's understandings as graduates

make their way in the world. This is one good reason (there are many specious ones) for increasing the student numbers. The proportion of enlightened minds – in the particular sense used here – in the general population is increased, and society's understandings are directly enhanced. But the university also promotes societal understanding more indirectly.

In reminding society that its cognitive orderings are always susceptible to scrutiny, the role of the university teacher is honourable in a connected sense. Not in terms of his or her individual efforts, but as part of a collectivity which together holds up for review the cognitive structure of society. The university is a supremely sceptical institution, refusing to take anything on trust.

Understanding does not kow-tow; it does not defer; it does not accept willy-nilly others' agendas. True understanding is tough and resilient. What counts is the better argument. True understanding is also not afraid to adopt an attitude of humility. Yet in saying 'I don't understand' or 'Help me to understand that point', one looks for a further substantiation. In turn, in that further substantiation, the base of reasoning is deepened or widened in general. The drive for personal understanding assists understanding in general.

Our starting point observed that understanding is a difficult term for the advocates of a competency-based approach to education. Competency stands for a prior determination of outcomes and of standards; it is a form of imposition. The fostering of real understanding can be none of these things. Since understanding has to contain elements of openness and evaluation, all the educator's starting points – aims, outcomes, intended mental states and even the standards – have to be provisional. The educatees can and do educate the educated.

Through understanding, personal enlightenment grows, as does society's understanding of itself. At best, competence will confine us to our present understandings; and, through its operationalism will, over time, come to confine even those. For understanding, read openness; for competence, read closure.

8

Critique

Introduction

Of critical thinking, we hear just a little in our contemporary age. Of critical thought, we hear even less. Of critique, we hear virtually nothing at all.

The world of work is ambivalent over critical thinking. For the most part, it is silent on the matter. Recently, however, critical thinking has begun to be seen by the corporate sector as part of the repertoire of the human capital to be supplied by higher education. Representatives of large corporations, at least, can be heard to say that they value critical thinking in the graduates they employ.

In the academic community, academics frequently proclaim their adherence to critical thinking as one of their main educational aims. Indeed, the promotion of critical thinking might be said to be a shorthand summary of what academic teachers see themselves in business for. Precisely what academics mean by this aim is rarely spelt out, however, even by the self-critical academics themselves.

Among educationalists – those members of the academic community who enjoy livings through critically reflecting on education – there has been for some time, especially in the USA, something of a critical thinking industry. Many of them, faced with a mass higher education system, are intent on developing critical thinking among undergraduates. It is hardly surprising if those paid to think of matters Educational – with a capital 'E' as it were – hold fast to the idea that there is a form of thinking that can be isolated and developed under the banner of critical thinking. Such a move supplies legitimacy for the educationalists to corner the critical thinking market, independently of the subject specialists. We can see the beginnings of such an interest developing in UK higher education.

The agendas of the first and the third of these interest groups come together in the notion of critical thinking *skills*.

Critical thinking in the world of work

For the world of work, critical thinking skills seem to promise an additional capacity in the graduate employees' repertoire of behaviours. They seem to offer a way of injecting additional power and capacity into the employers' human resources; and in two ways. Firstly, they bring, so it seems, a *new form* of productive capacity into human labour. Through its powers of critical thinking, the graduate workforce is no longer limited to the here and now. New possibilities – in design, production, product, service or customer – can be envisaged. New worlds can be created. The productive capacity can be multiplied, without additional input from the corporation. The workforce multiplies its own productive potential. Critical thinking skills take on the appearance of a form of continuous energy: they promise something for nothing.

Secondly, critical thinking skills offer a new form of flexibility among the labour force. Through critical thinking, more efficient strategies for meeting defined tasks are forthcoming. But more than that, through being encouraged to furnish those alternative strategies, human labour becomes a more flexible resource. Provided some of its creative ideas are taken up, a sense of identity with the enterprise will grow. In turn, as other ideas are produced – by others – so there will be a greater readiness to fall in with them; after all, one's own idea might be the next one to be taken up.

All this amounts to improving the total adaptability and productive power of the corporation in toto. The hope is that a kind of exponential momentum of creativity and human energy can be generated, and without intervention from on high. The labour force becomes self-adaptive; it provides its own cybernetic dynamic. However, this is a particular form of critical thinking.

Firstly, it is task-orientated. It is integrally linked to work, but work of a certain character, that of structured organizations having goals external to their operations (of profit-making, expansion, mere survival, or domination over competitors). This is not the work of the craftsman or even of the professional in command of his own labour: in those cases, work is determined and owned by the worker and has internal point and value. The mission of the corporation has no internal point.

In that milieu, critical thinking necessarily takes on a particular hue. The purpose of the critical thinking lies outside itself. The criterion of the worth of that kind of critical thinking is its success in bringing about more effective operations of the organization, effectiveness being determined in terms of the organization's goals. This form of critical thinking has to be seen for what it is, as a form of instrumental reason.

Secondly, particular thought items claiming the title of 'critical' might be produced by individuals, but in being orientated to tasks and operations owned by the corporation, and being judged in its effects on them, this form of critical thinking has its life in the corporation. Once produced, this thinking has no existence of its own. Either it is taken up by the corporation immediately or it is stillborn. This critical capacity is owned by the organization, not by the individuals who gave birth to the thought in question.

This form of critical thought does not offer the prospect of self-enlightenment to the individuals whose thinking generates it. It cannot do so. Organizational success is its aim.

Thirdly, in being concerned with external success, this critical thinking has a strategic role: not so much winning friends and influencing people (for that would confine it to the personal sphere) but more a matter of winning for and by the organization. What is being pursued is ultimately a kind of organizational domination. The task of critical thinking is to bring that domination ever nearer. Even organizational survival is a form of domination, since the corporation's survival presages another corporation's demise.

Fourthly, the critical thinking sought is a form of skill, and the term 'critical thinking skills' is often enough invoked.

The use of the term skill is particularly telling. Some point to the routinization of tasks and operations as being characteristic of skills. That may or may not be the case. Skills do not have to refer to identical operations. There is, though, a necessary ingredient of reliability, of performing within a range of acceptability and of meeting certain minima. There is a significant tension, therefore, between the ideas of critical thought and of skills. Critical thought – and particularly so in its radical form of critique – implies the possibility of breaking through any cognitive boundaries that may be present. Acquiring 'skills' necessarily implies that some criteria of skilfulness are present and have to be taken as given.

'Critical thinking skills', therefore, is a contradiction in terms. Its use in the corporate world is entirely understandable. The corporate world welcomes the boundary-breaking that critical thinking offers, but only up to a point. It shrinks from fundamental boat-overturning critique. In the end, critical thinking in the corporate world must be confined within manageable and predictable limits. But to do this is to bar real critical thinking.

The last characteristic of critical thinking in work extends that point. The barriers to critical thought can be quite insidious.

The organization has, we are frequently told, its own culture. The up side is an insistence on a sensitivity to organizational idiosyncrasy: the management of change has to take account of the particular culture to hand. The down side is that of norms and values imposing limits on the expression of any individuality as such. Those unspoken norms and values impose a pretty rigid framework on even the *utterance* of ideas.

Critical thinking may be desired; even welcomed. But limits are placed on it. It mustn't get out of hand. Critical thinking directed at the managing director's performance, the ethical character of the corporation's policies, the scope given to shareholders, the donation given to a political party, or which is aimed at the fundamental structure of decision-making: these kinds of critical thinking are not often encouraged. It is not for thoughts of this kind that the suggestions box is provided. Even critical thinking that, prima facie, seems to be within the corporation's own self-definition may, in practice, be off limits. An innovation may promise enhanced market share or even improved quality (Schon, 1982) but, if its implementation strikes at the in-house power structures or the received wisdom in doing things, it may equally receive short shrift.

In work, therefore, critical thinking is, at best, welcomed within limits. It has a certain scope: a set of boundaries in its forms, its analytic power, and its ideological force. One has to avoid being too clever by half.

Critical thinking and higher education

I have suggested that we are seeing signs of a common agenda developing between the worlds of work and education over critical thinking. And I have just argued that the underlying conception of critical thinking characteristic of the world of work is one of predictability, limits, boundedness, external criteria, and of effectiveness in producing external effects; in short, of instrumental reason. If this argument is to be sustained, a comparable analysis has now to be developed for academe.

Universities are becoming organizations and are beginning to exhibit the tendencies towards closure just picked out. As organizations, universities welcome or tolerate a degree of internal critique. But it has to be kept within limits; and this holds for both new and older universities. In both cases, it has to respect the traditions of the institution and it has to remain comparatively mute in the context of the new managerialism. Both kinds of institution will have their dominant, though markedly different, ways of going on; and critique had better know its limits.

Should the university invest in non-green or non-ethical shares? Should the university that has prided itself on the high A-level scores of its entrants lower its standards (as it may seem) and tangle with the assessment of prior experiential learning? Should the university accept research money from corporations that insist on retaining control over the findings and prevent publication in the journals? Might the university move towards a policy of ensuring that all its teaching staff gained some exposure to a programme aimed at improving their teaching effectiveness? Might the university bring students into academic decision-making in general, especially in the evaluation and redesign of the courses they are taking? Simply to ask some of these questions in many universities will run against the dominant interests and be the kinds of question that are better not asked. In other universities, different rules of the game may be followed; but some rules of the game there will be.

Certainly, universities have changed their policies on all those matters, even universities with long traditions. Even so, as organizations, universities retain a dominant culture within which the sheer posing of certain questions is unwelcome. The unwelcome questions will vary according to the 'mission', culture and traditions of the institution. Resistance to critique is by no means restricted to traditional universities. To wonder aloud in some newer universities whether a relatively open access policy or a modular curriculum framework is an unqualified good may also invite more than a raised eyebrow.

What is felt as critique varies, then, across universities. What is taken as given in one will rock the boat in another. In general, he who dares to put his head above the parapet and declare a position entirely counter to the vice-chancellor's had better have his forces well-positioned. To show, amid a university's demand that its staff should be heavily in the business of generating research income, that one has other values in academic life, is brave or foolhardy – unless one has other comparable goods to offer. To go even further and to argue, in *that* university, that (for example) the generation of research monies may just skew the university from the un-fettered pursuit of truth – if only because today's benefactors want some particular kinds of return for their money – would not be heard with any seriousness; and may not be heard with any politeness. Simply making the argument would appear to undermine the values that had become the driving motor of the university as an organization.

As organizations, universities are taking on the characteristics of organizational life in the wider society. That has long been the case. But the modern university, subject to the claims, financial uncertainties and inspections visited on it by the wider society, is more of a corporation than its earlier counterparts.

Staff are more definitely employees, with particular kinds of contract; their productions and activities are owned more by the university; they are required to work more in teams; more time is spent in negotiation with colleagues; an individual's own work is subject more to scrutiny and evaluation by colleagues (through staff appraisal, research ratings exercises and the establishment of course review systems); and financial considerations bear on many facets of the academic life. In so many different ways, academics are expected to take on a public persona in the university, and to identify with its larger project and mission. For yesterday's academic man, read today's organization person.

In this university of the new age, just as in organizations in the wider society, critique is bounded. Critique is valued if it is seen to be working in support of the university's declared (or even undeclared) mission. The university, as with private corporations, is having to succeed in a competitive environment. The boat cannot be rocked, at least not violently. Letters to the press may be scrutinized in advance; there can be no whistle-blowing in public. The relentless pursuit of truth has its limits, especially where the university's own sense of self-worth and direction is concerned.

In these circumstances, regret is hardly an appropriate response. The new managerialism will not lightly be dislodged from its task. The university, as a matter of fact, has taken on the character of an organization. What is unclear is whether the value-set underpinning the western university – of independent thought and speech, communicative reason, the dogged pursuit of truth, and evaluation of received wisdom – can serve still to provide a base for this new kind of institution.

The student as critical thinker

It is too soon to write an epitaph for critical thinking in the curriculum. Or if we do so, we would have to recognize its apparent re-emergence, albeit in different guise.

The curriculum is being professionalized. The days of the amateur are over. No longer is it *de rigueur* for lecturers without any formal educational background to put a bill of fare before the students. Careful thought has to go into the intended experience. The ends, the means, the technology of delivery, the learning experiences, the learning environment: all these, with their in-built changes in the higher education lexicon, have to be addressed separately.

Accordingly, critical thinking becomes just one aim among many. It has to fight its place among problem-solving, experiential learning, communications skills, groupwork, computer-aided learning, independent study, peer tutoring, enterprise-related tasks and so on. If critical thinking is re-membered, then – in this pedagogical genre – it will have to be addressed seriously. Efforts will have to be made to introduce students to the idea of critical thinking, and exercises carefully designed to develop these skills.

Critical thinking is dead; long live . . . It seems as if, under this regime, critical thinking may have an even *more* definite place in higher education. The international research on student learning and the low level of concep-tual understanding it has revealed, even among those achieving honours degrees, suggests that critical thinking was often more respected in the breach than in the attainment (Marton, 1984; Ramsden, 1992). Now, at last, critical thinking can be given explicit attention. Academics will be obliged to pay due deference to its development among their students.

However, there is critical thinking and there is critical thinking. Jurgen Habermas got it wrong; and implicitly admitted it. In his early magisterial work, *Knowledge and Human Interests*, he depicted critical reason as one of three dominant modes of thought, alongside instrumental or scientistic thought and thought orientated towards mutual understanding. Always more optimistic than his predecessors in the Institute for Social Research (such as Adorno, Horkheimer and Marcuse), Habermas believed that it was pos-sible to found a firm basis for a form of thinking outside the dominant positivism of the modern age. In that early work, the source of that alter-native rationality was located in critique.

The reason that this early foray had to be an unpromising tack is that every form of reason can be said to contain its own form of critique. If we do not posit the possibility of critique of some form, we cannot be said to be in the presence of reason. The question is what kind of critique is per-mitted: is it to be confined or relatively open? Positivism, scientific thought, bureaucratic modes of thinking, and managerialism of the current age all allow critique, but confined within certain limits. All modes of thought and action take place within frameworks; and their associated forms of critique are obliged to keep within those frameworks.

Karl Popper once referred (1970) to 'the myth of the framework'. He accepted, as the relativists were fond of pointing out, that all thought (and, we can add, action) takes place within some kind of framework. But, argued Popper, we are not thereby destined to be confined forever within those frameworks. The framework, too, can be examined, although Popper equivocated over whether only on a piecemeal basis or in toto. The problem that Popper evaded, and which lay behind Habermas' classification of cognitive structures, is that the practical rules of a particular framework all too often forbid a fundamental examination of the framework itself. To do so would be to run counter to the culture of the framework. The framework is continually having to be negotiated and lived: simply living within the framework is demanding enough (as Kuhn implied). The framework cannot easily be put in the dock without jeopardizing the whole enterprise.

When, therefore, we hear academics insisting on the importance of critical thinking among their students, there are questions to be asked about the seriousness with which academics take their own rhetoric. Are the students offered an educational experience in which they are encouraged to stretch their legs – intellectually speaking – and engage in their own evaluations of what they encounter? Are they forming a sense that it is their own thinking that counts, and that they should be keeping their own critical distance from all they experience on their course? Are they being given the confidence to form their own ideas and judgements and take up their own stances? A pedagogy of this kind requires that students be given both space, in which to form their own insights, *and* support, so as to achieve the confidence necessary for forming a viewpoint of their own when surrounded by the often intimidating weight of authority, in the tangible form of their lecturers and the library shelves (backed up by the computer catalogue).

These are important questions and increasingly so in an age of mass higher education. It is unclear whether the press of student:staff ratios is leading to the shrinking of the student's intellectual space and, by extension, space for critical reflection. There are also empirical questions to be raised about the extent to which quality assessment and the use of performance indicators such as non-completion rates and degree performance might lead to pedagogies that foster reproducing learning strategies on the part of the learner. It just may be that teachers and managers, seized with a heightened awareness of such performance indicators, will develop teaching approaches that present the student with a highly controlled learning environment. In this environment, risk will be minimized; learning will be safe, efficient, reliable and predictable. Critical thought will be squeezed out. There will be less failure or non-completion; but the scope for individual intellectual daring and personal initiative will also have been reduced.

Intellectual space

The notion of intellectual space may offer a fruitful way of analysing the contemporary changes in the higher education curriculum. That space can be interpreted psychologically: Does the student *feel* encouraged to branch out on her own? It can be interpreted pedagogically: Is the curriculum intended to promote personal risk-taking and independent thought? And it can be interpreted sociologically and epistemologically.

The sociological alternative?

If academics feel themselves to be at home in a particular framework, that comfort factor will spill over into their pedagogy. Pedagogical relationships will be fine so long as the student shows that she buys the academic's agenda, his set of problems, methodologies and dominant perspective. But in that culture, with those discipline-based and even intradiscipline-based boundaries, the student would be wise not to show too much interest in another form of intellectual life. Still less should she suggest in her conversations, whether in the lecture room or more privately, that there might be alternative and *equally legitimate* ways of looking at this problem. Resistance will be felt, the resistance of the sub-culture feeling that its way of looking at the world is being threatened.

If there are other equally valid perspectives, at the very least that will lessen the strength of this one. To admit as much is equivalent to admitting that there are other faiths that are just as worthwhile, even while I believe in *this* faith. The reason that that is unlikely is that that perspective requires the ability to step outside the framework and it is just that freedom that is withdrawn by the internal culture of a framework. An alternative *Weltanschauung* is rarely on offer.

Finding room for an epistemological edge

There is a necessary epistemological gap between a truth claim and any evaluation of it. The criteria framing the truth claim do not *have* to be the same as those framing the truth evaluation. The heated disputes of academic life are often of this sort: the parties to the debate talk across each other because they are working under different epistemic criteria. Major disputes within disciplines such as English literature, history, philosophy, psychology, geography and quantum physics turn on rival sets of fundamental concepts and theories. There is no rational way of deciding between the competing paradigms (Kuhn). The dominant assumptions of the disputants as to what a theory or a well-founded proposition is, or the way in which it is to be evaluated, turn out to be radically different. Consequently, even within a single discipline, the criteria by which a proposition is to be judged do not accompany the proffering of the proposition. The proposer is not free to determine in advance the ways in which others may come at his offering.

This point is linked to earlier points about frameworks (this chapter) and about understanding (Chapter 7). Frameworks are not given; they are not uncontroversial. We can always step outside the framework in which a proposition has its natural home and we can try looking at the phenomenon from a different point of view. Our understanding can be challenged; and radically so.

This is a characteristic of a genuinely *higher* education. Are students encouraged to recognize that what counts as truth can be viewed and evaluated from a number of perspectives? The available frameworks are not confined to the host discipline. It is entirely possible and may well be worthwhile to view or situate a scientific truth claim in a historical framework (Has this always been the case? How were phenomena such as this seen a hundred years ago?); or a sociological framework (What social interests might a theory of this kind serve? Why has this idea come forward at this time?); or a philosophical framework (What is the evidential basis for a truth claim of this kind? What assumptions and fundamental interests lie behind the framework in which the theory is offered?); or an aesthetic framework (To what extent does this theory meet the principle of economy? Is its relationship with the phenomenon it explains one of simplicity? Are terms like elegance, élan, daring, insightful, risky, profound, wit and so on at all helpful in characterizing this account?) (cf. Goodlad and Hughes, 1992).

Critical thought, therefore, has an epistemological *edge*. It places its object. It sets it *in* a framework. Critique asserts that no framework has priority, even if we cannot but place our observations in a framework of some kind. Critique, and a higher education founded on critique, obliges us to take responsibility for the framework we employ. Critique points up the epistemological insecurity of any truth claim. It denies the pretentiousness of knowledge represented as Knowledge. It deflates the epistemic cover of its object. It is an exocet into epistemic smugness.

It is hardly surprising if the newly found corporate willingness to embrace critical skills is nervous in the face of this kind of critique. This critique represents a subversive potential, epistemologically speaking. Those offering truth claims – whether in substantive form or simply through the practices of an organization – must know that their presuppositions, anchorings, implicit interests, implications and latent ideologies are liable to undergo the severest tests. The distorted communication structures of organizations (to pick up another Habermassian idea) will act to prevent such critique forming. The deformations of collective thought processes will diminish the chances of fundamental critique getting off the ground. And, even if formed, the distortions in the communication structure will act to prevent the potentially disturbing ideas getting a hearing.

The logic of our earlier remarks about the university qua organization is that fundamental self-critique is being limited in the very institution intended to promote critique. This observation has a particular resonance in an era in western higher education of quality assessment by external bodies. The central ingredient of such quality assessment at national level is that of an institutional critical self-assessment. But in an organization – the modern university – characterized by internal managerialism and institutional hierarchy acting within an external environment of competition, forces will be at work which will constrain the frankness of that self-critical analysis.

Limits to critical thought are also to be found at the centre of the intellectual life of the university. Disciplines are frameworks, albeit not entirely of a rigid construction. They provide security and identity for those who live and work in them. Accordingly, while in principle a framework can be left and another entered, such a move will happen rarely. The framework is a normative structure, exerting a strong pull. He who leaves it for another will experience the opprobrium of the inmates. He will be left in no doubt that he has sold out. Even if the move was only intended to be temporary, to see the world from another viewpoint, he should not expect a warm welcome back since his ease in transcending frameworks will be troubling to those of a narrower faith. That ability to hold in view more than one framework at a time will be sensed as a form of contamination in and of the purity of the tribe's collective beliefs. The academic world allows critique, but, again, within limits.

Critical moments

Critical thought is not to be characterized by any particular disciplinary modalities or any particular teaching method. It is not the case that literature or philosophy or biology or design (to take just some contemporary proposals) are especially potent in offering critical insight or in integrating synoptically the student's other studies. Nor is it the case that open learning or problem-based learning or independent study (to mention just some of the more obvious candidates) are, as teaching strategies, necessarily likely to produce critical thought. Yet, if critical thought lies neither in subject content nor in method, where then is it to be found?

As with understanding, critical thought comes in various shapes and sizes. Critical thought might be internal to a framework, seek to stretch it, or even (most radical of all) seek to stand outside it and to comprehend it from an external vantage point. Critical thought has both shape and size; and both of indeterminate character.

Yet even if what counts as critical thought is indeterminate, some criteria can be identified. Critical thinking is thinking about thought already formed. It is a second order form of thought. Technically, it is metacriticism (Habermas, 1978). It is thought that works on thought (Althusser, 1969a). And it is an educational process orientated to this end that we can properly term 'higher education'; that is, an evaluation of what already exists, whether in the minds of others including the thinking of the lecturer or other students or in the student's own mind. If the general point is taken, that thought can always be evaluated, then the first kind of critique should lead to the second. Having grasped that she can always conduct an evaluation of what she encounters in others, the student should recognize that the principle holds for her own thinking as well. From other-critique to self-critique.

Provisionality breeds provisionality. Once started on the path of recognizing the boundedness of all truth claims, the student is embarked on an irrevocable journey. With the recognition of boundedness, of a truth claim being embedded in a framework or *intellectual field* (to pick up a term from Bourdieu's writings), there can be no return to absolutism. To this extent, Perry, in his work on the student's intellectual progression to positions of increasingly sophisticated relativism, was stating a logical rather than an empirical truth (1970; 1988). Conceptually speaking, higher education *is* of this form and there must remain some presumption that institutions carrying the title (institution of 'higher education') will embody educational transactions of that kind.

We can identify four moments in a student's intellectual development in which critique exerts a progressive pull of an essentially epistemological character.

Firstly, there comes the recognition that all thought, including the student's own thinking, has a certain boundedness about it. To be understood, to be offered in a rational discourse, a proposition has to have an anchoring in a network of presuppositions and contextual givens. In a rational discourse, those other presuppositions and contextual givens could, in turn and in time, be taken up and critically examined. But not all at once; and certainly not at this moment. Academic discourse has a double character of explicitness *and* hiddenness. It is elaborate, at pains to make itself transparent in the sense of showing the grounds of its beliefs; yet, it never succeeds, for much remains – if only temporarily – in the shadows. The recognition by the student of this limited character of any claim to truth is the student's first critical moment. In taking this step, the student is freed from dependence on *any* truth claim at all.

Secondly, having grasped the necessarily limited character of all truth claims, no matter how apparently well-founded or how much backed up by tradition, the student is then freed to form his or her own judgements, own propositions and own truth claims. Naturally, the student will recognize, in turn, the necessarily limited character of *those* truth claims, but that is simply to recognize in her own thoughts what she recognizes in others. What is important, as Perry implied, is that the student is now willing to branch out, to put herself at risk (as it may seem to her), by forming and articulating her own position amid the countervailing positions of which she is perhaps rather dimly aware. The second critical moment, therefore, comes in being willing to take up a position of one's own *while* being aware of its necessarily limited character.

So far, we are with Perry. But Perry's nine stages of intellectual development stop at this point. To stop there, however, truncates prematurely the intellectual possibilities that higher education offers. Two further critical moments are possible.

The third critical moment is linked to our analysis of critical thought. We have distinguished between critical thought that is internal to a framework and that which is external to a practice or an epistemic sub-culture. We might label these CT(I) and CT(E) respectively. Minimally, a student's higher education will allow her to form critical judgements internal to a framework; that is critical thought of type CT(I). But a genuinely higher education will not be arrested within such a limited form. Fully challenged in her course of study, a student will be encouraged to view her objects of study in different ways. She will delight in taking up concepts and ideas from other frameworks and spontaneously testing them in her own work. Moving comfortably within contrasting critical perspectives of type CT(E), she will be a *practising* postmodernist (rather than being a mere discussant of it).

The fourth and final stage of a genuinely higher education process then awaits. The student comes to a felt and existential realization that not just the concepts and ideas, the primary evidence and the dominant methodologies are challengeable; but so too are the semantic and syntactical rules, the permitted logical moves and the forms of communication (for example, the use of diagrams). Realizing that, the student is well placed to exploit, to vary and to manipulate all those rules to her own ends, so far as she is able to within the policing tactics of her lecturers and examiners. In this sense, theory and practice can be united. The practice lies not outside the student's world qua student but is internal to it. The question is whether the student is going to be encouraged and will be willing to take the risks to be her own person, exploiting all the communicative resources at her disposal to form her own stories in her own way.

'The Student Charter'

The UK has recently seen published, by the National Union of Students, a statement entitled *The Student Charter*. Consisting of a series of demands concerning the organization, access to and funding of higher education, the document is a missed opportunity. Of the desirable character (even from a student's point of view) of higher education we hear little; and of student responsibilities we are told nothing at all.

This is a pity. The logic of this discussion has been that students in receipt of a genuinely higher education have the right not to be boxed in, so to speak; and in different ways. They have the right not to be limited to the demands of a particular species of academic life; the right to be able to form their own views and, even if it seems heretical, to import ideas and perspectives into their work other than those with which their tutors are comfortable; and the right to sufficient intellectual space to try out ideas their own way. All these are rights appropriate to the development of the students' critical thinking. But there are responsibilities too. The exercise of critical thought requires scrupulousness with others' work, with the views of other students, in the use of evidence, and in the way one puts a sentence together (even if one's chosen rules differ from those of the lecturer as the immediate audience).

There is much more scope for critical thought than higher education normally endorses, for all its insistence on giving high marks to critical thinking. Postmodernism helpfully reminds us of the conventional character of academic life and implicitly encourages us to break the conventions. Academe takes itself too seriously; postmodernism assures us that having fun is OK. But it cannot be the case that anything goes. There are limits. Academic life cannot be a solitary life: in the end, there has to be understanding. And understanding requires mutual respect and utterances that can be understood by *someone.*

A well-run programme of studies will give each student opportunities to find members of staff with different predelictions, so that the student's own voice will find a receptive audience. But if the student is to be part of a critical dialogue, she must be ready to be challenged to leave her own framework, if only temporarily, and see the intellectual world anew. That journey might be painful; it will almost certainly be uncomfortable. Critique might be awkward for the recipient (whether profession, university or the intellectual field); but its formation will often be stressful for the student. If there are no secure rules and positions, taking up a position of one's own calls for inner strength and toughness, or intellectual maturity. The more daring and the more risky the position, the braver the individual has to be. Standing out from the other students is never easy.

Conclusion

We return to our opening reflections. In calling for critical thinking skills, it is not very likely that corporations in the world of work have in mind the kind of emancipatory critique sketched out here. But there should be little worry in that quarter. Institutions of higher education have seldom been sites for an educational process characterized by open critique. Its disciplinary sects have seen to that. Now, with some alacrity, the university is embracing the language of critical thinking skills as it seeks to show its responsiveness to the wider world by shifting its curricula towards transferable personal skills. On the one hand, critique is confined within the epistemic frameworks of the academic community; on the other, critique is confined within the practical and ideological framework of the commercial community. Both communities speak the language of openness but continually betray it.

Emancipatory critique as sketched out here was always a marginal and a vulnerable form of higher education. Perhaps Hutchins' Chicago or Lindsay's Keele or Briggs' Sussex bore some witness to the idea. Today, the combined forces of discipline-bound research ratings and corporate survival suggest that its presence in the western university may soon be just a memory at best.

9

Interdisciplinarity

Introduction

Interdisciplinarity is another term fast fading from the higher education lexicon. It was always more a feature of the discourse of higher education than of its practice; but now it is disappearing even from the language of the higher education community. Sporadic attempts have been made to breathe life back into the idea but the task is now fruitless. The world of higher education has moved on and, with it, the idea of interdisciplinarity has almost disappeared. Our task is the seemingly less creative one of understanding why this situation has arisen.

The argument here is that interdisciplinarity is no longer possible because its axioms are being undermined. Interdisciplinarity (i) accepted the presence of disciplines as a fact of academic life; (ii) endorsed disciplines as the building blocks of undergraduate programmes. Interdisciplinarity paid compliments to disciplines: it did not seek to displace them but to build forms of integration between them.

However, both the axioms underlying interdisciplinarity are being challenged. Disciplines are no longer universally accepted as the fundamental social facts of academic life; policy studies (in all kinds of public, financial and social services), consultancy in professional fields and action research are being developed without any disciplinary anchoring. At the same time, disciplines are no longer uniformly endorsed as the building blocks of undergraduate programmes. Enterprise skills, communication skills, information technology skills, interpersonal skills and so on are reducing the hold of disciplines in the undergraduate experience.

Interdisciplinarity attempts to unify the student experience but new forces at work are fragmenting the student experience. We need, therefore, to try to understand the contemporary forces of fragmentation before assessing the place of interdisciplinarity.

Forms of fragmentation

To say that the higher education curriculum is faced with new forces of fragmentation is not to pretend to a golden age of general education. Renaissance man – or woman – never was an intended outcome of higher education. In the nineteenth century (save perhaps for some pools of Scottish enlightenment) the curriculum was dominated by the classics, and in the twentieth century it came to be dominated by the academics' research interests in their separate fields. Occasional efforts to reconstitute the curriculum so that undergraduates were exposed deliberately to a wide range of intellectual discourses – such as at Keele or Sussex or the former North East London Polytechnic – were weakened over time in the face of the dominant interest structure of academe. Cross-disciplinary curricula have never become a general movement across UK higher education.

Particularity has long been the hallmark of the British higher education experience. The student journey has been an initiation into a particular discourse; not of academe as such, but of history or physics and so on. Purity has been closely guarded as an internal value. The fissiparous disciplines have ensured fragmentation across the university but the individual student's programme has been characterized by purity and wholeness. What is significant about the new forces for fragmentation is that the purity and wholeness of the student's programme is itself being threatened.

Two contemporary forms of fragmentation have to be distinguished: internal and external. This distinction does not refer, as in our earlier discussions, to forces internal and external to the university. Rather, the terms refer to the student experience. On the one hand, fragmentation takes place *internally* in the student's mind: the contents of the student's programme are experienced separately and few, if any, links are made between them. On the other hand, fragmentation is present *externally* in the curriculum structures to which the student is exposed.

The main engines of this double fragmentation are the combined forces of modularization and credit transfer. Either development, by itself, would have limited impact on the student experience. In their combination, however, they present a force that compels a new mode of becoming for the student. The unitization of the curriculum (modularization), the summing of its parts (credit accumulation) and the transportability of the student's learning achievements (credit transfer) together represent several kinds of shifts.

Modularization and credit accumulation are increasingly found together in practice. They are, however, separate in their effects and, at times, we will need to pay separate attention to them in our discussion.

Let's go to market

Credit accumulation and credit transfer alter the market relations between producer and consumer. There always was a market in higher education, but it was a supplier's market in which the high status institutions could charge a premium for their products in the form of high A-level grades. Now the market relations are changing, with the students acquiring definite consumer power. If they are unhappy with the fare they are offered, as they accumulate their credits, they can go elsewhere. It appears that the UK is moving towards a national credit accumulation system (through work sponsored by the Higher Education Quality Council) although the practical problems have not been entirely solved. Even so, students are more easily moving across programmes in their own institution. The students exert at least local consumer choice and market pressures.

One upshot of this heightened form of market is that the notion of a course, as a predesigned programme setting boundaries to the student's learning experiences, is evaporating. Students increasingly frame their courses, or 'programmes', for themselves. Another is the arrival of an *internal* market, a market within an institution, as departments compete within an institution for the same consumers; and strive to hang onto them once in their clutches. Yet another is that, as the balance of power shifts away from the professional and towards the consumer, the academics pay attention to the expectations and reactions of their students. Student feedback becomes big business.

The banker's philosophy

'Banking' was a conception of education which was attacked by Paulo Freire (1972a). In a banking conception of education, recipients receive items of information and store them in the mind unchanged. Perhaps those items might be called up from the memory store at some point; and perhaps not. In contrast, Freire developed the notion of conscientization (1972b), in which the individual actively engages with her experiences and, in the process, transforms both the experience and herself. The test of education is whether experiences lead to personal transformation. Items lying inert in the recesses of the mind, as in the vaults of the bank, cannot count as education.

Credit accumulation points us back to the metaphor of banking but in a different and even more problematic sense. At least, in Freire's portrayal, items of knowledge were banked in the student's mind. The problem with credit accumulation is that the learning is banked by the institution or even by the higher education system. Credit accumulation points to a third party ownership of educational experiences. The experiences are not even owned by the student.

In a thoroughgoing credit accumulation system, curriculum units are clocked up sequentially, gaining credit in the system. The credits are banked securely in the system. The student knows that they can be cashed in at any time, enabling the student to transfer to another programme or even another institution. Trust, reliability and known currency values: these are the hallmarks of a credit accumulation system that works. This is educational banking *par excellence*.

Whereas, in Freire's conception, the knowledge gained was stored in the student's mind, in this technologized system, the hard-won gains are stored in the system itself. They can be forgotten about. For the moment, their purpose has been served in yielding the credits. Storing them, maintaining their currency and arranging for their retrieval at a later date are the responsibility of the institution concerned. If the institution should fall down on these responsibilities, the student would feel justifiably aggrieved. The institution would have failed to fulfil its side of the contract.

Credit accumulation, then, is a banker's philosophy *par excellence*, in which the banker takes control of the student's learning. The learning achievements are held by the institution or even by the system as a whole. Trusting the system to safeguard the worth of those achievements, the student can forget about them and move onto the next curriculum unit. What has been learnt can be put behind one. Out of sight, out of mind.

This fragmentation of experience is part of the logic of the system, albeit part of the hidden curriculum. Far from encouraging connections between educational experiences, this form of curriculum sets out to foster separateness. There are no credit points for attempting to bring one's separate units into a relationship with each other; so why do it? Such an effort would divert the student from the task of tackling the next unit; and the next one.

The dominant assumptions at work here are that knowledge is formed of discrete units in the mind and that no advantage is to be gained by attempting to link them. Storage and retrieval occur on a unit-by-unit basis. The worth of the units does not increase through their being opened to each other. The separate boxes in the vaults must remain closed. The bankers believe that the sum of the contents of the boxes is just that: bringing them together produces no added value. This is curious, even on the banker's philosophy; but it is the result of the monetary system they have adopted. The very thing that the bankers say they want to do – that is, to multiply the value of the contents – is denied to them by credit accumulation. This is an investment with a very low rate of return.

Promises, promises

Modularization and credit accumulation amount to a set of promises to students. Those promises can take a variety of analytical forms.

We could, for example, draw with profit still on Bernstein's sociological apparatus of the early 1970s, to develop a story employing the concepts of classification and framing. It could be argued that modularization produces a curriculum of strong classification because the contents of separate modules are well insulated from each other. However, it could be that modularization produces a *more* integrated curriculum because staff across different disciplines have to take account of each other's work, since they may have to display their wares to attract students widely from other domains.

So far as the pedagogical frames or relationships are concerned, it may be that, in modular programmes, reduced opportunities for a personal identification with individual members of staff are accompanied by more relaxed interpersonal frames. Doubtless, this has its benefits. On tightly bounded courses, built around single disciplines, there was always the danger of an over-intense discipleship breaking out, the student's intellectual development being confined to a limited set of experiences and interpersonal encounters. On a modular programme, the student will be exposed to a range of experiences, forms of inquiry, teaching approaches and sheer differences in understanding the world. As a result, her identity will be her identity and much less the result of a close identification with any one set of experiences.

Alternatively, an epistemological account could be developed: we could assess the extent to which the new curricula are embracing a wider sense of knowing. The argument could be that modularization is conducive to experimentation in knowing. With modular programmes, single modules that break the conventions of the dominant disciplines can more easily be started. Modularization is epistemologically subversive or liberating, depending on one's point of view.

We could also develop a psychological account of the current changes. The argument could be made that modularization presents the student with the greatest possibility of realizing her potential. Being able to make choices, being able to change choices once made, being able to pursue different personal agendas: modular programmes can offer options such as these, so liberating students from dependency.

Transparency and opportunity in educational offerings, freedom, independence and personal maturity: these, then, are some of the promises of modular programmes. There remains, however, an educational problem which the advocates of modular programmes have to address.

What of intellectual maturity?

In the list of educational promises just cited, personal maturity appeared but intellectual maturity did not. The omission reflects a distinction between having a sureness as a person and having a firm foundation for one's own intellectual position. Insofar as modular programmes require students to make their own choices and to form their own programme of study from the array on offer, their personal maturity is advanced. They are obliged to enter into the framing of their own educational formation. What is less clear are the implications for students' intellectual progression. It might be thought that personal maturity will lead willy-nilly to intellectual maturity. If students are coming to their own judgements about the educational route they are going to follow, they are surely likely to be more committed to their own studies; indeed, are more likely to have a sense of ownership of those studies. Consequently, their intellectual development is more rather than less likely.

In any case, this is surely an empirical matter. Whatever the curricular arrangements, students inevitably will advance at different rates and will be influenced to differing degrees by the opportunities that present themselves. Some will thrive in modular settings; some will be more comfortable in the structured settings of conventional courses. Nothing can usefully be said on the matter in general terms. Both of these arguments for intellectual maturity emerging from modularization are misguided. On the first point – the argument from ownership – one can own something, say a motor-car, without having a mature attitude towards it. Maturity does not automatically follow from ownership. The second point – the argument from contingency – evades the notion of intellectual maturity. The question is whether the logic of intellectual maturity and that of modular programmes inhabit the same educational universe. To answer that we have to delve into the notion of intellectual maturity itself.

Intellectual maturity refers to a state of intellectual security. Students reach this state when they (i) are able to articulate their ideas; (ii) are able to back up those ideas with reasons; (iii) are able to identify counter-reasons; and (iv) are willing to yield or modify their position; but (v) only on the basis of stronger reasons. Components of intellectual maturity, therefore, are commitment (to one's position and the reasons behind it), toughness (not to yield one's position except to the stronger reason), humility (to be prepared to yield a position to which one is committed), inquisitiveness (to continue a search for countervailing positions), and openness (being sensitive to the possibility that counter-arguments might come from quite unseen directions). The pedagogical condition of the realization of this intellectual maturity is intellectual space. (In the last chapter, we explored a fourfold analysis of the concept of intellectual space.)

The concept of intellectual maturity also links with the concept of understanding (Chapter 7). Both concepts point to a deep personal involvement on the part of the student with her epistemic experiences. In the end, those experiences have to be hers, her intellectual orderings. The western university has been an institution organized for the development of the metacognitive capacities which that deep existential appreciation calls for. The gradations of bachelor, master and (more recently) doctor reflect this *lengthy* process of coming to a personal realization of one's understanding and one's knowledge claims.

Michael Polanyi's term 'indwelling' and Richard Peters' term 'initiation' capture something of what was happening but neither does it justice. 'Indwelling' conveys something of the tacit dimensions of the educational person while 'initiation' picks up the interpersonal character of what is learnt; but neither sufficiently connotes the personal dynamic at work. Our notions of intellectual maturity and understanding point to an active personal realization, a bringing in of the external sense data to make it one's own. These two ideas also carry the sense that this is a continuing process, over time. Profundity, depth, integration, linkages, differences, tensions, dissonance: a wide range of epistemic associations have to be identified by the student. They have to be the student's associations; and there has to be time for them to develop.

Are modular programmes prima facie more or less likely to promote *these* dimensions of intellectual maturity? That is a test, at least, which the advocates of modular programmes have to meet. And this test is not to be met by the response that institutional managers, students and national policy makers all favour modular programmes. Each of those groups will have its own agenda, none of which is likely to hinge on intellectual maturity as just defined.

A new kind of straitjacket

Talk of personal realization, existential appreciation and indwelling injects more than a psychological dimension into our discussion. What is at stake is the developing relationship between students, ultimately as autonomous cognitive persons, and the form of intellectual life with which they are grappling. The thinking characteristic of those working in civil engineering, or nursing, or theology, or literary criticism is a social structure standing externally to the student's development. Further, the educational and pedagogical process is itself a social process (even if pursued through a distance learning mode).

Recognizing these predominantly social characteristics of epistemic formation and pedagogy does not solidify academic forms of life as unchanging traditions. To that extent, Oakeshott underestimated the problem. An 'engagement' (Oakeshott, 1962: 310) with some important clustering of ideas there has to be but the engagement is far from straightforward. Not only do academic traditions change over time, as paradigms and even truth criteria succeed each other. Even more significant, when judged from the student viewpoint, the framework lived by this lecturer and by this department differs from the framework lived by that lecturer and that department. These differences can be markedly different as this lecturer or group have one orientation towards the definition of the subject while others have yet other definitions. But to remind ourselves of these differences in the form of life only emphasizes that the student biography is a problematic engagement with a set of ideas, methodologies and even perspectives. The student's *habitus* (Bourdieu, 1971) has to be constructed, often in painful struggle, by the student. In any modular framework, the unitization of curricula threatens to arrest the possibilities for deep and persistent engagement.

It may be said that these worries are unfounded and that well-constructed modular programmes will have none of these anti-educational characteristics. The Open University and the former polytechnics have demonstrated that. Well-constructed modular frameworks can provide both personal and intellectual maturity (to pick up our earlier distinction). Modular schemes can enable students to break out of the confines of individual epistemic frameworks. Cognitive freedom and personal responsibility are enhanced by modularization as students are implicitly encouraged first to determine the composition of their programmes and then to form connections between their experiences. With well-constructed modular frameworks, backed up by sound student guidance systems, a proper balance can be struck between an immersion into valued forms of intellectual life and the student's independence *of* those experiences. Well-run modular programmes should both offer multiple perspectival transformation *and* give the student the epistemic power to manipulate that repertoire of perspectives. Renaissance man is possible, after all.

But this set of hopes begs all sorts of questions. The frequent and necessary insertion of the phrase 'well-run' in that last paragraph betrays some of the suppositions at work. With modular programmes, are such elevated cognitive achievements, *in principle*, likely to come about? Is there a prima facie case for believing that they will? The answer must be no.

Modular programmes represent a profoundly different educational offering compared with more conventional fare. That is their underlying intention. The division of learning into discrete components, each with its own set of learning outcomes and assessment, provides certainty where previously there was uncertainty. Students know what they are getting, and where they should be getting to. No longer is there any vagueness of the purposes of the curriculum; no longer are there mysteries to be 'caught, not taught' (as Richard Peters put it). Now the relevant knowledge and skills are identified, and are to be taught and acquired. This is efficient *and* transparent. In the long run, it also reduces the control that academics have over their pedagogical encounters, since the degree of control of others – students, managers and the state – is increased. No wonder that the state, the institutional managers and the students are all in support of it.

The motivations, interests and structural dynamics associated with modular systems are *not intended* to bring about a deep personal immersion in epistemic discourses. They have other motivations and purposes, none of which is deliberately orientated in that educational direction. We have already encountered some of the reasons but it is worth identifying them more explicitly.

In whose interests?

Firstly, modular systems were introduced with the educational intention of expanding student choice over their programmes of study. It is right, on this view, that students as adults should be enabled to have a significant degree of control over the substance of their studies.

Secondly (and related to the first point), through modularization, institutions could appear to be more responsive to student preferences. In this sense, modular programmes are a sign of institutions responding to students as customers. In turn, they accentuate the element of consumption in the educational process. However, they also turn higher education into even more of an individual's collection; the interpersonal element is forgotten.

Thirdly, modular systems produce more visibility of the teaching effort. Individual lecturers are minimally required to provide some kind of specification of their curricular offerings so that the total array of units can be made known to potential consumers. Further, they may be required, as part of that exercise, to articulate the objectives of each module; and this may necessitate a measure of self-clarification if that degree of explicitness has not been called for in the past. Modular programmes offer a means of surveillance.

Fourthly, they extend greater control by the institutional management (King, 1994). With a unitization of curricula, modules or units can more easily be started and terminated. Modules are products or 'lines', with stock control rendered more immediate. Modular systems also reflect a view of staff as human resources. Through unitization, staff can more easily be switched away from unattractive offerings to more appealing ones. Modular programmes allow a penetration of the curriculum by managers; they provide a curriculum function *for* managers. The whole organization becomes more manageable.

Lastly, modular systems point towards organizational integration. Institutions of higher education across the world are loosely coupled institutions with high degrees of autonomy at the level of the operating units (Clark, 1983; Becher and Kogan, 1992). In a world in which universities are being required rapidly to meet the demands upon them (of the market, of mission definition, of quality assurance, of financial probity), new levels of organizational integration are called for. Modular systems provide a way of meeting that imperative but one which avoids a direct assault on academic freedom. Freedoms to admit students, to teach and to examine might only be curtailed at the margin. Yet the bringing of the total curriculum offer under a single framework is to inject institutional, organizational and managerial dimensions into the teaching function in significant ways. Modularization brings vertical integration into the teaching function: willy-nilly, lecturers become institutional and organizational actors.

The message of these observations is straightforward. It is that the contemporary shift towards modular structures is being driven not by educational motivations but by interests external to academe. To say this is not to downvalue the motivations in question. The academics have usurped their power, insisting on over-narrow discipline based frameworks of experience. But we still have to understand the contemporary changes at work.

Under new management

Historically, the fare put before students was controlled largely by the academics. Power and control lay with them. Modularization represents a shift in power in four directions: towards the state, the labour market, the student as consumer and the institutional managers. Of these four, the most assertive interest is that of the institutional managers. Each of the other three interests are beginning to show themselves but are, as yet, rather weakly developed. The state is gently encouraging moves in the direction of modular systems but that influence is a form of action at a distance. The labour market gives out ambiguous signals, wanting both focused technical skills and general personal abilities. Although it knows it wants more than a discipline-dominated curriculum, it is unsure about the economic value of modular degrees. Students are only just beginning to develop their consumer power: while particularly evident in postgraduate programmes where many are self-payers, there is little evidence of a student demand for modular programmes at first degree level. So while real, those first three sets of interests could not account for the general modular movement.

Some will say 'What movement?', for many academics have not fallen in with the modular agenda. Particularly in the older universities, modular systems have not entered the corporate consciousness, especially at the undergraduate level. As Gaie Davidson has shown in her recent study (1992), a majority of older universities have joined the newer universities in establishing a policy to bring their programmes under a modular framework. There is often, though, a gap between the manifest policy and the academic life of the university. The values-in-practice do not always correspond with the values-in-policies.

This tardiness to fall in with the university's written declaration fits the analysis we have been developing. In the contemporary era, the main drive for modular programmes comes from the institutional managers, the last of the four groups identified. This is different from the introduction of modular systems in the polytechnics in the 1970s, when their initiation was often due to the efforts of academics, even if backed by institutional managers. In the new regime, there are no safe academic havens.

The end of interdisciplinarity

We can now turn back to the topic of interdisciplinarity. If the analysis of modularization and credit accumulation just offered is sound, interdisciplinarity is dead; at least, as a policy option. The term can no longer do any work for us in describing possible curricula in higher education. This turn of events is readily explicable.

The idea of interdisciplinarity implies a bringing together of epistemic elements normally held separate. On this view, it may seem as if there is a greater need for interdisciplinarity than ever before. If modular programmes are supplying a centrifugal force to educational experiences, interdisciplinarity may seem to provide a counter – and even corrective – centripetal force. But modularization and interdisciplinarity are not so easily brought into a relationship with each other.

Interdisciplinarity suggests the possibility of integrating disciplinary frameworks but, under modularization, there is no necessary disciplinary framework. A modular programme is not necessarily based on disciplines. A discipline is an epistemic ordering of a sub-culture of the academic community; but modular programmes, we have seen, also reflect sets of interests held by other interest groups. What is at stake is not just a contingent fact about shifting patterns of curricula but the rival and underlying interplay of forces at work.

We have identified the forces at work as the producers (the academics), the clients (the state), the consumers (employers) and the customers (the students). The interests of academics as producers (if not as educators) may turn around disciplines; but these other interest groups have alternative interests. In this setting, interdisciplinarity will have a thin time of it. Simply finding disciplines that might be integrated is going to be tricky. Curricula are being defined by quite other orderings. 'Transferable skills', 'competence', 'experiential learning' and 'capability' are simply symptoms of the contemporary struggle in which the university curriculum is being presented with alternative conceptions of student development, conceptions that owe nothing to disciplines as orderings of human consciousness. The *disciplinary* ground on which interdisciplinarity works is being broken up.

Certainly, academics have not en masse bought the managerial or vocational agendas that underlie the contemporary movements. Disciplines remain as the sub-strata of academic life; the research endeavour largely continues to be situated within disciplines. The trouble is that strata can be dislodged or even overlaid by new ones; there may be upheavals. Over time, quite new layerings may be laid down. For instance, pure research is overlaid by applied research, which is overlaid by policy studies, which in turn is overlaid by development projects or action research. Nor are these trends narrowly confined: they are found across fields as diverse as biotechnology, health studies, transport studies and historical studies (the last, for example, in local history projects linked to income-generating exhibitions). So the character of what passes for legitimate research changes. And funders want results yesterday. Disciplines, with their inbuilt norms of steady, patient, rule-governed work, are losing their grip as the unrivalled orderings of academic life.

Interdisciplinarity is losing its potency, then, because interests other than disciplines are coming to influence what counts as a valid mode of student formation. Enterprise, capability, competence, modular programmes, credit accumulation and other shifts are eroding disciplines as the dominant substructure of the curriculum. The force of these challenges is derived from the concatenation of interests that they represent, all of which reflect – to pick up the sub-title of this book – the changing pattern of relationships between higher education, knowledge and society. They are indicative of the growing incorporation of higher education into society.

Different readings of this situation are possible and plausible. The image of beleaguered academics, holding fast to their internal agendas in the face of overwhelming external forces, is beguiling. But it is an inadequate representation. Many of the innovations just mentioned are being embraced with some alacrity within institutions of higher education. Admittedly, the pattern is uneven, both across disciplines and across institutions. Across disciplines, we can hypothesize that responsiveness will be a function of the market position of a discipline, 'market strength' being understood in terms both of the economic and the cultural capital supplied by different intellectual fields. Across institutions, a greater readiness to sponsor new forms of programmes and curricula innovation appears to be present in the former polytechnics. These two dimensions, of institutional and discipline responsiveness, need to be superimposed one on the other for a fuller picture.

The fundamental point remains. Forces are at work in UK universities which are cutting across disciplines and which represent a considerable weight of forces. They have added power because while they may spring from external agendas or influences (of the state, the economy, civil society or even the residues of a liberal educational lobby), they have also found allies *within* a large segment of the academic community. No longer is it possible to characterize higher education and society as squaring up to each other. Higher education has become representative to some extent of societal and state ideologies. It is no longer possible, too, to characterize the academic community *in toto* in terms of allegiance to particular disciplines; other modes of discourse and ideas of student development now claim the allegiance of some 'academics'.

Missed connections

Interdisciplinarity is dead, at least as an idea with any pragmatic purchase. Interdisciplinarity was a notion born of the internal agenda of academics as educationalists. It was always a long shot. It required academics – typically vice-chancellors – who had educational vision, a perspective not tied to any single discipline, organizational flair to effect significant change, and leadership qualities to win the support of reticent discipline-based academics. Now, the dominant sources of curriculum momentum are seeking to displace disciplines as bases of student formation.

En passant, we can note that general education met a similar fate. There, too, we find a curriculum idea coming from within the academic community and intended to transcend particular disciplines. Whereas interdisciplinarity looked to bring disciplines together, ultimately to produce a new cognitive perspective in which individual disciplines were exploited as resources, general education sought to inject a common form of understanding across all programmes.

Interdisciplinarity offered integration of the individual psyche through a personal apperception of the relative contribution of the separate disciplines; general education promised integration of the student body through common intellectual experiences. The one promised integration of the corpuses in the student mind; the other promised integration of the students collectively as educated persons.

Not surprisingly, general education has suffered a fate similar to inter-disciplinarity. Both had their origins in the internal agendas of the academic community, albeit of those who worked against the academic currents to effect cross-disciplinary integration and an academic community of some kind. In an age in which the dominant sources of curriculum innovation are coming at academe from the state and the wider society, both forms of curriculum development are *passé*. It is not just that they are of a former time, but that they are not of *this* time.

We are witnessing a fundamental shift in which higher education moves from being a form of cultural transmission to one in which it becomes a means of generating economic capital. The disciplines were a vehicle for *both* endeavours: as sophisticated forms of cognition, practice and under-standing, they supplied cultural capital in a society – 'modern society' – in which everyone was literate; and, as bodies of technical and professional knowledge, they produced economic capital. Disciplines have been able to enjoy their long innings precisely because they have been able to fulfil *both* the internal interests of the academic community and the external interests of the wider society. Individuals could take their degrees and pass into society both with a securer hold on the labour market *and* a social standing not otherwise available.

The marginalization of interdisciplinarity and general education is a sign that this dual legitimacy enjoyed by disciplines (within academe and the wider society) is ending. Cross-disciplinary strategies will fail to get a hearing because, while they are an attempt to reduce the force of disciplines, they nevertheless keep disciplines intact. Coming from within the academic community, these doctrines were never seriously going to dislodge the dominance of disciplines. Disciplines as the bedrock of academic life were acknowledged; the only question was whether an additional, integrative, element could be sustained.

Conclusion

An argument in this book is that transferable skills should not be under-stood as a reincarnation of these old-fashioned cross-disciplinary ideas. The generality of the one is not the generality of the other. They represent competing educational codes. We now have an additional strand to this argument. Interdisciplinarity and general education were devices to de-velop integration across academe. That they never managed to obtain a secure foothold not only was indicative of the reluctance of discipline-based academics to grant them legitimacy but was also a sign of the doubts of the wider society that they offered either cultural or economic capital. The cross-disciplinary movements failed because they lacked friends both in academe and without. In the end, they failed because they treated disci-plines with too much respect and left them untouched.

In contrast, the transferable skills of the current age are precisely an attempt to displace disciplines. The problem that *their* advocates have to face is that these forms of educational process rest on a fundamental interest in driving up economic capital and are lacking in cultural capital. Consequently, the disciplines will not be entirely dislodged so long as they supply cultural capital. In a market situation, cultural capital will often trump economic capital. Students will insist on studying history before acquiring engineering 'competences'. Because of their cultural capital, law and medicine could probably sustain a competency approach; but precisely because of their cultural capital will not be first in the queue to nod in that direction.

As a result, we are seeing signs of a strange admixture in higher education: disciplinary reinforcement coupled with technical specificity and general competences for economic renewal. This is an unstable and uneasy combination. Interdisciplinarity and its relatives are dead; so no succour is available there. What is less clear is whether there is any form of cross-disciplinary education available to us. I shall later argue that there is and that there has to be.

10

Wisdom

Knowledge is increasingly divorced from wisdom
(Midgley, 1989: 18)

Introduction

Midgley didn't get it quite right. Knowledge is increasingly being divorced from action. In the process, both knowledge and action are impoverished and diminished. Knowledge becomes, as Midgley demonstrates, mere information; and action, so we might say, becomes simply labour (cf. Arendt, 1958). *As a result*, the chance of attaining wisdom is severely reduced, if not made impossible. We can see signs of this loss in the university, at the levels both of the institution and of the student experience. That, at any rate, is the argument of this chapter.

Wisdom goes beyond knowledge but it is never free of some anchoring in knowledge. We begin our discussion, therefore, by looking at some contemporary views of knowledge. If knowledge is problematic – and it is – wisdom, too, must be problematic.

There is an alternative

In his book *Thought and Change* (1964), Ernest Gellner constructed an essay about thought and modern society *and* their interrelationships. In typically pungent Gellnernian style, he argued that each age has a characteristic mode of thinking. For modern society, that form of thought is essentially scientific, this society being fundamentally science-based. It could not be otherwise. The ratchet will not allow society to slip back. Nor, in their hearts, do most citizens wish it any other way. Those nations not yet in this happy state are striving to reach it as quickly as possible. The adoption of the scientific mode of thought is both a fact and a matter devoutly to be wished. No alternative is seriously possible, Gellner argued. We cannot jump out of our psychological and sociological skins. We are wedded to this form of society and its dominant forms of thought. It is only in marginal activities, such as Oxford philosophy, that we see expressed the fanciful belief that a state of pure thought is possible.

Several of those ideas have permeated Gellner's writings over the last quarter of a century and, with them, their question-begging character.

Firstly, is it really the case that societies cannot slip back, cannot regress in their mode of conduct or their frames of thought? A *fin de siecle* war in central Europe with its near-imagery of concentration camps gives pause for thought. More locally, the UK has seen a growing disparity in the distribution of incomes over the past fifteen years or so. And, on an altogether more parochial level, the autonomy of universities has diminished as they have been formed into a system under state tutelage. Whatever one's reading of these and other developments, Gellner's faith in modernity to offer unquestionable and one-way progress cannot be left to stand as a self-evident fact.

However, even if the ratchet theory is correct, we are hardly any better off when it comes to understanding the fate of wisdom. Wisdom implies not just progress in our thinking and actions, but deliberate progress. If the tram is ascending just under an inner impulsion, it can hardly be the result of the application of wisdom.

Secondly, we should not readily accept Gellner's assertion that we cannot step outside our psychological and sociological skins. Gellner's argument contains a sophistication within a sophistication. He is right to caution against the belief that there is any pure redoubt readily available. Oxford philosophy claimed a purity for itself, Gellner observes, that it never possessed. Its consequent 'finishing school' character reflected not only its social function but also its intellectual mission. Its strategy of conceptual clarification, as Gellner pointed out, could never solve problems but at best could only expose them (even if *it* thought that conceptual clarification was an end to the matter).

No position of absolute cognitive purity is available. On this point, Gellner was, and still is, right. Yet we are not condemned only to describe the situation in which we find ourselves. It is possible to critique one's own and others' situations, and with a straight face.

Gellner is hoist with his own petard. His argument contains an assertion (that we are wedded to this society) and a value position (that this society is the best possible, if only in the sense that no alternative can seriously be conceived). Gellner's position fails by his own standards since it offers evaluations, albeit evaluations in praise of the contemporary state of affairs. If positive evaluations are legitimate, so too are more critical ones. It may not be possible to jump out of our psychological and sociological skins but we can, snake-like, look back on ourselves and even, over time, deliberately shed our skins in favour of a more agreeable wrapping. Wisdom, indeed, consists precisely in the identification of alternatives. It implies that we can and on occasions will be prepared to divest ourselves of our psychological and sociological skins.

So far as higher education is concerned, we are not ineluctably tied to the system we have. There *is* always an alternative, even if it is convenient to the dominant powers for us to believe to the contrary. We can always ask critical questions. What are the dominant interests at work behind the changes taking place? What values do they represent? How might we rationally ground our activities in higher education, both at institutional and at course level? What possibilities are open to us? That there are difficulties in grounding our higher education practices does not mean that we have to accept the status quo. The present arrangements and those looming into view reflect uneven forces. Believing that things are ultimately for the best will surrender higher education to the big battalions.

Wisdom and traditions

A third strand of Gellner's argument to be addressed is his ready endorsement of science as the supreme form of knowing. Given that stance, it is not surprising to see Feyerabend and Gellner locking horns in bloody combat (Feyerabend, 1978: ch. 2; Gellner, 1979: ch. 10). Feyerabend has persistently argued that science is not the rational enterprise it takes itself to be, that its belief in its own supremacy and its dominant place in modern society are forms of ideology, and that alternative rival traditions of knowing are unreasonably ruled out of court. In his *Farewell to Reason* (1987), Feyerabend draws a distinction between theoretical and empirical traditions of knowing. 'Theoretical traditions' are represented above all in modern science which seeks to offer universal truth claims, universal in the sense that they are intended to cover all instances of events of a certain class. 'Empirical traditions', on the other hand, are those that focus on the particular: the individuality of events and persons and concrete human responses to them are what are valued in these forms of knowing.

This distinction has point in today's university. For example, it bears upon the current incorporation of health studies into higher education as nursing and other professional schools are assimilated into universities. Midwifery education presents a particular case in point. Historically, midwifery has been an essentially human practice in which the midwife has interacted with empathy with the mother-to-be. It is a nice example of an 'empirical tradition' (in Feyerabend's terminology) in which key aspects of the knowing are embodied in human action and are transmitted to new recruits to the profession through the practical example set by those experienced in the field. Knowledge traditions of this kind are being challenged and potentially undermined as forms of professional development in the process of bringing these traditions into the mainstream of higher education. This undermining is the direct result of the high marks that higher education accords to science and theory based traditions of knowing.

This is a point not just about the legitimacy of science – of formalized explicit codified corpuses of knowledge – to set the standards by which aspirants to the academy are to be judged. Rather, the criteria of sound knowledge are always controversial and *no* single set of criteria has the right to insist on the high ground.

That valid ways of knowing come in a variety of forms is becoming a commonplace in the literature. It is apparent in the influential work of Donald Schon, who has pointed out that competent professional practice is built around 'knowledge-in-action' and that its development depends upon 'reflection-in-use'. In teacher education Paul Hirst, drawing upon the work of Schon among others, came to sense that his earlier insistence upon the primacy of theoretical knowledge was misplaced and recanted that philosophy. Instead, professional knowledge in school teaching was a matter of identifying and appraising the 'practical principles' inherent in the teacher's professional activities (Hirst, 1983). Wisdom may be captured in enlightened action just as much as in the deployment of formal knowledge.

Anything goes

We have, then, the Gellner–Feyerabend debate ('row' would be a better description). On the one hand, there is the claim (of Gellner) that the high marks given to science are entirely appropriate: not only socially but also epistemologically, the superior status of science in our culture is warranted. On the other hand, there is Feyerabend's claim that the superior status of science is without epistemological foundation and represents the domination of a narrow cognitive grouping in society and, thereby, an unwarranted closing of our cognitive options.

Such an opposition of views prompts questions. I have identified three problems with the Gellnerian position; but problems loom immediately with Feyerabend's position too.

Feyerabend is associated with the phrase 'anything goes', a phrase which percolated his first major book *Against Method* (1975). In a subsequent book, *Science in a Free Society* (1978), he became coy about the phrase. He shouldn't have done. The phrase is an admirably neat precis of the logical end of his position. But if serious human thought is not to be constrained by any set of rules, if all rules are there to be broken, on what basis can we move forward? How can we distinguish the charlatans and the quacks from the serious knowledge claimants? An open market of ideas is all very well, but the democracy of the market-place usually turns out to be a pretty uneven contest. The better argument can easily be that which is put from a prior position of power or put with more ideological force. Indeed, in his writings (in his analysis of the way in which Galileo operated, for example), Feyerabend argues that science and more especially scientists work in just this exploitative, rhetorical or resourceful way. The better argument is precisely that which wins.

Unfortunately, Feyerabend does not sufficiently distinguish truth criteria apparent in the historical process of the growth of knowledge from truth criteria that we might wish to formulate in an attempt to govern the full range of *future* such efforts. Even if limited traditions have been developed so far, and even if the stated rules of procedures are often broken, it by no means follows that a policy of rule-lessness should govern our future attempts to advance human understanding.

The cognitive anarchy to which Feyerabend's position logically leads – as an outcome of an antipathy to rule-following – connects with the situation in which the postmodernists are placed. If there are no general underlying rules of right reason, on what basis can we reason? The logic of an incredulity towards metanarratives (Lyotard, 1984) ought surely to be an incredulity towards *any* narrative. In a fully postmodern world, progress in human understanding cannot be on the cards. Wisdom implies that some judgements, some uses of knowledge, are better than others. An 'anything goes' policy would deprive us of wisdom.

We seem, in our discussion, to have reached something of an impasse. Both Gellner's underwriting of modernity as a given, with its characteristic forms of thought, *and* Feyerabend's radical alternative in eschewing any form of cognitive rules as a basis for rational thought would rule offside any attempt to hang onto the notion of wisdom. However, both writers share a feature on which we can build. In the writings of both authors, thought is a social phenomenon and works through having social legitimacy (cf. Gellner, 1974; Feyerabend, 1987). It also embodies social interests. If we want to understand how and why forms of thought are on offer in our universities, we have to comprehend their forms of thought in the context of the interests they reflect in the wider society.

Knowledge and wisdom

At this point, we can turn helpfully to Nicholas Maxwell's work, *Knowledge and Wisdom* (1987). Maxwell argues that the process of knowledge advancement has lost its way, having taken a wrong turn in the Enlightenment. The Enlightenment sought to put social progress on a sure foundation by anchoring the attack on social problems in science as a secure means of obtaining knowledge. Unfortunately, science has taken on an agenda of its own. Science has grown through an empiricism which has been supremely efficient at securing just that end, namely the growth of science. What it has been much less successful at is addressing social problems. The strength of Maxwell's argument lies in his offering us not only an insight into the basis of science but also in his setting out a schema for a knowledge enterprise orientated towards social problems. However, the implication of Maxwell's analysis for our present discussion is that a large-scale societal enterprise, scientific enquiry and education, has been hijacked *internally* by the scientific community.

This is a bold conclusion and not one to be accepted entirely without qualification. Firstly, Maxwell overlooks the point that scientific knowledge is far from immune to social influences. The 'strong programme of the sociology of science' (Bloor, 1991) asserts that there is no difference in substance between scientific propositions and any others in terms of their status as social utterances. This view denies any cognitive purity to science. Scientific propositions gain recognition and legitimacy in scientific circles by adhering to conventions which are essentially social in character and we can understand those conventions in just the same way as any other sets of social conventions. Science does not occupy a neutral social space in society but, as a major social institution, draws on themes, issues, and even ideas as resources at large in the wider society (Bloor, 1991; Barnes, 1974).

Secondly, while science as a social institution has enjoyed a measure of social autonomy, that has to be read in part as a freedom granted by the wider society. Organized science has grown at a considerable rate since the 1930s because the state assumed it was getting something for its money. A vigorous science base was seen as the key to the post-industrial society (Bell, 1976), providing the necessary intellectual capital that that society called for. Autonomy and growth are conditional upon fulfilling the mission set for it.

Thirdly, science has come to be seen by the state as a force of economic production. The allocation of resources to science, the general direction, and the terms and conditions under which science is prosecuted are all heavily circumscribed, either directly by the state or by the multinational corporations (many of which have developed their own scientific capacity). Publication in the journals of findings from research projects is curtailed, either because of sensitivity in the defence field or because of corporate competition. Accordingly, there has arisen a 'new politics of science' (Dickson, 1988).

On all three counts – taking in societal imagery and themes, becoming a force of production, and being directly controlled by external forces – science has to be understood in terms of its relationships with its wider society. Maxwell's analysis is provocative but, in the end, leaves science and society as far too separate from each other. Any call for a new form of science can only have cash value if it addresses the sociopolitics of science in the modern society.

The title of Maxwell's book is *Knowledge and Wisdom*, but it is long on the deficiencies of organized knowledge and rather short in its analysis of wisdom. Maxwell does argue that wisdom will not be forthcoming unless we explicitly reorientate our knowing activities in the direction of solving particular human problems. However, a proper appreciation of wisdom has to comprehend the external forces at work which would reduce the exercise of wisdom.

Knowledge and human interests

Knowledge and Human Interests is the title of Jurgen Habermas' (1978) major early work. Despite its density and length, the essence of that book can be summarized fairly readily. The drive for knowledge on the part of human beings is powered by an inbuilt momentum, deriving from fundamental human interests. Habermas' claim is that there are three sets of interests behind our knowing efforts and that, in turn, they give rise to three separable forms of knowing. The interests in question are not ephemeral, characteristic of a particular form of society or a definite moment. Rather, they are so deep-seated as to be almost anthropological in nature, even if the interests in question have developed with the evolution of human society.

Firstly, human beings have an interest in predicting the workings of the environment in which they find themselves and in controlling it, so far as they are able. This *instrumental* interest sponsors purposive forms of knowledge in general and science in particular. Science is here understood as a system of structured knowledge independent of the world and which objectifies the world. Through that objectification, control and prediction are made possible.

Secondly, human beings have an interest in comprehending each other and in communicating with each other. This is a *hermeneutic* interest in knowledge, giving rise to forms of thought such as the humanities and the expressive arts. Their inner purpose and (therefore) character lies not in controlling the world – not even the human part of it – but in understanding its meanings, meanings that are injected by human beings themselves and in their own interchanges. This understanding of understandings is built on a framework of open and uncoerced interchange. These hermeneutic circles of mutual interpretation are necessarily open and never conclusive.

Thirdly, human beings have an interest not just in controlling or comprehending the world they live in but also in freeing themselves from dependence on it. This *emancipatory* interest gives rise to critical or evaluative modes of thought. Particular contenders as forms of critical thought are (so Habermas suggests) Marxism and Freudism: they are contenders precisely because they offer views of the world which lead to changed self-understandings and so, in turn, to new – and emancipated – forms of human action. Whatever we may think of these two claimants, the general point remains. Through our knowing efforts, we can come to see ourselves in radically different ways and, as a result, be conceptually enabled to take up different stances in and even against the world.

Wisdom and human interests

If wisdom is connected with knowledge, and if knowledge is structured by different human interests, then wisdom might appear in different modes. In principle, wisdom could be based in instrumental, communicative or emancipatory forms of human interests and their associated forms of knowing. This is not an empirical matter. It rests on what we take wisdom to be.

One ingredient of wisdom is reflection and, in principle, reflection could be found in each of the three forms of knowing just outlined. However, reflection is a *necessary* component of communicative and emancipatory forms of knowing whereas it is merely a *contingent* aspect of instrumental knowing. Indeed, it is implicit in Habermas' analyses that instrumental knowing is generally lacking in reflection. In objectifying the world, in seeking to predict it with a view to its control, reflection is largely repudiated.

Communicative knowledge, on the other hand, necessarily calls for reflection. A university which is genuinely functioning as a learning community is a self-learning community. Such collaborative learning calls for an unconstrained exchange, freed from the distorting components of power and money. It has to resemble, in Habermas' terminology, an 'ideal speech situation' in which participants have equal dialogical chances. Without the instruments of power and money, participants have to take account of each other's viewpoint. Mutual reflection is, therefore, built into the realization of communicative knowledge.

Correspondingly, reflection is also a logically necessary component of emancipatory knowledge. It is part of what is meant by emancipation. Emancipation is achieved through a combination of knowledge about the social and psychological environment, a personal understanding of that knowledge and critical self-reflection, so that through that understanding one can see new possibilities for one's own life world. Knowledge, understanding, self-reflection, critique and imaginative construction, and self-renewal: if these are the components of emancipation, the key lies in self-reflection. Through self-reflection, knowledge and understanding are introjected so as to have self-transforming power.

Reflection, therefore, is necessarily built into communicative and emancipatory knowing but is, at best, merely a contingent feature of instrumental knowing. Accordingly, wisdom – as some kind of integration of knowing, reflection and action – has a strong and even a tight connection with communicative and emancipatory knowing but a flimsy and ephemeral link with instrumental knowledge. Indeed, the logic of the analysis just sketched out is that, given the general self-reflective blankness of instrumental knowing, wisdom is rarely on the cards in that domain.

Wisdom in the university

Our discussion has been conducted at a high level of generality and its bite on practical matters in higher education may seem opaque. In filling out the argument, a cardinal distinction has to be made between wisdom as a characteristic of persons and as a characteristic of processes. We may want our students to develop wisdom and our teachers in the universities to display it; but we can also hope, not unreasonably, that universities themselves will act wisely. We begin with that latter possibility, that wisdom might be an attribute of universities as such.

To what extent do universities exhibit wisdom? We can attack the question by picking up the threefold analysis just offered and considering the extent to which universities' policies and practices are characterized by instrumentalism *or* communicative mutuality *or* self-critical professionalism. In other words, do we see the internal dynamics of universities revolving around the dimensions of power, prediction and control, the fulfilment of goals set by others (managers or the state), and objectives that turn on efficiency, extrinsic value and surveillance? *Or* are we witnessing varied signs of collaboration across departmental and disciplinary boundaries, an effort to work towards a sustained and collectively owned institutional mission, *and* a determination critically to form principles and a policy framework within which the management can act but under which the institution as a community can unify?

Under, but only under, the latter set of circumstances, which admittedly amount to a severe set of criteria, we can begin to talk of *institutional wisdom*. To emphasize the point, where the institutional members are working together (which implies that they are allowed to work together) in an unconstrained spirit of mutual collaboration and supportive self-critique, we are in the presence of a combination of knowledge, understanding, reflection, policy formation and action *at the level of the institution*. In such a situation, it is no strain on our conventional use of language to talk of an institution – faced with some kind of financial crisis, say – acting wisely. Wisdom can be an attribute of institutions, just as of persons; but in order to qualify for the description, severe criteria of openness, non-coercion, and mutual forward-looking dialogue have to be present *and* lived by the institution's members.

To shift the level of interpretation, wisdom might also be said to characterize our curricular intentions. That this sounds odd is indicative of some deep-seated aspects of modern curricula that run the other way.

Earlier, I argued that understanding could be more or less broad in scope. Wisdom, in contrast, is *necessarily* broad in its make-up. Wisdom is the grasping of a range of different possibilities, seeing things under different aspects, and distancing oneself from one's immediate object. Going some way towards wisdom in the course of one's studies would require from the student an ability to form a view about her studies and to do so through alternative cognitive frameworks. It would require the student being able to comprehend the different uses to which her knowledge may be put, the different interests that it might serve, and – more radically still – different approaches to her studies depending on the interests being served.

In looking for signs that wisdom is important in the framing of a curriculum, a range of questions suggest themselves. Is the development of understanding seen as a form of inter-communication with others, with authors of texts to be read and tutors and other students on the programme, or is it seen simply as an assembly of facts, data and information to be mastered whether for reproduction in the examination or for exploiting in the world? Does the student take the value of her knowledge as given (and her principal frameworks of disciplinary perspective and skill within it) or is it viewed with some degree of critical detachment, the student being aware that there are always questions that can be turned on the intellectual field itself and the interests it serves? Is the capacity of knowledge for enlightenment understood? Knowledge, as well as offering technical means of achieving given ends, can pose critical questions of those ends and so transform action.

If the notion of wisdom seems strange as a description of 'learning out-come' in the university, it is an indication that the relationship of the student to her studies is unduly limited. To the extent that students are not encouraged in their studies to embrace such far-seeing perspectives or enabled to see their understanding as a form of communication with others (dead and living), or to comprehend knowledge as a challengeable social institution rather than a given corpus of data and information: to that extent, wisdom will rightly seem an otiose term in higher education.

Mere technique

Wisdom is some kind of relationship between knowing and action. 'Wisdom' implies limits to both knowing and action.

On the knowing side of wisdom, I have argued that there are tendencies in modern society, reflected in higher education, to favour forms of know-ing skewed in the direction of that which yields results. Science and tech-nology come highest in the knowledge policies of the state: funding formulas are developed to encourage the growth of student markets in those sub-jects. Generally, students in all disciplines are encouraged and, in some institutions, required to develop a familiarity with computers. The educational process becomes dominated by a wish to secure those knowledge forms which seem to promise prediction, control and (therefore) power.

But if the knowledge side of wisdom is being unduly skewed in higher education, so is the action side. Action is being shorn of reflection and, in the process, is being reduced to mere technique. Again, the work of Jurgen Habermas is helpful here.

Embryonically in his early writings and as a substantive part of his later work, Habermas has argued that the three human interests (outlined on p. 146) are not equal players in the epistemological stakes of modernity. In particular, the communicative/hermeneutic and the critical/emancipatory interests are being squeezed out by the instrumental/purposive interest. In his terminology, the life world and critical forms of discourse are being 'colonized' by the objective and controlling forms of thinking. In higher education, at the level of the state, we see this development in policy terms through the increased means of surveillance by national bodies in general and the use of numerical performance indicators in particular. Both are indicative of the forms of thinking characteristic of state bureaucracies in wishing to predict and control rather than to allow individual institutions room for their own self-definition and collective formation.

These tendencies on the part of the state are being paralleled in universities as they become organizations. Characteristics of organizations are common identified purpose, lines of authority, clear superior-subordinate relationships, forms of accountability, and definite means of decision-making. All these developments are being now seen in the university.

Symptomatic of this trend is the recognition that collegiality is being expunged as a feature of university life. One sign is the reduction in the number of committees and the associated drift to concentrate strategic decision-making in the centre. Management information systems relying on computers and quantified data become more central in institutional processes. The loss of collegiality is also evident in the impoverishment of our language. The notion of 'academic community', for instance, seems to be entirely *passé*.

The apologists will say that such changes in the internal decision-making arrangements of universities are necessary for institutional survival. Managers have to manage. The effect of this ideology is profound, however, and strikes directly at the character of the university. Historically, the university has been a collectivity of freely associating individuals. Its development into an organization, with a hierarchical line-management structure, is new. A consequence is a tendency towards a 'proletarianization' of the academic members of universities (Halsey, 1992). Indeed, to pick up a distinction from Hannah Arendt, academics are being reduced to labourers. Real work is owned by the worker; in the modern university, however, the academic's priorities are increasingly defined by the head of centre, head of department and pro-vice-chancellor – all of whom may be in conflict over the proper use of her labour while in the university's employ. Wisdom is ruled out of court since the sense of agency and autonomy it carries is extinguished.

Wisdom and values

Action in the university is being reduced in another equally profound way, namely 'decisionism'. Drawn from the work of Jurgen Habermas, and characteristically awkward as it is, the term is nevertheless illuminating of a feature of the modern university. The idea of decisionism reflects a movement in ethics and a spirit of the age that we cannot talk seriously about values. Value talk is off-limits. All we have are our own intuitions, emotions and values: essentially, these are non-discursive entities. We can express them but we cannot rationally discuss them. Consequently, our decisions in our working lives cannot and, on this view, should not be guided by values. Indeed, talk of values is itself unsettling to those inhabiting an organizational ethos. It falls outside the discourse of management, planning and organization.

Adopting a discourse that excludes values is itself to take up a value position. It is also, again, to pick up another Habermassian idea, to embrace a form of strategic rationality. Measurement, costings and efficiency assessments *are* a form of rationality: but their exclusive application to human affairs at the expense of judgemental evaluations and an explicit recognition of the presence of values is, in the end, to treat human beings as objects. It is to deny their ownership of their own projects and enterprises, embodying particular and personal values. And it is to deny that, in higher education at least, decision-making takes place in the midst of institutions and activities reflecting contested values. Although there *cannot* be final end-points to a value-focused discussion, a rational discourse around values – to follow Habermas further – can certainly be present provided that it follows the general rules of *any* rational discourse.

Decisionism, then, has the effect of reducing rather than (as it pretends) expanding the pool of rationality under which universities might work. It extends strategic reason into areas where we should see communicative reason at work. Strategic rationality is maintained at the expense of open- ness, values debate, dialogue and thorough-going critique. In the effort to gain control over its affairs, and to generate flexibility of response, in the end the university loses collective control over its fate. Qua organization, it may change but it will do so with a certain blindness for the ultimate ends and values it is serving are not open for debate.

What this means is that wisdom is going to be thin on the ground as the university becomes more of an organization. Wisdom as a characteristic of communities would imply a willingness seriously to consider institutional ends collectively. As management extends its range, even taking the cur- riculum into its embrace (Chapter 9), the scope of collective decision- making will be reduced. It is often said that, in meeting the challenges coming at it, the modern university has to be willing to keep its goals under review, redefining its mission and niche in the market as necessary. How- ever, the exploration of ends is likely to be limited. It will be framed within a strategic consideration of what will work, of what will ensure institutional success or even survival. Further, the processes by which the mission is defined are likely to be controlled by management. Less likely is an open debate of the values that the institution should serve in which the outcome of that debate is unknown before it is started. A genuine debate about values reduces the power and control that managers and administrators have in orchestrating institutional affairs.

Accordingly, the discomfort we feel in using the term 'wisdom' as a description of academic life is entirely explicable. Wisdom points to an openness of reflection and vision, but what we are seeing is a closing of the interior discourse of the university. The very human interest lacking in wisdom – purposive/instrumental – is colonizing alternative interests which would otherwise have encouraged wisdom.

Conclusion: the loss of the virtues

Wisdom is not the only virtue that is having a poor time of it in the modern university. Patience, humility, generosity, perseverance, thoroughness, carefulness, quietness: these might once have been felt to be signs of a strength of character. No longer. In an age of self-promotion, self-presentation, visibility, efficiency, work-rate, personal performance indicators and sheer competitiveness, character traits such as these come to be seen as signs of personal weakness. But the changing fortunes of the virtues do not just affect personal characteristics but also strike at the heart of what is valued in academic life.

For example, scholarliness is hardly a prized virtue in an age in which an institution's publications output has to be improved year on year. No longer is the scholarly life, in which one produces four or five major works in one's academic career, appropriate. Wittgenstein produced one major work in his lifetime and one posthumously; and that rate of productivity would raise more than an eyebrow in an institution conscious of its research ratings. (His teaching techniques were not much to write home about either.) The result is a change in the character of the academic text. A short text, packed full with bibliographic references, which has the appearance of engaging with the mood of the moment is the outcome. Not yet a coffee-table academicism, style and immediate effect are what count. After all, performance indicators can hardly record lasting impact. A short shelf-life is the order of the day, and so on to the next text with a clear conscience. Even mere output is not enough, for the real high marks go to research income. Scholarly output is hardly going to ensure economic survival, after all.

We are clearly witnessing a change in the character of academic life. The question is, how is this change to be understood? This development could be read as just another phase in the long history of the university to adapt to the requirements coming its way from its host society. For most of its history, the university has been tolerated and indeed supported by crown, church or state on the condition that it acted the part set for it. Other functions were allowed provided that they did not affect the larger and dominant mission. The current realignment is merely that: simply an adjustment to a new level of requirements from the wider society.

But we should pause before accepting such a benign view. For the argument so far is that we are seeing a profound shift in the value-base of academic life and, with it, a withering away of the virtues which the university has supplied in and to society.

In an institution in which the curriculum is being defined in terms of competence-based outcomes, in which accountability mechanisms are taken on as external agendas and so are felt as imposed, in which mass higher education coupled with required efficiency gains reduces the academic's non-determined time, in which increasingly sophisticated management information systems open professional activities for inspection, and in which power both increases and concentrates in the locus of newly emerging managers, the sum of human activity increases and is more productive. But in this general busy-ness, the character of the cognitive effort of students, of lecturers, of professors and of managers changes. Problems are posed and even 'solved'; skills develop; policies are shaped; and techniques are refined. But wisdom, as a form of deep reflection, collective exchange, and a recognition and even a critique of inner values, is put in jeopardy. Indeed, it ebbs away; it is surplus to requirements.

Part 4

Competence Reconsidered

11

Two Rival Versions of Competence

Introduction: speaking of assimilation

We can now pull together the strands of our analysis so as to prepare the ground for a concluding proposal in the final chapter.

Our task has been one of exploring the emerging relationships between higher education, knowledge and society, especially as reflected in the changing language of higher education. En route, we have examined only some of the new terms and ideas coming into widespread use. For a comprehensive examination, in addition to terms examined here – competence, capability, enterprise, outcomes, modularization, credit accumulation and skills (whether 'transferable' or not) – we would have to add others such as experiential learning, problem-based learning, open learning and even 'the student experience' *and* we would have to reflect on ideas such as profiling and learning contracts. That we have had to limit ourselves to a less than total examination of the contemporary lexicon is not especially problematic since our main concern has been to use these semantic explorations as a way into a broader analysis.

The method adopted here has been, as we might term it, socio-conceptual archaeology. Language typifying a social practice such as higher education does not change without cause. Nor are the causes simply a matter of idiosyncratic innovations. Language is social and terms come to be taken up in a widespread way because they have societal resonances and uses. The changes to the higher education lexicon are not mysterious but are explicable. An adequate explanation, however, has to be built on a sense of the changing character of higher education in modern society. In this book, a view has been offered which can be readily summarized.

Higher education is a social institution: that much has always been the case, ever since its mediaeval foundations. Recently, however, the modern university has seen a radical shift; and that shift – set against a near-thousand years' history – is particularly sudden and rapid. From being a small institution on the margins of society, the university is quickly becoming a major institution incorporated into the mainstream of society's institutions.

The university was long sponsored by the dominant agencies of society – crown and church – but has now been taken up by the modern state in its efforts to promote economic and productive capacities. This process started in an arm's-length way in the period of major growth in higher education post-Second World War. Now, however, we are witnessing the inner sanctum of the curriculum and the learning process coming under the gaze of the wider society. The state, the market and the economic institutions of modern society now exert a direct influence on the character of higher education whereas formerly it was, at most, indirect. Higher education, to repeat an earlier assertion, has changed from being an institution in society to becoming an institution of society.

That process of assimilation continues to unfold. It takes varied forms across different institutions, different subjects and different modes of study. An honours physics course in an élite university taken on a full-time programme might exhibit a minimum degree of assimilation. Factors at work include the purity of the discipline and the societal capital it offers, the status of the institution and the extent to which the student experience is framed by the institution. (The poles of this last dimension are a full-time programme on a residential campus and a part-time programme built around work-based learning.) Any variation on one of these dimensions will alter the extent of the assimilation. The assimilation of academe is uneven. Resistance and accommodation are both apparent.

Unevenness across the system is indicative of underlying power structures and sites of varying vulnerability. Physics is able to resist in a way that the humanities are not (and so we find a readiness in humanities programmes to demonstrate their 'enterprising' character). At the institutional level, an élite university is able to resist in a way not open to an institution attracting less social prestige. Programmes in a new university may feel a greater need to respond to the claims of the student market than at an older university whose market is assured.

Precisely how these exchanges between academe on the one hand, and the state, economy and market on the other, are being played out is not our concern here. That story awaits a detailed empirical examination (although see Boys et al., 1988; Brennan et al., 1993). Such a story would have to include an account of the changing character of the welfare state, and it would have to embrace some analysis of the shifting stance of the state itself. It appears that we are seeing not so much the rolling back of the state but a new managerialism on the part of the state itself, exploiting the market as a proxy for state planning (Pritchard, 1994). Again, the substance of that story is not at the centre of our interests. Even so, that sociopolitical context cannot be entirely forgotten for it is a contributor to the semantic structure which we have been unravelling.

Our main concern has been the changing set of dominant ideas and meanings which are configuring the general understanding of higher education. The ideas and their associated curriculum developments have their anchoring, as with all language and institutional shifts, in social interests.

Since a central thesis of this book has been that the relationships between higher education and society are changing (essentially becoming closer), it follows that those ideas and developments can only properly be understood through exposing their connections with that wider societal surround.

This is not to reduce meaning to social interest, philosophy to sociology. It is to recognize that meanings are influenced significantly by social interest. That point, in turn, cuts two ways. We understand the meanings that attach to our social institutions by having a sense of the general traffic between the institution and the wider society. And, more radically, we gain insight into the constitution of contemporary society itself by excavating the central concepts of its key institutions.

As we have seen, the language of higher education is taking on the language of society. Empowerment, consumer, efficiency, audit and competence: these are terms having currency (if not always recognized) in society. That they also now have currency in higher education is testimony to the latter's penetration by wider ideologies.

We can press our analysis forward by polarizing two contrasting ideologies, paving the way for a third perspective to be set out in the final chapter.

Two rival conceptions of competence

The idea of competence has been a running theme in these explorations. That it has been a theme and less a point of attack is important. Competence as such has not been the issue in this book. What has been at issue is the interpretation given to competence. To repeat an earlier point: competence is an entirely acceptable aim for the academic community. We want our doctors, accountants and even philosophers to be competent. We may want more than competence from them but, still, competence remains a near-universal virtue.

Competence, then, is not problematic in itself as an educational aim, even in higher education. It becomes problematic when either or both of two conditions are fulfilled: firstly, when competence becomes a dominant aim, so diminishing other worthwhile aims; or, secondly, when competence is construed over-narrowly.

Competence is a contested concept. The argument here has been that there are two versions of the idea jockeying for position in academe: one is an internal or *academic* form of competence, built around a sense of the student's mastery within a discipline; the other – now being pressed robustly – is an *operational* conception of competence, essentially reproducing wider societal interest in performance, especially performance likely to enhance the economic performance of UK Inc. From cognitive culture to economic performance: the changing definitions of competence are a microcosm of the changing definitions of the university.

All the distinctions in Table 11.1 below have been made and developed in our earlier discussions. Here, therefore, just some brief notes on each polarity may be in order.

Table 11.1 Two rival versions of competence

	Operational competence	Academic competence
1. Epistemology	Know how	Know that
2. Situations	Defined pragmatically	Defined by intellectual field
3. Focus	Outcomes	Propositions
4. Transferability	Metaoperations	Metacognition
5. Learning	Experiential	Propositional
6. Communication	Strategic	Disciplinary
7. Evaluation	Economic	Truthfulness
8. Value orientation	Economic survival	Disciplinary strength
9. Boundary conditions	Organizational norms	Norms of intellectual field
10. Critique	For better practical effectiveness	For better cognitive understanding

Epistemology

The 'know that'/'know how' polarity is admittedly crude; and is one that higher education has lived with for some time through the gradual development of professional education. For those of an operational frame of mind, the test of worthwhileness of a form of knowing is: 'What does it enable us to do?' Valid knowledge here takes a pragmatic turn. For those preferring an academic variant of competence, the test of worthwhileness is: 'Is our knowledge of the world being advanced?' Both are narrow conceptions of knowing and both are flawed, pretending a spurious separation of thinking and doing (with each putting its money on a different one of the two runners). Doing at any level of complexity involves thinking, and thinking conducted with any seriousness is a form of action; but both points are sophistications often forgotten by the ideologists.

Situations

The operational spirit defines situations pragmatically. To some extent, situations define themselves – or may appear to do so. A more accurate account would be to say that situations are defined by the interests being brought to bear. And these will vary, depending on the outcomes of power plays in the wider society. For the academic spirit, situations are framed at least by the intellectual field of the academics present. This, too, is a matter of interests at work; but here the interests are cognitive in contrast to the operational interests of the opposing camp.

Focus

Within the operational ideology, the focus of any particular activity or interest is on outcomes. Outcomes may be in the past, present or future. Much effort is invested, especially against a context of the globalization of risk, in reducing risk by attempting to forecast outcomes. The kinds of outcome in question are changes in operational situations or in situations affecting operations. Competence is a function of an ability to control outcomes or to compensate for them. In contrast, the focus of competence in the academic domain is that of meaningful propositions. In the teaching domain, indications of propositional thinking are called for; in the research domain, public indications of *new* propositions are prized. The idea of 'focus' here turns on a distinction between pragmatic results and cognitive offerings.

Transferability

Both ideologies value transferability across domains of skill, or at least claim to do so. Operational competence looks to a transferability across domains of performative skill. (Whether such transferable skills exist remains, we noted earlier, another matter.) Academic competence is partly defined in terms of intellectual skills in transfering understandings from one cognitive situation to another. In both ideologies, skills are resources to be brought to bear with discrimination on new or challenging situations. The skills vary in kind, however. We have here a contrast between metaoperations and metacognition. It is a difference captured by the two questions: 'Did she really realize what she was doing?' and 'Did she have a sense of how she was trying to advance her understanding?'

Learning

In the academic version of competence, in both teaching and research, learning is essentially propositional in character. Many will say that individual facts, propositions and items of information are neither here nor there. What counts is the imparting of what it is to think as a historian or physicist and so on. Higher education is a matter of acquiring the outlook of the discipline. That is said, certainly. But it is doubtful if many students could recognize the claim in their curriculum experience. The reason is clear. By and large, the disciplines lack the reflexivity that a curriculum built around a disciplinary perspective would require. After all, the academics' own learning is of a propositional kind. It is not of a deeper, richer understanding of the nature of their own discipline. What fires academics is precisely the latest findings or heated controversy over new concepts. It is not concerns over the fundamental character of their discipline. The learning contained in both the work of academics and their teaching is essentially propositional in kind.

In the operational variant of competence, learning is characteristically experiential in nature. Recently, that learning has been given a public profile and higher education has been encouraged to recognize it as a valid form of learning. This development is merely a footnote to the key point, for it points up the fact that experiential learning has always been the dominant form of learning in the operational mode of human activity.

The notion of experiential learning is incoherent, since all learning is experiential. Strictly, we should be putting quotation marks around 'experiential'. What its proponents have in mind is the justifiable point that learning takes place other than in formal settings labelled as learning situations. However, there is an equivocation in the argument. On the one hand, it is said that: Look, here is a form of learning, valid in itself but different to that prized by the academic community. On the other hand, it is claimed that there is a correspondence between the two forms of learning, sufficient to allow a translation to be made between the two. If you can describe your experiential learning, I can tell you its equivalent in academic terms and so determine the appropriate amount of academic credit coming your way. Experiential learning is both different and the same. You can have your cake and eat it.

Communication

Communication is vital to both conceptions of competence but the sense given to communication differs radically between them. The form of communication associated with the operational sense of competence is that of winning over and influencing people. (The absent 'friends' is deliberate. There is no sense of winning friends here.) It is a form of communication intended to yield results; and acceptable results can include a change in attitude and a willingness to embrace a new organizational culture, just as much as putting a signature on a contract. In either case, communication is for the sake of the organization and its success, growth or even sheer survival.

Communication in the academic mode is for the sake of the discipline. The pedant will say that disciplines have no sake. That is not quite true. Disciplines wield a force of their own. We do not have to reify disciplines into given things: disciplines are the territory of fierce disputes and even battles, much more than students are often led to believe. But the communication structure of the discipline is not entirely up for grabs. Some give-and-take there can be; mavericks can be allowed to take some liberties. The earring in one ear on the conference platform, the occasional diagram where usually none is permitted, the rare use of colloquialisms: there is some tolerance, normally. But to admit this is simply to underline the main point, that disciplines do have a certain genre, a characteristic mode of expression which had better be understood and practised.

I suggested earlier that, irrespective of the communicative norms of individual disciplines, there are cross-disciplinary requirements of communication, built around norms of truthfulness, sincerity, commitment and authenticity. In the corporate world, on the other hand, truthfulness, sincerity, commitment and authenticity are not *necessary* conditions of doing business. Communication may produce results without such ingredients. They may even get in the way of effective communication. The salesman who believes that his company's products are competing against superior rival products had better not have too many qualms about sincerity if he wants to keep his job.

Evaluation

The primary test of operational competence is economy. Efficiency and effectiveness are often put together with economy as standards by which performance is to be judged, but they are subsidiary when compared to economy; and are derivative of it. The question to be asked in the sphere of operational competence is: How much profit will this operation generate? Or, more appropriately in a public service like higher education (but only just), how much money will this operation save? Efficiency is, in the end, a function of economy: more output is promised per measure of input; in other words, a more economic operation. Effectiveness looks different; engineers want their bridges to stand up. But effectiveness is measured against price: all bridges corrode. The question is, how quickly and at what cost? The interest in money can be analysed further in terms of, for example, the power relations that stand behind it. All that concerns us here, however, are the immediate motives at work.

The primary test of disciplinary competence is veracity. Truth is not absolute. Truth claims are assessed against the disciplinary tribe's norms and values, paradigms and dominant truth criteria. And all these change over time.

Both are narrow sets of standards against which competence is to be judged.

Value orientation

Operational competence is orientated towards economic survival: sheer unalloyed survival. The ethics of the market-place is not quite a contradiction in terms; but the instances of ethics, as in 'his word is his bond', are confined to specific situations and are highly structured. Their formality both reduces their ethical element and reflects their pragmatic character.

Disciplinary competence is founded on a will to achieve truthfulness. Plagiarists and cheats will not be forgiven; although (as Feyerabend points out) a strict admonition of cheating would render epistemic progress somewhat difficult. (As we noted, on Feyerabend's analysis, Galileo was a supreme cheat among cheats; but there have been more recent notable examples.)

The disparity between these two value orientations was captured by Minogue (1973), in remarking that the survival of the planet or of the human species is not a matter of interest within the academic frame of mind. That Minogue got things askew as a matter of fact is clear enough. Medical scientists, we might reasonably assume, commonly do have an interest in securing increased longevity for the human species; they are not only interested in advancing knowledge. These days, too, they may have an interest in taking out a patent in biotechnology with a view to making their personal fortune. That reflection indicates that the values of the commercial world are increasingly to be found in the academic world and is another example of a point made in our explorations, that the world of academe is playing its part in the assimilation of values from the world of work. There are, though, necessary limits to this charitable disposition. If unchecked, pecuniary advancement would lead to the dissolution of the discipline. The academic life demands that the discipline be itself maintained and preferably enhanced relative to other disciplines. A bit on the side is all very well, so long as it is just that.

Boundary conditions

Actions derive their meaning by being interpreted within a larger framework or set of boundary conditions. With operational competence, the boundary conditions are those of the organization. Sanctions arise when those norms are contravened, whether they be symbolic (such as in the mode of dress), in the realm of values (as reflected in the internal operations or the effect of policies on the external environment) or in the sphere of operations as such. In each case, what is at stake is the internal coherence of the corporation as framed – whether explicitly or, more often, tacitly – by the corporation itself.

For disciplinary competence, on the other hand, the boundary conditions are those of the relevant intellectual field. To pick up again one of Bourdieu's terms (1971), the intellectual field provides a *habitus* to the individual working in it, that is to say, a set of taken-for-granted dispositions and attitudes. The individual stands at an intersection of concepts, ideas, theories and genres, which together constitute a discourse. There is an intellectual struggle in making sense of it, but it is a struggle within the limits of a largely familiar and comfortable terrain.

Operational boundary conditions are local in character whereas the intellectual field supplies a near-universal terrain. 'Universal' in two senses: in principle, anyone can enter and participate provided they have the necessary minimum intellectual competence; and the rules are impersonal to a large degree. '*Near*-universal' because both principles must be qualified. The academic world is not noted for its tolerance and openness, the rules being interpreted and sometimes implemented so as to distort their supposed even-handedness. Journal editors may not always act scrupulously and academic references may sometimes reflect personal bias. Nevertheless, in general, the boundary conditions of academic life stand independently of persons and organizations whereas in corporate life they are integral to organizations and their personnel.

Critique

Everyone is in favour, or so it seems, of critical abilities. Workers are to be empowered critically to assess their working environment and come forward with new ideas; students are to be encouraged critically to reflect on their programme of studies and to shape its development. The nature, however, of critique varies between academic and organizational life.

The form of critique demanded by operational competence is, as just implied, a form of reflection intended to bring about greater effectiveness. Critique works within a horizon of utility; that is to say, critique is tolerated provided it points towards changes with a use-value which are located within the relevant boundary conditions. Those tempted to critique current operations – to raise their head above the parapet of norms and operations – have, in short, to be prepared to face the response: 'But what is the point of your objection? Where does it get us?' Critique is not valued in itself: it has to promise tangible rewards within the boundary conditions.

It is not true, therefore, to say that the academic world revolves around critique whereas the corporate world does not. The corporate world recognizes that it is facing a wider environment of change and that organizational responsiveness requires a measure of critical reflection from employees generally. Neither is it correct to say that critique characteristic of the academic world faces no restraint. Academic critique is subject to a number of conditions, both general across disciplines and specific to disciplines. There are rules of the game to be observed: discourses are (following Foucault) sites of power and those who wish to be taken seriously in the discourse had either better be prepared to fall in with the rules or be excommunicated.

A difference in the two versions of competence emerges in their treatment of understanding. Understanding is present in operational critique, but it is an understanding of operations. We want to know whether things work, rather than why they work; and even less, what counts as working. In the sphere of academic critique, it is an understanding of concepts, ideas, evidence and theories that counts. This is critique in several senses. Picking up a Kantian sense of critique, it can include reflection on the limits and constitution of understanding, even if that reflection is confined to reflection on the form of understanding offered by a single discipline. (To cull examples from contemporary academic debate: What is the study of international relations? What is this thing called science? What are feminist studies?) It may also include understanding operations, happenings, events, organizations and policies in the 'real world'.

So academic critique is reflection orientated towards understanding better the already existing understandings. On the other hand, critique in the operational sense is an understanding that enables us 'to go on' with greater confidence. This is *not* to be downplayed, as the academic world is tempted sometimes to do. Professionalism, following Schon, can be said to embody valid 'knowledge-in-use', the result of a myriad of real-time experiments in thought and action.

Critique internal to operations can and does have issue in improved performance. But the notion of improvement only has application through the generation of some standard external to the performance. For that standard to be secure, we have to have recourse to an independent reflective discourse. Greater rationality in our operations requires sustained reflection *on* those operations but it also calls for the independent perspectives and insights provided by the disciplines to be turned onto those operations. In the end, operational critique has to be underpinned and evaluated by the cognitive critique of the disciplines.

We have, then, two distinct forms of critique in the domains of operations and of academic reflection. Both have their limits and both have a contribution to make towards more insightful and, therefore, more rational action. Neither, by itself, can supply a comprehensive account of critical thinking.

Having sketched out some differences between the two ideologies of competence – operational and academic – we can now turn to some general themes prompted by this analysis.

On transferable skills

A fundamental question before us throughout this book can now be answered. The question has been: are the general skills of the world of work the same as the general skills of the academic milieu? When employers ask higher education to produce graduates with transferable skills and academics retort that they have always been in that line of business, or even say that they intend to bring transferable skills higher up their teaching agenda, are the voices of the labour market and of academe expressing similar points of view? Is the same thing being meant, for example, by 'communication skills'? The answer is apparent from our analysis: they are not the same thing at all; or, at least, *ought not* to be the same thing. The interest in truth internal to academe cannot be forsaken, unless academe is entirely to fall in with Foucault's line. Communication in the wider world may typically revolve around power and securing results; but the academic world has a responsibility (the term can be used without embarrassment) to seek truth and to give higher marks for verisimilitude than for overt components of communicative competence, necessary as it is for the academic to be able 'to communicate'.

To continue with this example of 'transferable skills', communication skills are not all of a piece across the two definitions of competence but their differences are by no means obvious. The public presentations of the corporate world appear to be mirrored by the showy conference presentations of the academic globetrotter, but their internal point and standards differ. Certainly, understanding is present in the corporate world but it is understanding gained within a power structure and within an interest structure of success. What counts in the academic world is enlightenment based on truth. The mode of presentation may assist or hinder understanding – whether the form of interaction is face-to-face or through the written word – but the 'quality' of the presentation is an issue only insofar as it enhances or lessens the understanding of the argument being made.

That strategic communication is being incorporated into the curriculum has been a sub-plot of this book. The curriculum is changing not just to admit but even to be formed in a major way by skill development, orientated directly to a labour market characterized by change and uncertainty. But it is also apparent that strategic communication is being seen increasingly in universities. As universities become organizations, become bureaucracies, hierarchically arranged and with lecturers becoming 'human resources', communication is less dialogical and more strategic in character. Put simply, it is concerned to get things done, to produce institutional responses to the pressing challenges of the environment in which the university is operating, and less concerned to arrive at views of the world characterized by the better argument.

This colonization of a realm of dialogic communication by a realm of strategic communication invades the academic sphere. In competing for research contracts, academics are being asked to participate in 'beauty contests' in which (politely speaking) they parade their wares or (less politely) they sell themselves. The slick presentation with the well-prepared overhead slides is what counts. But strategic communication is to be found within academe as well.

In procedures organized for appointing new lecturers, for example, it is becoming common for short-listed applicants to be asked to give presentations to a group of staff. Correspondingly, in moves towards appraising teaching effectiveness and in quality assessment exercises, staff are being judged by their ability to perform. In both cases, this weight given to the character of the performance as such is symptomatic of strategic reason at work. The counter view will be put that, in both cases, evidence is being sought of the ability of the performer to be sensitive to context and to respond to the views and positions of audience members. Dialogue is important, after all. But this is to mistake the real intent of the appraisal. Suppose that our performer, applicant or observed teacher, was simply to invite questions and then to respond to them or even to set the assembled groups tasks for mutual self-learning: in either case, the intentions of the appraisers would be thwarted. It is, after all, the performance that counts.

Communication skills are simply the most popularly acclaimed of the transferable skills. If there are doubts about the correspondence of communication skills in the two realms of academic and operational competence, then there have to be doubts about the common nature of transferable skills as such.

Transferable skills betoken generality; but it is precisely their generality that is in doubt. The so-called transferable skills, even if they exist, turn out to be skills with a currency in the corporate world. The transferability associated with getting things done and with having effects on people and on organizations cannot be the transferability of intellectual skills associated with winning through to the better argument. These are two contrasted forms of human competence overlying fundamentally different interests in control and in understanding.

The academics either deceive themselves or, more probably, are trying unconsciously to deceive their detractors when they claim that they have been in the same business as their detractors all along. After all, if that were so, why are graduate employers so insistent that their graduate employees are deficient in transferable skills? The proper response is not that we have always been in that business but that 'Our transferable skills are not your transferable skills; and we are going to hang onto ours'.

Openness and closure

A theme not far under the surface of our discussion has been that of openness and closure. It is apparent that no simple categorization of operational and disciplinary contexts in terms of open or closed can be sustained. Both contexts have elements of closure in them, as must be the case with any systematic set of human interactions. Indeed, disciplines are, in this sense, more susceptible to closure than operational contexts precisely because they have a necessarily high degree of systematicity. While their truth criteria, paradigms and modes of procedure all change over time, the time-span of major change tends to be on the long side. They have a degree of durability and even inertia which organizational operations, faced with the challenges of the 'real world', do not.

Yet, for many commentators (such as Popper from an epistemological perspective and Horton from an anthropological perspective), western thought is characterized by significant elements of openness. There are no absolute authorities: only the even-handed demands of reason and evidence. Yes, there are party lines; but there are no three-line whips. Contrary views can be heard and are even welcomed.

Another reading of openness is rationality combined with dialogue, and this is the reading brought to us by Jurgen Habermas. Through adherence to the norms of rational discourse one is necessarily engaged in a dialogue, for part of that normative structure lies in offering truth claims with a view to engaging with others in dialogue over the worth of those truth claims. A corollary of a dialogic structure orientated towards truth is that the dialogue is not constrained by unequal power relations.

It will be urged that just as much can be said of operational competence: there, too, contrary views are increasingly welcome, to a point. If the modern corporation is to survive, it has to be a learning organization; and a learning organization is necessarily an open organization, with all its members being encouraged to form their own evaluations of their immediate circumstances. Yet it is openness of a truncated kind. Permissible openness here will turn upon an interest in furthering the fortunes, even if only the survival, of the organization. That this is coming to have meaning and, indeed, application to our universities is indicative again of the extent to which universities are becoming organizations. The point remains that organizational openness will tend to curtail opportunities for significant cognitive challenge from the organization's members.

The reasons for tendencies towards closure are already to hand in the analysis just given of what it is to conduct a rational discourse. Organizations are of their nature hierarchical and characterized by power relations. (Admittedly, there are signs of organizations adopting flatter internal formations and, in this sense, coming to resemble universities of yesteryear just as universities are coming to resemble old-style organizations.) Secondly, unequal power relations *do* produce the equivalent of three-line whips. The limits of opposition are more tightly drawn than in the academic domain. We do not often find permitted the equivalent of the kind of continuing debate quite typical of academic journals, in which contestants are given space to set out their alternative views of the very nature of the discourse itself. It would be the equivalent of the corporation's house magazine giving space to employees to argue that the corporation should be in a quite different business. This may happen; but its occurrence would be a case of the exception that proves the rule.

The question remains, therefore, for those who are urging higher education to incorporate operational competence in its programmes of study: is openness really going to be tolerated? And to what degree, in what proportion and of what kind?

Technique

All forms of competence are a matter of technique, although that statement has to be qualified immediately. In the domain of academic competence, technique is a necessary but quite insufficient condition of being recognized as 'one of us'. A number of other attributes are called for, including a determination to get to the bottom of things (as Richard Peters put it), a willingness to give oneself to the demands of the discipline (in other words, a self-discipline), a personal toughness in developing and propounding one's own thinking, a commitment to and ownership of one's offerings, and an ability to put an individual stamp on things. In short, academic competence calls for ethical qualities, for certain kinds of human *being*. Technique, in contrast, can be evident without such human qualities.

To say of a concert pianist only that she possessed technique of a high order is pretty damning. Technique is, at best, a resource to be put to the service of other values. Doubtless, its significance varies across fields of human activity. Clients rightly want the professionals who serve them to be competent, whether doctor, surveyor or lawyer. Getting the notes right on the concert platform is less important as a criterion of effectiveness than getting the drug dosage correct.

But even though its value varies, technique can never be a sufficient desideratum by itself in any human activity of value. Yet operational competence drives up the value of sheer technique and even places it above all other considerations. Competence, skill, knowing-how, getting things done, technique, effectiveness, operation: all these are coming to form a constellation of concepts marking out a discourse and a set of interests.

A concern for technique above other kinds of criteria drives out a concern for values; or appears so to do. In fact, it does not do so since it represents itself a penumbra of values founded, as we have seen, in a dominant interest in manipulating the environment, understood in its most general terms. Technicism seems to be value-free but is shot through with values. What it does is to rule out of order *explicit* attention to values. Admittedly, academic discourse often falls into this same trap; but that reflection only underlines the general point, that operational competence and disciplinary competence are *both* ideologies.

Conclusion

Higher education is seeing two sharply opposed definitions of competence. The two definitions, termed here *operational* and *academic*, contain alternative clusters of related ideas, turning on different interpretations of transferability, skill, communication, situations, focus, orientation, critique and epistemology. Each definition is coherent in itself but, in being opposed to the other definition, is inevitably narrow in character. We have here polar opposites (even if the ice is melting and the waters are merging).

The two definitions of competence are Weltanschauungs, sets of beliefs and values marking out a total project on the part of their adherents. The project – operational or academic – is a kind of claim on higher education. It seeks to protect or even advance a cause. Accordingly, there can be no simple rapprochement between these two views. They each gain their legitimacy (insofar as they have any) in part from their being opposed to the other definition. They are, therefore, *rival* versions of competence.

Even more, they are both ideological in the strict sense of the term. The two definitions of competence reflect structured social interests (roughly, the one external and the other internal to the academic world); they are attempts to define a social activity (higher education); they are normative projects intended to bring about allegiance among the believers; and – representing their definition as the one valid view – they contain a significant element of distortion. Both camps, therefore, are claiming to tell us about a portion of the world (higher education) in a way that restricts the possibilities open to it, and in a way that reflects sets of social interests. These elements of the descriptive coupled with the normative, social interests and distortion are all classic hallmarks of ideology (Eagleton, 1991).

Ideology should not be seen as a rational project, even if it has rational elements (Gouldner, 1976). Rather than countering it head-on, we have to box a little more cleverly. We can side-step them (Maginot-like) by opening up another front, conceptually and pragmatically. That, at any rate, is the prospect of our last chapter.

12

Beyond Competence

Dreams and minds

In a dream, a huge pelican-like bird swoops down and scoops up in its beak a young woman from the deck of a yacht which she is crewing. Is the dream to be explained as the result of a condensation in the brain of certain images that had presented themselves to the dreamer over the last twenty-four hours, including advertisements for *Jurassic Park* (a film about pre-historic monsters); a news item about airplanes used in firefighting on the south coast of France which scoop up water from the Mediterranean; and another news item about an open-sea yacht race? Or are we also to see the dream as carrying some semantic content, warranting some kind of inter-pretation and possibly revealing some hidden and even repressed state of mind?

Is a dream, in other words, simply an indication of a brain processing information, computer-like? If so, there can be no imputation of meaning to mental states: they are just the outcome of neurological events, a full description of which would consist of identifying some neurones as being in a state of electrical excitation and others as not. *Or* is a dream only fully understood when we can understand its contents as carrying meaning? By 'meaning', all that we need imply here is that the contents have to be describable using concepts (bird, swoop, scoop, youth) which have human import and that there is some personal association with those concepts at work, however ill-formed.

In higher education, are educators to be understood simply as those who bring about a change in the brain-state, influencing (if not causing) some neurones to be switched on and others off? Or are they to be understood as bringing about changes in mental states, with minds being influenced to take on new concepts and to form intentions or, at any rate, capacities in relation to those concepts? Are students just the possessors of supremely adept computers-as-brains so that the task of the teacher is to enable the computer to function at full power: processing sense data, forming new neural nets and acting on those transformed brain-states, perhaps even producing new formations of that information? Or are students also the possessors of minds, capable of supplying meaning to their brain-states, taking up stances towards their own mental furniture, and acting in the world – whether in professional life or in other settings – through a conceptual framework that they have made their own?

Partly at issue in this book has been precisely this mind-brain problem. The philosophers and the neuropsychologists continue to debate it (cf. Searle, 1992). No matter: educators, implicitly or deliberately, have to adopt a position on the subject.

The argument of this book has been that we are currently faced in higher education with two rival ideologies of competence, an operational definition and an academic definition. Strikingly, both have inbuilt tendencies to veer towards the brain end of the mind–brain axis, much as each will protest to the contrary.

Reproduction, not transformation

Operational competence proclaims its acceptance, at the higher levels of competence, of the idea of coping with unpredictability. After all, we live in an unpredictable age, and corporate life is one of living effectively with continuous change. This sounds like minds at work, making sense of the world and coming forth with new ways of tackling the world. The verb is the giveaway: 'tackling', not thinking about the world or reflecting on it or forming judgements on it. Mind, therefore, is at best boxed into an instrumental orientation; and is at worst merely a function of the conditions and environment within which it is obliged to operate.

The notion of 'outcome' is peculiarly and unwittingly apt in this perspective. What is sought is a response to a given situation: an input-output notion lies not far under the surface of operational competence. What is prized is not a genuine personal interpretation of a situation (for that could lead to an unduly challenging world-view) but a *re*processing of presented sense data. Real independence of mind cannot be tolerated. Real minds would be liable to challenge the given definitions of competence and outcomes. 'Mind', therefore, falls outside the constellation of concepts containing competence and outcomes.

But 'mind' tends also to be excluded from academic definitions of competence, at least as represented in the higher education curriculum. Much international evidence, accrued over the past twenty years, indicates that a significant proportion of students adopt a *processing* orientation to their learning. They construe the learning task as one of assimilating and reproducing the sense data they have had put their way. They do not see it as their responsibility to engage in a way that is personally meaningful with that which they encounter. Still less do they wish to seek out quite different kinds of cognitive experience, and so to frame their 'student experience' for themselves.

Occurrences of this kind cannot be laid solely at the door of the students. A central message of that research is that teachers have a responsibility for the way in which students take up their learning stances. Gibbs (1992) cites the case of a single student taking a joint honours programme who adopts a surface or reproducing learning approach for one subject and a deep or meaning approach for the other, this strangeness being explicable through the teaching approaches and the educational experience as framed by the tutors concerned.

In an early paper, Ramsden (1983) produced evidence to back up his contention that the English polytechnics were more likely to promote learning approaches based on a meaning rather than a processing orientation. Whether such a case would find evidential support today is, of course, uncertain. What can be said is that there is a logic to a situation where an academic culture that prizes research (literally where the prizes go to those who excel in research) also promotes a reproducing culture. In such a culture, *both* teacher and taught may all too easily construe their respective roles as one of coming into contact with the latest research findings and assimilating them. Students end up with a reproducing attitude because that is the implicit attitude of those who stand before them.

The centrality of the reproducing mode in academic life is one of the messages of Kuhn's classic text (Kuhn, 1970). Scientific knowledge works quite happily for most of the time within accepted paradigms or exemplars. The scientific mode of inquiry is not to inquire very far at all. It is to take as given the ways of thinking, boundaries of thought, conceptual schemas and frames of reference that contemporaneously define the immediate intellectual field. This is a reproducing mode of thought *par excellence*; not a transformatory mode of thought at all. The 'revolutionary' mode of thinking – Kuhn's word was apt – is reserved for rare occasions and even rarer thinkers. And, when offered, it normally encounters resistance.

It is, then, reproduction rather than transformation that comes most easily to the academic turn of mind. It is hardly surprising that we find so many fundamental intellectual revolutions being wrought outwith academe (Wittgenstein, Einstein, Darwin, Freud, Marx). Accordingly, it is not students who should be in the dock when we find them adopting reproducing learning approaches, for they are only *re*producing the reproducing learning approaches of those whom they take to be epitomes of the learning enterprise.

There are, then, reproducing tendencies in *both* operational and academic forms of competence. This surprising situation is explicable in the following way. All forms of life look to their own reproduction. Forms of life are essentially conservative, creating boundaries within which they might be perpetuated. What actually counts as being competent will differ across forms of life; and the modes of existence of operations in the commercial world and of thought in the academic world are – in their extremes – strikingly different. Nevertheless, each will have a sense of what it is to be competent; and a notion of competence necessarily has closed components. Reproduction and closure go together in perpetuating a form of life.

The objection will come that this makes no sense, so far as operational competence of the kind sketched out in this book is concerned. Far from wanting reproduction of given competences, the learning society wants capacities in the labour market that will produce spontaneously new forms of human capital. We all have to be ready to take on two, three or even four kinds of career, so we are told; and we had better be prepared in advance. We should acquire both 'transferable skills' and a preparedness to face confidently entirely new situations, and even to bring about new situations (providing that they have capital generating power). Far from being characterized by reproduction, the learning society is founded on continuous change. Not so much getting on one's bike; more getting on one's motor bike to keep ahead of the changes before one.

The discontinuity of contemporary society is not to be downplayed. This, after all, is part of the character of *post*modernity, as distinct from mere modernity. But postmodernity is as much a cultural project as it is a reading of human capital formation. And, as with cultural movements generally, it is hardly surprising if there is a lag between the changes in meaning structures developing in society and those still embedded in the labour market. The forces of production are, in this sense, superseded by the relations of production. International conferences and seminars for national planners and bureaucrats may speak the language of postmodernism but the employers have not heard the message; and nor have certain state agencies. What counts in the pragmatic world of labour markets *and* in the ideological world of state educational policies is a determination to increase productive capacity.

It follows that we do not yet have a higher education for the learning society. Nor is it in sight, even in the narrow sense of 'learning' given to 'the learning society'. Reproduction still rules OK: the corporate world wishes to see itself reproduced in its own image. The state, being unable to envisage an alternative, is an accomplice in this strategy. Operational competence, as reflected in the work of the National Council for Vocational Qualifications, remains essentially a strategy for reproduction rather than for transformation. It does not dare to be otherwise.

Mind and body

If a mind/brain tension lurks in this situation, so too does a mind/body problem.

It is striking how many authors of competence-orientated texts are today calling up Gilbert Ryle's classic book of 1949, *The Concept of Mind* (e.g., Schon, Eraut, Hirst, Birch). (The present author was even telephoned and asked for the reference to Ryle's text while this manuscript was being written.) In that text, Ryle sought explicitly to exorcise the ghost in the machine. Western philosophy had been bewitched by a 'legend' of the human being

as being composed of two separate entities, mind and body. There are
no two such separate entities, Ryle argued. 'When I do something intelligently, i.e. thinking what I am doing, I am doing one thing and not two'
(p. 32).

How does it happen that a text known mostly just by those who have
taught or passed through philosophy courses is suddenly picked up by
those working in other domains; and a text which is over forty years old?
What we have here is a developing discourse in Foucault's sense of the
term. Ryle's text reemerges to serve a purpose, to bolster a particular cause.
Whether read or not, the supposition is that (for example, in distinguishing
knowing-that from knowing-how) Ryle has somehow written a script that
legitimizes giving high marks to performance. Knowing-how contains its
own components of intelligence after all. Ryle's text becomes a rallying cry
for the competence lobby. Operationalists of the world unite!

Unfortunately, for all its lucidity, Ryle's argument is inadequate. In
exorcising the ghost from the machine, Ryle has left us with not much
more than an intelligent machine. He is right: knowing-how cannot be
defined in terms of knowing-that; but that leaves us with knowing-that and
knowing-how. Instead, Ryle proceeds as if human being is just a matter of
intelligent knowing-how. Notice, too, *his* invocation of 'intelligent': how are
we to classify an act as intelligent if all we have by way of conceptual apparatus
are the ideas embodied in the action? The use of the term 'intelligent' is
to import from the now expunged world of knowing-that both criteria and
factual knowledge relating to intelligence. In other words, Ryle's position
is incoherent. Yes, knowing-how cannot be reduced to knowing-that but
neither can knowing-that be reduced to knowing-how (as Ryle and now our
contemporary operationalists wish to do).

Any possible weakness in Ryle's argument, still less any possible incoher-
ence, is of course never countenanced by those who call him up in support
of their operational apologias. The sheer existence of such a text, rightly
accepted as a classic of its genre, is sufficient for their cause. It apparently
legitimizes a movement which – in its non-intelligence – Ryle would have
surely disowned. (That philosophy departments have been and are being
closed due to the onward march of that operationalism is an irony lost on
these advocates.)

While they are eager to call up Ryle, these authors are never to be seen
calling up another philosopher who has written extensively about the mind-
body problem, and of even more recent vintage. I have in mind Michel
Foucault.

In *Discipline and Punish*, Foucault explains how:

> The classical age discovered the body as object and target of power. It
> is easy enough to find signs of the attention then paid to the body –
> to the body that is manipulated, shaped, trained; which obeys, responds,
> becomes skilful and increases its forces.
>
> (Rabinow, 1984: 180)

In our context, this passage is extraordinary; it could have been an appraisal of operational competence as currently being instantiated in UK contemporary educational policy. But Foucault goes on:

The Great Book of Man-the-Machine was written simultaneously on two registers: the anatomico-metaphysical register, of which Descartes wrote the first pages . . . and the technico-political register, which was constituted by a whole set of regulations and by empirical and calcu-lated methods relating to the army, the school and the hospital, for controlling or correcting the operations of the body. These two regis-ters are quite distinct since it was a question, on the one hand, of submission and use and, on the other, of functioning and explanation: there was a useful body and an intelligible body.

(Rabinow, 1984: 180)

This passage contains two messages and an irony. The first, and major, message is that the body has been a focus of the exercise of power in much of western society. As Foucault puts it, there is a 'political economy of the body' (p. 172) and a 'political technology of the body' (p. 173). The minor message is that state institutions, including educational institutions, have been sites of the exercise of such power.

The irony is that Ryle, currently called up in the service of operationalism, saw himself as waging war on Descartes; and here Descartes is in the dock for legitimizing this kind of body politics. As we have seen, Ryle never escaped from Descartes' model of mind and body; he simply neglected any serious account of mind, despite the title of his book.

What I am suggesting is that Foucault offers a way into comprehending the contemporary operationalism facing us in UK education. With its neglect of 'understanding', and its stress on operations, training, perform-ance and the increase in productive forces, we have here the makings of just such a site of surveillance and control that Foucault was describing in his accounts of institutional life in historical France.

Rather than calling up Ryle as a remembrance of past philosophy, we might wonder why another, and even more recent, classic text is never mentioned in the same breath. Stuart Hampshire's *Thought and Action* (1970) tackles ground similar to Ryle's book but provides a much more subtle argument. Admittedly, paragraphs up to four pages long do not help its accessibility, but the argument is penetrating and runs quite counter to the operationalism being advocated today.

In part, Hampshire seems to be going in the same direction as Ryle. He warns against assuming 'too simple an opposition between speech and action and between thought and action' and he questions 'the naive dualism that divides, within a person's history, the internal and the mental from the external and physical'. But whereas Ryle tries to squeeze the internal and the mental into the external and the physical, Hampshire maintains a sub-tle interplay between them. As he pointedly asks: 'Is a conclusion that I reach in my own thought, the assent that I give to a statement in my mind, an action?' (p. 90). After all, 'An ordinary human action is a combination of intention and physical movement. But the combination of the two is not a simple additive one' (p. 74). As he adds, 'The thought that accompanies and precedes action is inextricably connected with the processes of deciding and trying' (p. 106).

These brief quotations cannot do justice to the complex and tightly interwoven argument that Hampshire gives us (a style of considered and careful intellectual argument that is, by the way, now out of fashion, a point not unconnected with the story we are unravelling here). Nevertheless, the quotations are representative and point to a constellation of terms that provide the framework for Hampshire's discussion: 'thought', 'action', 'mind', 'assent', 'intention', 'deciding', 'trying' and even 'I'. These terms reflect a sensitivity to human freedom, embodied especially in the use of language.

Putting Hampshire's argument in the context of the present argument, we might say that action cannot be construed as mere performance. As Hampshire insists, where action is present, it is always possible to ask of an individual, 'But why did you act as you did?', where only the individual concerned can supply a valid answer. To reduce human action to a constellation of terms such as 'performance', 'competence', 'doing' and 'skill' is not just to resort to a hopelessly crude language with which to describe serious human endeavours. In the end, it is to obliterate the humanness in human action. It is to deprive human being of *human* being.

Beyond competence

In the last chapter, I summarized the analytical part of this book by counterposing two conceptions of competence, the operational and the academic; and in elaborating the two conceptions, I tried to show that *both* were impoverished. We can now build on those remarks by sketching out an alternative conception of human being which might furnish us with new kinds of educational aim for the new century.

Table 12.1 shows the analysis offered in Table 11.1 together with an additional column.

The third column captures a view of human being located neither in operations and technique, nor in intellectual paradigms and disciplinary competence but in the total world experience of human beings. The term 'life-world' is that of Jurgen Habermas and it captures the point that what is at issue is an education for the world of human life. The life-world is broader than the world of either corporate competence or academic competence; and the objection will come from both camps: 'But how can a higher education for life be justified?' From the perspective of corporate competence, we are likely to receive questions, meant to be penetrating, such as: 'How can it be justifiable to spend taxpayers' money on such an education?' or 'How will such an education help to generate an economy capable of withstanding the challenge of the Pacific rim?' From the

Table 12.1 Beyond competence

	Operational competence	Academic competence	Life-world becoming
1. Epistemology	Know how	Know that	Reflective knowing
2. Situations	Defined pragmatically	Defined by intellectual field	Open definition (with use of multiple approaches)
3. Focus	Outcomes	Propositions	Dialogue and argument as such
4. Transferability	Metaoperations	Metacognition	Metacritique
5. Learning	Experiential	Propositional	Metalearning
6. Communication	Strategic	Disciplinary	Dialogical
7. Evaluation	Economic	Truthfulness	Consensus
8. Value orientation	Economic survival	Relative strength of discipline	The 'common good' (defined consensually)
9. Boundary conditions	Organizational norms	Norms of intellectual field	Practicalities of discourse
10. Critique	For better practical effectiveness	For better cognitive understanding	For better practical understanding

perspective of disciplinary competence is likely to come the questions: 'But how can a higher education for life generate a basis for knowledge and understanding equivalent to that of the disciplines?' and 'Isn't one of the values of disciplinary inquiry that it provides a vehicle for overcoming prejudice and false belief?'

Note that both ideologies feel able to fire these salvoes. They both feel that they are on secure ground, even though they are on quite different and even opposing ground. They cannot both be right, although both may fall short of the mark. As we have seen, their questions spring from a restricted perspective; indeed, from an ideology. So while their questions have to be treated seriously, they have also to be seen for what they are: reflective of an ideological position. The challenge before us, accordingly, is as much to develop a position that is less ideologically saturated as it is to produce a theoretically sound position.

Epistemology

Against the know-how of operational competence and the know-that of academic competence, an epistemology orientated towards the life-world is that of reflective knowing. This is an epistemology that treats knowing seriously and sceptically: its central motivation is double-barrelled, to embrace knowing but also to query it. Life-world becoming is more epistemologically sensitive than either operational competence or academic competence, both of which tend to take their own epistemologies for granted as supreme epistemologies. These two ideologies claim to be interested in knowledge but are so only on their own terms.

Reflective knowing is relaxed about forms of knowing: it does not strike a fixed position about favoured epistemologies but accepts that all kinds of knowing can help us to understand our world better. At the same time, it adopts an ironic stance in relation to all forms of knowing (cf. Rorty, 1989). It *knows* that all forms of knowing are partial and so keeps a jaundiced eye on them all. No one form is allowed a privileged status. Science is not granted special favours; and nor is practical know-how.

Correspondingly, *all* other claimants for knowledge can be acknowledged as serious candidates so long as they are prepared to submit themselves to continual scrutiny. Tacit knowing (Polanyi), knowing 'without a knowing subject' (Popper), knowledge-in-use (Schon), non-propositional knowledge (Hamlyn), traditions in knowledge (Feyerabend) and the rest can be recognized as carriers of worthwhile knowledge and, therefore, worth exploiting in a university curriculum provided they are willing to submit themselves to being placed under permanent review. Periodic cycles of quality assessment and quality audit are feeble processes of review in comparison. The price of epistemological admission to the academy is continuous scrutiny.

Situations

In the life-world, situations are open-ended. Life-world *becoming* requires that we are able to take up alternative perspectives and so bring a range of human and value concerns to bear on the issues that face us. Operational competence and academic competence are just resources, albeit valuable, that we might wish to employ; but there are others. Human concerns, aesthetic sensitivities, collective will-formation, action-based understanding, value choices: these are indicative of the much wider range of resources of understanding which we might wish to marshal in the life-world.

Such resources may also, from time to time, bring about a transformation in the way in which those situations are themselves perceived. Through such a flexible and imaginative use of resources, we can both transcend the power structures embedded in knowledge frameworks and create anew the situations before us.

Focus

Capability for the life-world requires a focus on the process of dialogue and argument as such. That is to say, dialogue and argument are so central to progress in the life-world that they cannot be taken for granted but have to be continually reworked and even renewed, taking on more refined forms as circumstances suggest or allow.

Interactive computer systems may allow for dialogical processes literally unimaginable (Ainley, 1993); but their development can easily slide into becoming an extension of operational competence. New technologies may herald the dawn of new forms of democratic interaction but may also bring more refined means of bureaucratic and power-led control. In their democratic development, we would see new roles for higher education in distributing knowledge more widely across society: a kind of twenty-first century version of the nineteenth century universities' extension movement (Gordon and White, 1979; Bell and Tight, 1993). But such interactive capability could also provide opportunities for the articulation and development of discourses held in and more properly representative of the life-world itself.

Transferability

The existence of transferable skills of any kind has been in question throughout this book. The argument has been that *if* transferable skills exist, then we should distinguish the transferability of operations (metaoperations) from the transferability of cognitive processes (metacognition). The two sets of transferability are different, neither being reducible to the other. The logic is that neither offers a comprehensive approach to transferable skills.

Insofar as there is a transferability to be identified in the life-world, it is that of metacritique. That is, capability in the life-world requires the capacity to take up an attitude of 'passionate scepticism' (to borrow a phrase from Bertrand Russell). In this attitude, *nothing* is taken on trust, not just because it might be flawed or deficient in some way but because life-world capacity calls for a personal ownership of one's experiences. Ideas, statements, symbols, ethical stances, institutions and ideologies – the totality of one's experiences, both immediate and mediated – must come under continuous scrutiny. What passes for evaluation, belief and evidential practice must itself be subject to one's own evaluation.

Metacritique cannot rest. It is a form of continuing self-surveillance. Surveillance cannot be excluded from our contemporary world but it can take the form of self-surveillance. External surveillance will tend to close off opportunities; self-surveillance, in contrast, is a necessary prolegomenon to emancipation.

The transferability here, then, is less an operational skill (as with metaoperations) or even a cognitive capacity (metacognition) but is more a state of mind. The transferability in question is one of comparing, contrasting, exchanging, reviewing and experimenting across the manifold domains of one's own human projects. Collaboration or at least interchange with others will be helpful in these tasks. No romantic notions of personal integration and coherence need be at work here. The aim, rather, is to maximize one's chances for personal emancipation by exploiting all the cognitive and personal resources at one's disposal. Challenge, resilience, daring, risk and maturity all come into play. Are the educators *willing* to educate themselves?

Metacritique is much more than an internal dialogue. It takes the form of a continuing and parallel array of consultancy reports, self-commissioned and conducted by oneself, all emerging with definite recommendations which go into the next round of personal – and even interpersonal – projects.

Learning

As against the experiential learning of operational competence and the propositional learning of academic competence, life-world becoming looks to a learning best characterized as metalearning. Society *is* changing, and individuals will be obliged continually to renew their cognitive state; in short, to go on learning. But that point is ambiguous, even if it is commonly made. As a form of operational competence, it could mean that individuals should be willing to take on new skills aimed at enhancing productive capacity; or, as a form of academic competence, it could mean that individuals should be prepared to tackle new intellectual fields as the definition of their professional field changes. Neither is what is intended here.

Rather, metalearning for the life-world is a willingness critically to examine one's learning. Putting it grandly, what is indicated here is a form of continuous action learning, where one's projects and practices are ruthlessly evaluated by oneself, and jettisoned where appropriate. Tests of appropriateness would be open and subject to evaluation themselves. Learning, therefore, is learning about oneself but in a rigorous fashion, a process that can have no end. We learn from our mistakes; but the purposes of the projects, the criteria of 'mistakes' and the learning to be extracted are all themselves kept under review. The guardians *can* guard themselves.

Communication

Whereas operational competence looks to strategic forms of communicative competence and academic competence looks to communicative competence framed by disciplinary norms, life-world becoming looks to a dialogical form of communication.

If experiences have ultimately to be recreated, if values have to be constructed, if projects have to be formulated, communication is a paramount feature of the life-world. This point seems simple and innocuous enough but it has profound implications. It calls, in the first place, for an ideal speech situation (in Habermassian terminology) where the only communicative act that counts is that of the better argument. Communication of this sort is a direct assault on power structures, whether of the kind inherent in operational competence or in disciplinary competence; and both forms of power structure are, as we have remarked, to be found in higher education. A higher education that understood this point, therefore, would offer a pedagogy characterized by a relatively even dialogic discourse between teacher and taught.

This is not, of course, to say that anything goes. Rules of rational discourse of the kind mentioned earlier (essentially Habermassian validity claims of rational discourse) would need to be safeguarded. But, in short, what would be developed in the teaching situation is a learning community in which everyone was communicating with and, therefore, learning from each other.

Evaluation

Whereas profit and truth are the cardinal criteria of operational competence and academic competence, here the cardinal virtue is that of consensus. Truth is not outlawed but is displaced. It is understood that what counts as truth is itself debatable. There is, at any one time, an infinite number of ways of carving up the world and of construing it. It is not quite right to say, *a la* Rorty, that all we have are our stories of the world, for we have an obligation if they are to be taken seriously to try them out on each other. We have both to take others' stories seriously and to try to secure assent to our stories.

Truth is worth seeking, even if we cannot be sure that we have reached it. However, other values are worth upholding in pursuing our projects. Aesthetic values, sensitivity to others, ecological sensitivity, ethical principles and many other matters may be worth taking into account. Others will lob in rival values such as wealth creation, orderliness, predictability and security. But this only adds to the complexity of the debate and drives up the significance of trying to reach a consensus, even if, again, that end too is unattainable.

Value orientation

The value orientation of operational competence is that of economic survival while that of academic competence is that of sustaining or even enhancing the relative strength of the discipline. For life-world becoming, what is ultimately at issue is the common good. But it follows from what has been said that the common good cannot be defined a priori, but has to emerge out of and be challenged within a genuinely open dialogue. It is an improvement in the life-world as such that is the fundamental motivation.

A capability orientated to this end, therefore, will look to marshal the total complex of resources available, including ideas and perspectives as well as technologies, and deploy them in a dialogical setting. The means are subservient to the ends; and the ends are kept under permanent review.

Boundary conditions

Capability for the life-world has to operate in the world and, therefore, is exposed to definite boundary conditions. The life-world is less structured than the corporate world or the academic world, but it has its own dimensions of politics, interests, power-plays, unexamined values and motivations. All these hedge in the life-world, exerting pragmatic limits to what might be achieved. At one level, effectiveness in the life-world is 'the art of the possible'; at another level, it is a function of the available discourses. What is possible owes much to the ideas, myths, hopes, fears, and imaginative possibilities that are entertained. These, in turn, are constituents of the concepts present in the local discourses *and* are an outcome of the kind of discourse. A genuinely unconstrained discourse will furnish ideas and imaginative possibilities not available in a discourse that is ideologically saturated or distorted by power relations (and, for Habermas, these two dimensions are different sides of the same coin).

Capability in this domain, therefore, will consist of widening or relaxing the conditions under which the discourse takes place. The boundary conditions are moveable. Capability here looks to see that all have a hearing, that different viewpoints are permitted and, indeed, that quite different approaches to understanding a problem are given a fair wind. This form of capability looks to make real communication possible and to encourage all to work at it to ensure that it goes on happening. But it also recognizes that discourse is politically structured; so it does not rest content with working immediately on the level of discourse but seeks, perhaps surreptitiously, to change or circumvent the political structures that are impinging on the discourse.

For example, an institutional quality assurance system may have a managerial motivation but, brought under the control of the faculty, can come to serve self-improving professional purposes. While the power structures are weighted on one side, the faculty are hardly likely to be honest in their self-evaluations. The discourse will be distorted. So the faculty need to work to gain political control over the process; only then will the distortions of the discourse be minimized and only then will the imaginative possibilities of self-evaluation be realized.

Critique

If operational competence tolerates critique provided that it supplies a greater effectiveness and if academic competence sees critique as improving understanding within a disciplinary framework, critique in the life-world is aimed at improving our understanding of our life-world itself; in short, of ourselves. Critique here takes on the attributes of *this* capability that we have been discussing: it is practical, multiperspectival, consensual and dialogical in character. It is intended to enable us together to handle our situations better – better, that is, in every sense: with sensitivity to others, a sense of the conflicting values present in a situation, an aesthetic appreciation, a concern for the environment *and* to see those situations in new ways.

Critique is not simply critical, but is constructive and is organized to develop solutions, or at least imaginative possibilities, for discussion. Critique is intended to move everything – purposes, situations and persons – forward.

Conclusions: implications for higher education

What are the implications of all this for higher education? The implications are straightforward. They are that the process of higher education should be arranged so as to promote the kinds of life-word becoming just outlined. For example, higher education should provide experiences to every student which encourage:

1. systematic reflection on one's own actions (action being interpreted to include one's own thinking);
2. reinterpretations of the presenting 'situations'; a curriculum is not a set of impositions on the student but is a set of possibilities and practical hopes in part framed by the student;
3. genuinely open dialogue, with the student being encouraged to develop his or her dialogical competence;
4. adherence to the rules of rational discourse, yet a mutual recognition that the rules are conventions and themselves should be interrogated from time to time;
5. a willingness to develop arguments for the appraisal of the other participants on the course;
6. an openness to possible forms of analysis, perspective and argument; a determination not to be hedged in by any particular 'method' but to embrace every possible perspective and approach;
7. the development and potentially continuous expression of a sceptical outlook;
8. attention (by the students) to and maintenance of the character of the dialogue; being sensitive to the claims of others who wish to enter the dialogue and encouraging *them* to do so;
9. a continuing reappraisal of one's own learning (aided by peer interaction);
10. testing the implications of and (where appropriate) the validity of the argument in pragmatic situations, where tests of validity include ethical evaluations;
11. exploring the implications for our social, political, economic and other institutions of the arguments held to have (some) validity.

At first glance, this list may not seem controversial; yet it runs counter to the positions of either academic or operational competence. In the first case, there is no mention of disciplines, truth, knowledge, objectivity or even autonomy, teaching or learning: nor is this an accident. The assumptions of academic competence are deliberately being called into question. In the second case, there is no mention of skills, competence, outcomes, and all the conceptual baggage that goes with the mind-set of operational competence. Both are limiting ideologies, and contain impoverished views as to what it might be to develop interactive minds engaging with the world and searching collaboratively for wisdom. *Both* ideologies show the limits of competence in addressing the task in front of the university if it is to offer a higher education appropriate to the twenty-first century.

Retrospect and Coda

Retrospect

This book could have been read as a number of educational stories, stories about vocabularies, being and becoming.

Vocabularies

Language can constrain thought and action; and it can open them to new possibilities. Our explorations have drawn attention to the vocabularies that attach to contemporary educational ideologies. Those vocabularies are limiting in more than one way.

Firstly, many of their central terms point to limited views of thought and action. 'Competence', the central notion of our discussions, is par excellence a limited concept. Of anyone's competence, we want to say, very well but is that all he has to offer? Competence is not to be derided, but the idea of education has offered the promise in western culture of a much more complex development of human beings.

On competence, we have distinguished two warring interpretations, an operational and an academic interpretation. Both reveal their limitations in their very terminology: within the operational conception of competence, terms like 'skill' and 'outcome'; and within the academic definition of competence, terms like 'discipline' and 'objectivity'. Both sets of terms constrain *both* thought and action, although respectively they take pride in exerting different limitations in those two fields. In both cases, the silences count more than the explicit agendas in determining the limitations at work.

Skills and outcomes explicitly limit action but, in being largely silent about thought, exert their greatest limitation in that domain. As we saw, the language of skills and outcomes is completely unable to handle the idea of understanding; that silence accordingly exerts its greatest influence in the domain of thought. Correspondingly, a concern with disciplines, objectivity and truth appears to be over-focused on thought and therefore limiting *of* thought; but, precisely because it is silent about action, is devastatingly limiting in that domain.

We have seen, too, that terms in widespread usage in a public service such as higher education do not just float around like individuated linguistic odds and ends. Indeed, to the contrary in two ways: first, rather than coming along separately, they are clustered in constellations of concepts, and second, these constellations of concepts are vigorously at work, defending and attempting to advance particular agendas serving identifiable social interests.

In developing the argument of this book, we have focused on one clustering of terms – including competence, outcomes, skills, transferability, enterprise and credit accumulation – which together constitute (as I have termed it) an operational definition of competence. This operational conception of competence is, as we have observed, an ideology in the strict sense of the term. That is, it gains its power by offering a definition of reality that at the same time furthers a set of societal interests. Perception, partiality and programme are all carried forward together.

Ideologies appear to be rational. They appear to be open to debate. Their protagonists appear to be offering propositions that are genuinely open for examination. This apparent rationality is how they win over adherents. No-one wants to feel gullible. One wants to feel one has come to take on one's new view of the world as a result of a dispassionate view of the evidence. Ideologies are a great help here by seeming to do that work for one, yet in a thoroughly dishonest way. One way of doing this is to rubbish the opposition; or, rather, to show up the flaws in the opposition's viewpoint.

The ideology of operational competence gains its legitimacy by seeing off the ideology of academic competence. It is a victory won rather easily. The ideology of academic competence never put up much of a fight; and, in any case, it has had little strength on its side. In this book, we have concentrated on examining the case for operationalism. There are two reasons for concentrating our attentions on just one of the definitions of competence in question.

Firstly, the academic idea of competence *was* long flawed, both philosophically and sociologically. Philosophically, the idea of objective knowledge has been long abandoned as a sure linchpin of cognitive progress (even if some still hanker after it). Sociologically, the notion of autonomous institutions in which pure cognitive pursuits could be conducted was made *passé* over a generation ago, as financial responsibility for higher education passed from the Treasury to the Department of Education and Science and became subject to state planning. This double undermining – epistemological and sociological – of the idea of liberal higher education has meant that the notion of academic competence is seriously flawed. Academic competence is the pedagogical statement of liberal higher education, a specification of the kind of outcome that liberal higher education was supposed to produce. In the modern world, assailed philosophically and sociologically, academic man, or woman, is a creature without any kind of home.

Secondly, and more significantly, it is the operational definition of competence that is making the running at the moment. It is the language of competence, enterprise and transferability that we hear rather than talk of objectivity, truth and the disciplines. That latter vocabulary has taken on an old-fashioned ring. The language of operationalism, by contrast, has become the dominant vocabulary of higher education, a dominance entirely explicable in terms of the forces of the state backing it. It is *that* definition of competence, therefore, that has been our main target.

Being

Higher education is a process of human development orientated towards some conception of human being. The two conceptions of competence identified here contain markedly different views of human being; and these views amount to alternative sets of values. Operationalism looks to develop human beings who have an apparent ease in performing effectively in the world; it values such individuals. Academicism, in contrast, looks to develop human beings who are cognitively comfortable living on the inside of a discipline (or two), who care about its contours, who understand its demands, and whose conceptions of the world are shaped by that cognitive framework. Academicism values that kind of individual, the kind of individual who takes a particular delight (to use Marjorie Reeves' term) in shaping ideas according to the canons of the discipline.

It will be said that these are caricatures, pictures of ideal forms of human being nowhere to be found or even imagined. Both barbs miss their target. The argument here is that operationalism and academicism constitute two competing conceptions of human being, which are locked deep in our language and in our social practices in higher education. They do not *have* to be found or imagined in their pure forms. However, both conceptions of competence are very much alive, albeit in different ways. Academicism is perhaps dying, but it is a long time a-dying, refusing to give up the ghost: less a matter of its struggling on and more a matter of its not easily being put down. Operationalism, in contrast, is struggling to come into the world. It is demonstrably alive and kicking, and indeed keen to flex its muscles. Both conceptions have sizable interests, although academicism lies quiet, vainly hoping that operationalism will suffer a stillbirth.

These two conceptions of competence are polar opposites, turning on different senses of the relationship between thought and action. For academicism, action is subservient to and is reducible to thought; that is, formal, systematic, elaborated thought. For operationalism, thought is subservient to and is reducible to action. Legitimate thought is evident in action.

Both positions are incoherent. Action worthy of the name (as distinct from movement or behaviour) has to draw on independent thought *and* to be susceptible to evaluation by thought drawing on cognitive frameworks other than that in which the action was couched. Thought, correspondingly, has to be expressed, articulated, shared, offered and exchanged. In other words, thought is a complex of form*s* of action.

If both positions are incoherent, any viable third position will not be found by trying to locate some happy midpoint. What is required is a quite different conception of human being to guide our pedagogical practices in higher education. Certainly, thought and action have to be brought together but not in any facile sense. Both operational competence and academic competence are representative of comparatively closed worlds, respectively of work and instrumental action on the one hand and of formal thought and cognitive interaction on the other hand. If we are to find a notion of competence adequate to the demands before us as we move into a new century, it will have to be framed by quite different kinds of cognitive and social interest, which are much more open to the challenges of human life. We need a conception of higher education guided by a conception of human being which is as unconstrained as possible.

The domain of human interaction as such, termed by Habermas the 'life-world', provides just such an open world and one in which both thought and action are jointly necessary. A higher education that takes as its guiding aim a conception of human being capable of contributing effectively to the life-world provides a third and a different sense of competence.

Becoming

A higher education is necessarily a process of becoming. The question is, what kind of becoming? Operational and academic versions of competence look to different kinds of becoming. However, they are both similar in that the form of becoming required of students is a realization of states of being outside themselves.

Academic competence looks to students entering the disciplines, being 'initiated' into them (in Richard Peters' evocative term). The disciplines are seen as standing independently, corpuses in their own right, and it is the duty of the student to yield to their demands. The notion of 'discipline' reflects something of this process of giving oneself up to those external demands.

Operational competence looks to students obeying the 'standards' of external competences, marked out in the world of work. Instead of the structure of disciplines, it is now the occupational structure that imposes its demands. The use of the term 'standards' does similar work to 'disciplines', indicating that here are external desiderata to which the student has to conform if she is to make any progress.

In contrast, the suggestion made here is that we should think of the process of higher education as involving quite a different kind of becoming. Instead of asking the student to respond to and to fulfil the demands of standards externally present, higher education should be conceived as a process of fulfilling *internal* demands. In the higher education sketched out here, students come into themselves. The challenge on the educator is to provide an experience in which the student can be released into herself. Instead of imposing external demands, the task is one of enabling students to free themselves from the constraints under which they are already thinking and acting.

Insofar as disciplines or general intellectual skills or occupational standards or transferable skills *or any other external framework* is thought to have any use at all, if we are in the presence of higher education, those frameworks have to be seen by the students themselves *as* frameworks. That they are human constructions will be understood by both teachers and students. That they are potential forms of the imposition of power over students will also be understood. Disciplines, objective knowledge, occupational standards, skills and the whole ragbag have to be seen for what they are: ideologies exerting power and constraint, requiring a certain form of human development. In this sense, both the academics and the operationalists are in league in framing *their* conception of ideal human being and in requiring the student to conform to it. If we see higher education as a form of becoming in which students become *themselves*, an altogether different notion of becoming is required.

The seemingly paradoxical idea of students being released into themselves is the only way forward. Students have to be given the confidence – and, admittedly, the conceptual wherewithal – to work things through for themselves. Nothing can be taken as given, even the forms in which they are allowed to express themselves. The trouble is, of course, that their teachers are also their examiners; or, increasingly, their likely employers. So the external frameworks will often bind tightly. Nevertheless, if we seriously want higher education to be adequate to the demands of the new century and if we really want to create a learning society, ways will have to be found of maintaining significant amounts of space in which students can develop for and by themselves.

Some who think along these lines use a range of terms such as 'emancipation', 'empowerment' and 'self-realization' to describe the intended process of becoming. None of these is quite right. Emancipation suggests a freeing from constraint but, while students have their own inner constraints, there has also to be continual vigilance that students do not yield and succumb to entirely new constraints (in the form of disciplines or declared competences). Empowerment suggests that students be given power over their own affairs but, while we want them to have a measure of control, the notion of power is otiose in the conception of becoming suggested here. Self-realization suggests that students be given freedom to realize themselves but, while the sense of personal space is helpful, the additional implication that there is a pure self waiting to be realized is not.

Higher education as self-construction

There is probably no single term available to capture neatly the sense of becoming being sketched out here. Perhaps that is as it should be. Any single word is potentially apt to become a slogan and in its turn to become another binding framework.

It is worth noting that the idea of becoming being put forward here is not a free-for-all: it neither permits students an intellectual licentiousness nor grants them complete autonomy. On the contrary, it is highly demanding. It requires not only that they form their ideas, develop their modes of address and pursue their own activities; in short, construct their own voice. It requires also that they submit those ideas, patterns of expression and ways of doing things to the scrutiny of their peers. This means overcoming two forms of fear: a fear of articulating one's own viewpoint and a fear of submitting it to scrutiny by one's peers (a much more fearsome process than submitting it to a socially defined authority such as a lecturer or professional representative).

The becoming in question here, therefore, is a winning through to one's own position, expressing it in the way one wants (whether mainly in thought or in action) but being able to defend it in open dialogue. It is a seeing through of all frameworks, not so much a kicking them into touch since (as Popper remarked) we cannot do without frameworks, but of exploiting them as resources for one's own purposes and not because other authorities are requiring one so to do. It is a bringing to fruition, to articulation, that of which one was dimly aware but in a form that stands up to examination.

This is neither a selfish form of becoming nor even selflessness. This is a construction of the self through critical dialogue and mutual reflection, a process requiring toughness and resilience on the part of the student, so as to produce a self separate from external frameworks (of thought or action, of work or intellect). This self-construction is anathema both to the academics and to the operationalists since it stands independently of the worlds both of academe and of work. And the severity of its demands are not self-evidently attractive to students-as-customers. It is a process of becoming, therefore, that is unlikely to find many takers.

Coda: Recovering the idea of 'educator'

As the unit of resource falls and as consumerism descends on higher education, a drive to student-centred learning arrives. Teachers are told to become facilitators of learning, mentors, counsellors, curriculum managers; anything but teachers. The idea of educator vanishes at the same time.

It will be apparent that a pedagogy and a curriculum of the kind argued for here places definite and considerable responsibilities on academics as educators. In an education for academic or operational competence, the responsibilities are definite but limited; on the one hand, to enable individuals to live comfortably in disciplinary territories and, on the other hand, to bring students to a mastery of the identified skills. In a higher education for life, the educator's responsibilities are not merely expanded but are susceptible to continuing redefinition and expansion and even challenge.

In essence, the role of the educator implied by our explorations here is that of turning a cohort of students into a learning community, with the students being interactive and participatory, mutually supportive but self-critical. It does not follow that the educator's role is that of a specialist in group dynamics. To the contrary: the group must find its own dynamic. Nor does it follow that learning and interaction will happen successfully without structure. The interactions have to have point; and they will have point with a definite structure to the programme. Nor does it follow that academics as teachers have to be experts in the latest theories on student learning (helpful as that can be).

The educators' first responsibility remains to be fully on the inside of their own disciplinary calling: they have to keep faith with their vocation, provided that they can view it with the critical detachment that a pedagogy for life calls for. It is no part of the present case that university teachers can simply concentrate on the techniques of teaching: to go down that road is inevitably to fall in with the thinking of the operationalists. Life-world becoming points to seeing one's intellectual habitus as one habitus among many.

To put it sharply, being a university teacher of the kind envisaged here is complicated stuff. It entails bringing off an extraordinary set of transactions with, and modes of development in, a heterogeneous group of students. It is extraordinary because it consists of transactions that enable the students to come into themselves, to become more fully themselves, and to develop within frameworks of understanding made available to them but which do not constrain them. It is an opening up without closure, an *interaction* between teacher and taught, a situation in which everyone gains. One person's development is not at the expense of the others but positively helps the others. It is an education for collective self-transcendence.

Bibliography

Note: John Searle comments in his recent book, *The Rediscovery of the Mind* (1992), that 'I have come to believe that philosophical quality varies inversely with the number of bibliographical references, and that no great work of philosophy ever contained a lot of footnotes'. Deliberately, this work contains no footnotes and the text is relatively free of bibliographic references but a bibliography can hardly be avoided today.

Bibliographies are always something of a fraud. In any work of substance, drawing on reading over decades, it is impossible to be sure of the sources of one's ideas. The items in the list that follows, accordingly, have been chosen with four considerations in mind. Principally, I identify those sources with which I engage explicitly in a positive spirit in this book. There are, in addition, residual groups: first, those sources which, while not necessarily identified explicitly in the text, have been helpful in developing these ideas; secondly, other texts which are directly relevant to the text and which constitute, as it were, additional reading; and, only lastly, those texts at which I aim my attack. Fortunately, the ritual of the bibliography does not necessarily require one to separate one's sources under these categories.

Adorno, T. and Horkheimer, M. (1989) *Dialectic of Enlightenment*. London, Verso (first edition 1944).

Aggar, B. (1991) *A Critical Theory of Public Life: Knowledge, Discourse and Politics in an Age of Decline*. London, Falmer.

Ainley, P. (1993) *Class and Skill: Changing Divisions of Knowledge and Labour*. London, Cassell.

Althusser, L. (1969a) *For Marx*. Harmondsworth, Penguin.

Althusser, L. (1969b) Ideology and ideological state apparatuses. In B. Cosin (ed.) *School and Society*. London, Routledge and Kegan Paul.

Arendt, H. (1958) *The Human Condition*. London, University of Chicago Press.

Baird, J.R. (1988) Quality: What should make higher education 'higher'? *Higher Education Research and Development*, 7 (2), 141–52.

Ball, S.J. (ed.) (1990) *Foucault and Education: Disciplines and Knowledge*. London, Routledge.

Barnes, B. (1974) *Scientific Knowledge and Sociological Theory*. London, Routledge and Kegan Paul.

Barnes, B. and Edge, D. (1982) *Science in Context*. Milton Keynes, Open University Press.

Barnett, R. (ed.) (1992) *Learning to Effect*. Buckingham, Open University Press.

Barnett, R. (ed.) (1994) *Academic Community: Discourse or Discord?* London, Jessica Kingsley.

Barrett, W. (1979) *The Illusion of Technique*. London, William Kimber.

Becher, T. (1989) *Academic Tribes and Territories*. Buckingham, Open University Press.

Becher, T. (1994) Interdisciplinarity and community. In R. Barnett (ed.), op. cit.

Becher, T. and Kogan, M. (1992) *Process and Structure in Higher Education*. London, Routledge.

Bell, D. (1976) *The Coming of Post-Industrial Society*. London, Penguin.

Bell, M. and Tight, M. (1993) *Open Universities: a British Tradition?* Buckingham, Open University Press.

Bergendal, G. (ed.) (1983) *Knowledge and Higher Education*. Stockholm, Almquist and Wiksell.

Bergendal, G. (ed.) (1984) *Knowledge Policies and the Traditions of Higher Education*. Stockholm, Almquist and Wiksell.

Bernstein, B. (1971) On the classification and framing of educational knowledge. In M.F.D. Young (ed.), op. cit.

Bernstein, B. (1992) *Pedagogic Identities and Educational Reform*. Paper given to Santiago conference, mimeo.

Bernstein, R.J. (ed.) (1985) *Habermas and Modernity*. Cambridge, Polity.

Bernstein, R.J. (1991) *The New Constellation*. Oxford, Polity.

Birch, W. (1988) *The Challenge to Higher Education*. Buckingham, Open University Press.

Black, H. and Wolf, A. (eds) (1990) *Knowledge and Competence*. London, HMSO/COIC.

Bloom, A. (1987) *The Closing of the American Mind*. London, Penguin.

Bloor, D. (1991) *Knowledge and Social Imagery*. London, University of Chicago (second edition).

Bocock, J. and Watson, D. (eds) (1994) *Managing the University Curriculum*. Buckingham, Open University Press.

Bonefeld, W. and Holloway, J. (eds) (1991) *Post-Fordism and Social Form: A Marxist Debate on the Post-Fordist State*. Basingstoke, Macmillan.

Bourdieu, P. (1971) Intellectual field and creative project. In M.F.D. Young (ed.), op. cit.

Bowles, S. and Gintis, H. (1976) *Schooling in Capitalist America*. New York, Basic Books.

Boys, C., Brennan, J., Henkel, M., Kirkland, J., Kogan, M. and Youll, P. (1988) *Higher Education and the Preparation for Work*. London, Jessica Kingsley.

Bradshaw, D. (1985) Transferable intellectual and personal skills, *Oxford Review of Education*, 11 (2), 201–16.

Brennan, J. (1985) Preparing students for employment, *Studies in Higher Education*, 10 (2), 151–62.

Brennan, J. and Silver, H. (1988) *A Liberal Vocationalism*. London, Methuen.

Brennan, J.L., Lyon, E.S., McGeevor, P.A., Murray, K. (1993) *Students, Courses and Jobs*. London, Jessica Kingsley.

Bridges, D. (1993) Transferable skills: a philosophical perspective, *Studies in Higher Education*, 18 (1), 43–52.

Brosan, G. (1971) A polytechnic philosophy. In G. Brosan, C. Carter, R. Layard, P. Venables and G. Williams (eds) *Patterns and Policies in Higher Education.* Harmondsworth, Penguin.

Burke, J.W. (ed.) (1989) *Competency Based Education and Training.* Lewes, Falmer.

Carr, W. and Kemmis, S. (1986) *Becoming Critical.* London, Falmer.

Clark, B.R. (1983) *The Higher Education System: Academic Organization in Cross-National Perspective.* London, University of California Press.

Collier, G. (1993) Learning moral judgement in higher education, *Studies in Higher Education,* 8 (3), 287–98.

Davidson, G. (1992) Credit accumulation and transfer and the student experience. In R. Barnett (ed.), op. cit.

Derrida, J. (1992) Mochlos; or the Conflict of the faculties. In R. Rand (ed.), op. cit.

Dickson, D. (1988) *The New Politics of Science.* London, University of Chicago.

Downie, R.S. (1990) Professions and professionalism, *Journal of Philosophy of Education,* 24 (2), 147–60.

Drucker, P.F. (1992) *The Age of Discontinuity.* London, Transaction.

Duke, C. (1992) *The Learning University.* Buckingham, Open University Press.

Eagleton, T. (1991) *Ideology.* London, Verso.

Eggins, H. (ed.) (1992) *Arts Graduates, their Skills and their Employment: Perspectives for Change.* London, Falmer Press.

Elliott, R.K. (1975) Education and human being. In S.C. Brown (ed.) *Philosophers Discuss Education.* London, Macmillan.

Employment Department (undated, c. 1990) *The First Year of Enterprise in Higher Education.* Sheffield, Employment Department.

Eraut, M. (1992) Developing the knowledge base: a process perspective on professional education. In R. Barnett (ed.), op. cit.

Feyerabend, P. (1970) Consolations for the specialist. In I. Lakatos and A. Musgrave (eds) *Criticism and the Growth of Knowledge.* Cambridge, Cambridge University Press.

Feyerabend, P. (1975) *Against Method.* London, Verso.

Feyerabend, P. (1978) *Science in a Free Society.* London, Verso.

Feyerabend, P. (1987) *Farewell to Reason.* London, Verso.

Fleming, D. (1991) The concept of meta-competence. In *Competence and Assessment,* Issue 16. Sheffield, Employment Department.

Fleming, D. (1992) Vocational expertise and the contingency of value. In *Competence and Assessment,* Issue 20. Sheffield, Employment Department.

Frank, A. and Schulert, J. (1992) Interdisciplinary learning as social learning and general education, *European Journal of Education,* 27 (3), 223–38.

Freire, P. (1972a) *Pedagogy of the Oppressed.* Harmondsworth, Penguin.

Freire, P. (1972b) *Cultural Action for Freedom.* Harmondsworth, Penguin.

Fromm, E. (1960) *Fear of Freedom.* London, Routledge.

Fuller, T. (ed.) (1989) *The Voice of Liberal Learning: Michael Oakeshott on Education.* London, Yale.

Galbraith, J.K. (1969) *The New Industrial State.* Harmondsworth, Penguin.

Gellner, E. (1964) *Thought and Change.* London, Weidenfeld and Nicolson.

Gellner, E. (1974) *The Legitimation of Belief.* London, Cambridge University Press.

Gellner, E. (1979) *Spectacles and Predicaments.* Cambridge, Cambridge University Press.

Gellner, E. (1991) *Plough, Sword and Book: The Structure of Human History.* London, Paladin.

Gellner, E. (1992) *Reason and Culture*. Oxford, Blackwell.

Gibbs, G. (1992) *Improving the Quality of Student Learning*. Bristol, Technical and Educational Services.

Giddens, A. (1991) *The Consequences of Modernity*. Oxford, Polity Press.

Giroux, H.A. (1983) *Theory and Resistance in Education: a Pedagogy for the Opposition*. London, Heinemann.

Gless, D. and Herrnstein Smith, B.H. (eds) (1992) *The Politics of Liberal Education*. London, Duke University Press.

Godley, A.D. (1908) *Oxford in the Eighteenth Century*. London, Methuen.

Goodlad, S. (1976) *Conflict and Consensus in Higher Education*. London, Hodder and Stoughton.

Goodlad, S. (1985) The sociology of reductionism: administrative reductionism. In A. Peacocke (ed.), op. cit.

Goodlad, S. and Hughes, J. (1992) Reflection through action: peer tutoring as service learning. In R. Barnett (ed.), op. cit.

Gordon, C. (ed.) (1980) *Michel Foucault: Power/Knowledge*. Hemel Hempstead, Harvester Wheatsheaf.

Gordon, P. and White, J. (1979) *Philosophers and Educational Reformers*. London, Routledge and Kegan Paul.

Gorz, A. (1989) *Critique of Economic Reason*. London, Verso.

Gouldner, A. (1976) *The Dialectic of Ideology and Technology*. London, Macmillan.

Gouldner, A. (1979) *The Future of Intellectuals and the Rise of the New Class*. London, Macmillan.

Griffin, A. (1994) Transferring learning in higher education. In R. Barnett (ed.), op. cit.

Grundy, S. (1987) *Curriculum: Product or Process*. Lewes, Falmer.

Habermas, J. (1976) *Legitimation Crisis*. London, Heinemann.

Habermas, J. (1978) *Knowledge and Human Interests*. London, Heinemann (second edition).

Habermas, J. (1979) *Communication and the Evolution of Society*. London, Heinemann.

Habermas, J. (1987) *The Philosophical Discourse of Modernity*. Cambridge, Polity.

Habermas, J. (1989) *The Theory of Communicative Action*, Vol. 2. Cambridge, Polity.

Habermas, J. (1991) *The Theory of Communicative Action*, Vol. 1. Cambridge, Polity.

Hague, Sir Douglas (1991) *Beyond Universities: a New Republic of the Intellect*. London, IEA.

Halsey, A.H. (1992) *The Decline of Donnish Dominion*. Oxford, Oxford University Press.

Hamlyn, D.W. (1971) *The Theory of Knowledge*. London, Macmillan.

Hampshire, S. (1970) *Thought and Action*. London, Chatto and Windus (first edition 1959).

Handy, C. (1985) *Understanding Organisations*. London, Penguin.

Harris, K. (1979) *Education and Knowledge*. London, Routledge and Kegan Paul.

Heyck, T.W. (1982) *The Transformation of Intellectual Life in Victorian England*. Beckenham, Croom Helm.

Hirst, P. (1983) Educational theory. In P. Hirst (ed.) *Educational Theory and its Foundational Disciplines*. London, Routledge and Kegan Paul.

Hodgkinson, P. (1991) Liberal education and the new vocationalism, *Oxford Review of Education*, 17 (1), 73–88.

Horton, R. (1971) African thought and Western science. In M.F.D. Young (ed.), op. cit.

Howard, C.C. (1991) *Theories of General Education: A Critical Approach*. Basingstoke, Macmillan.

Huber, L. (1992) Towards a new *Studium Generale, European Journal of Education,* 27 (3), 285–301.

Hyland, T. (1992) Meta-competence, metaphysics and vocational expertise. In *Competence and Assessment,* Issue 20. Sheffield, Employment Department.

Jarvis, P. (1993) *Adult Education and the State.* London, Routledge.

Jessup, G. (1991) *Outcomes: NVQs and the Emerging Model of Education and Training.* London, Falmer.

Kenny, A. (1992) *The Metaphysics of Mind.* Oxford, Oxford University Press.

Kerr, C. (1972) *The Uses of the University.* Cambridge, Mass., Harvard University Press.

King, R. (1994) The Institutional Compact in J. Bocock and D. Watson (eds), op. cit.

Kuhn, T.S. (1970) *The Structure of Scientific Revolutions.* London, University of Chicago.

Lakatos, I. and Musgrave, A. (eds) (1970) *Criticism and the Growth of Knowledge.* Cambridge, Cambridge University Press.

Lawson, H. and Appignanesi, L. (eds) (1989) *Dismantling Truth: Reality in the Post-Modern World.* London, Weidenfeld and Nicolson.

Lyotard, J-F. (1984) *The Postmodern Condition: A Report on Knowledge.* Manchester, University of Manchester.

Lyotard, J-F. (1992) *The Postmodern Explained to Children.* London, Turnaround Press.

MacIntyre, A. (1982) *After Virtue.* London, Duckworth.

MacIntyre, A. (1990) *Three Rival Versions of Moral Enquiry.* London, Duckworth.

McPeck, J.E. (1981) *Critical Thinking and Education.* Oxford, Martin Robertson.

Marcuse, H. (1968) *One-Dimensional Man.* London, Sphere Books.

Margetson, D. (1991) Why is problem-based learning a challenge? In D. Boud and G. Feletti (eds) *The Challenge of Problem-Based Learning.* London, Kogan Page.

Margetson, D. (1994) Current educational reform and the significance of problem-based learning, *Studies in Higher Education,* 19 (1), 5–19.

Marton, F., Hounsell, D. and Entwistle, N. (eds) (1984) *The Experience of Learning.* Edinburgh, Scottish Academic Press.

Maxwell, N. (1987) *From Knowledge to Wisdom.* Oxford, Blackwell.

Midgley, M. (1989) *Wisdom, Information and Wonder: What is Knowledge For?* London, Routledge.

Minogue, K. (1973) *The Concept of a University.* London, Weidenfeld and Nicolson.

Mulkay, M. (1991) *Sociology of Science: a Sociological Pilgrimage.* Buckingham, Open University Press.

Neave, G. (1992) On instantly consumable knowledge and snake oil, *European Journal of Education,* 27 (1/2), 5–28.

Newman, J.H. (1976) *The Idea of a University.* Oxford, Oxford University Press.

Niblett, W.R. (1974) *Universities between Two Worlds.* London, University of London Press.

NFER (1991) *Enterprise in Higher Education: second year national evaluation, final report.* Slough, NFER.

NUS (1993, but undated) *Student Charter.* London, National Union of Students.

Oakeshott, M. (1962) *Rationalism in Politics.* London, Methuen.

Passmore, J. (1980) *The Philosophy of Teaching.* London, Duckworth.

Peacocke, A. (ed.) (1985) *Reductionism in Academic Disciplines.* Guildford, SRHE and NFER-Nelson.

Perkin, H. (1969) *Key Profession.* London, Routledge and Kegan Paul.

Perry, W.G. (1970) *Forms of Intellectual and Ethical Development.* New York, Holt, Rinehart and Winston.

Perry, W.G. (1988) Different worlds in the same classroom. In P. Ramsden (ed.) *Improving Learning.* London, Routledge.

Peters, M. (1991) Habermas and the question of modernity. Mimeo.

Peters, M. (1992) Performance and accountability. In Post-industrial society: the crisis of British universities, *Studies in Higher Education,* 17 (2), 123–40.

Peters, R.S. (1966) *Ethics and Education.* London, George Allen and Unwin.

Phillips, D.C. (1987) *Philosophy, Science and Social Inquiry.* Oxford, Pergamon.

Polanyi, M. (1962) *Personal Knowledge: Towards a Post-Critical Philosophy.* London, Routledge and Kegan Paul.

Polanyi, M. (1966) *The Tacit Dimension.* New York, Doubleday.

Popper, K.R. (1961) *The Poverty of Historicism.* London, Routledge and Kegan Paul.

Popper, K.R. (1970) The myth of the framework. In I. Lakatos and P. Musgrave (eds), op. cit.

Popper, K.R. (1975) *Objective Knowledge.* Oxford, Oxford University Press.

Premfors, R. (1991) *Knowledge, Power and Democracy.* Studies of Higher Education and Research, Stockholm, Council for Studies of Higher Education.

Pritchard, R. (1994) Government power in British higher education, *Studies in Higher Education,* 19 (3), forthcoming.

Rabinow, P. (1984) *The Foucault Reader.* London, Penguin.

Ramsden, P. (1983) Institutional variations in British students' approaches to learning and experiences of teaching, *Higher Education,* 12, 691–705.

Ramsden, P. (1992) *Learning to Teach in Higher Education.* London, Routledge.

Rand, R. (ed.) (1992) *Logomachia: The Conflict of the Faculties.* London, University of Nebraska.

Reeves, M. (1988) *The Crisis in Higher Education.* Buckingham, Open University Press.

Reid, L.A. (1986) *Ways of Understanding and Education.* London, Heinemann.

Robbins, L. (1963) *Higher Education: Report of the Committee.* London, HMSO.

Rorty, R. (1980) *Philosophy and the Mirror of Nature.* Oxford, Blackwell.

Rorty, R. (1989) *Contingency, Irony and Solidarity.* Cambridge, Cambridge University Press.

Rosenau, P.M. (1992) *Post-modernism and the Social Sciences: Insights, Inroads and Intrusions.* Princeton, Princeton University Press.

Roszak, T. (ed.) (1969) *The Dissenting Academy.* Harmondsworth, Penguin.

Russell, C. (1993) *Academic Freedom.* London, Routledge.

Ryle, G. (1949) *The Concept of Mind.* Harmondsworth, Penguin.

Sartre, J. (undated) *Being and Nothingness.* New York, Philosophical Library.

Schon, D. (1982) The fear of innovation. In B. Barnes and D. Edge (eds), op. cit.

Schon, D. (1987) *Educating the Reflective Practitioner.* London, Jossey-Bass.

Scott, P. (1984) *The Crisis of the University.* Beckenham, Croom Helm.

Scott, P. (1990) *Knowledge and Nation.* Edinburgh, University of Edinburgh Press.

Scott, P. (1991) *The Postmodern Challenge.* Stoke-on-Trent, Trentham Books.

Scott, P. (1994) Divide and rule. In R. Barnett (ed.), op. cit.

Searle, J.R. (1992) *The Rediscovery of the Mind.* Cambridge, Mass., MIT Press.

Shils, E. (1984) *The Academic Ethic.* London, University of Chicago Press.

Siegel, H. (1990) *Educating Reason: Rationality, Critical Thinking and Education.* London, Routledge.

Silver, H. (1991) *A Higher Education.* Basingstoke, Falmer.

Snow, C.P. (1964) *The Two Cultures: a Second Look.* Cambridge, Cambridge University Press.

Squires, G. (1990) *First Degree.* Buckingham, Open University Press.

Squires, G. (1992) Interdisciplinarity in Higher Education in the United Kingdom, *European Journal of Education*, 27 (3), 201–10.

Stephenson, J. and Weil, S. (1992) *Quality in Learning: A Capability Approach in Higher Education*. London, Kogan Page.

Stronach, I. (1990) Education, vocationalism and economic recovery: the case against witchcraft. In G. Esland (ed.) *Education, Training and Employment*. Wokingham, Addison-Wesley.

Tapper, T. and Salter, B. (1992) *Oxford, Cambridge and the Changing Idea of the University*. Buckingham, Open University Press.

Tavistock Institute of Human Relations (1990) *The First Year of Enterprise in Higher Education*. Sheffield, Employment Department.

Taylor, W. (1991) *The Ethics of Authenticity*. London, Harvard.

Test, K. (1992) *Civil Society*. London, Routledge.

Thompson, D.L. (ed.) (1991) *Moral Values and Higher Education*. Albany, NY, Brigham Young University.

Training Agency (1989, 1990) *Enterprise in Higher Education, 1988–89; 1989–90*. Sheffield.

Trow, M. and Nybom, T. (eds) (1991) *University and Society: Essays on the Social Role of Research and Higher Education*. London, Jessica Kingsley.

Turner, B.S. (ed.) (1990) *Theories of Modernity and Postmodernity*. London, Sage.

Unit for the Development of Adult Continuing Education (1989) *Understanding Learning Outcomes*. Leicester, UDACE.

Unit for the Development of Adult Continuing Education (1989) *Understanding Competence*. Leicester, UDACE.

Walsh, P. (1993) *Education and Meaning: Philosophy in Practice*. London, Cassell.

Weiner, M. (1981) *English Culture and the Decline of the Industrial Spirit 1850–1980*. Harmondsworth, Penguin.

White, J. (1982) *The Aims of Education Restated*. London, Routledge and Kegan Paul.

Whitehead, A.N. (1934) *The Aims of Education*. London, Williams and Norgate.

Winch, P. (1963) *The Idea of a Social Science and its Relationship to Philosophy*. London, Routledge and Kegan Paul.

Winter, R. (1992) The assessment programme – competence-based education at professional/honours degree level. In *Competence and Assessment*, Issue 20. Sheffield, Employment Department.

Wolf, A. (1990) Unwrapping knowledge and understanding from standards and competence. In H. Black and A. Wolf (eds), op. cit.

Wright, P. (1990) Strategic change in the higher education curriculum: the example of the enterprise in higher education initiative. In C. Loder and G. Williams (eds) *Quality Assurance and Accountability*. London, Kogan Page.

Young, M.F.D. (ed.) (1971) *Knowledge and Control*. London, Collier and Macmillan.

Young, R.E. (1989) *A Critical Theory of Education*. Hemel Hempstead, Harvester Wheatsheaf.

Index

Note: This book is partly an interweaving of certain terms:

capability
communication
competence
critical thought
curriculum
disciplines
enterprise
higher education
ideologies

knowledge
learning outcomes
skills
society
students
transferable skills
understanding
university.

For these terms, only major references are cited below in the index, together with their first occurrence where appropriate.

The Society for Research into Higher Education

The Society for Research into Higher Education exists to stimulate and co-ordinate research into all aspects of higher education. It aims to improve the quality of higher education through the encouragement of debate and publication on issues of policy, on the organization and management of higher education institutions, and on the curriculum and teaching methods.

The Society's income is derived from subscriptions, sales of its books and journals, conference fees and grants. It receives no subsidies, and is wholly independent. Its individual members include teachers, researchers, managers and students. Its corporate members are institutions of higher education, research institutes, professional, industrial and governmental bodies. Members are not only from the UK, but from elsewhere in Europe, from America, Canada and Australasia, and it regards its international work as amongst its most important activities.

Under the imprint *SRHE & Open University Press*, the Society is a specialist publisher of research, having some 45 titles in print. The Editorial Board of the Society's Imprint seeks authoritative research or study in the above fields. It offers competitive royalties, a highly recognizable format in both hardback and paperback and the world-wide reputation of the Open University Press.

The Society also publishes *Studies in Higher Education* (three times a year), which is mainly concerned with academic issues, *Higher Education Quarterly* (formerly *Universities Quarterly*), mainly concerned with policy issues, *Research into Higher Education Abstracts* (three times a year), and *SRHE News* (four times a year).

The Society holds a major annual conference in December, jointly with an institution of higher education. In 1992, the topic was 'Learning to Effect' with Nottingham Trent University. In 1993, it was 'Governments and the Higher Education Curriculum: Evolving Partnerships' at the University of Sussex in Brighton, and in 1994, 'The Student Experience' at the University of York. Conferences in 1995 include, 'The Changing University?' at Heriot-Watt University in Edinburgh.

The Society's committees, study groups and branches are run by the members. The groups at present include:

Teacher Education Study Group
Continuing Education Group
Staff Development Group
Excellence in Teaching and Learning

Benefits to members

Individual

Individual members receive:

- *SRHE News*, the Society's publications list, conference details and other material included in mailings.
- Greatly reduced rates for *Studies in Higher Education* and *Higher Education Quarterly*.
- A 35% discount on all Open University Press & SRHE publications.
- Free copies of the Precedings – commissioned papers on the theme of the Annual Conference.
- Free copies of *Research into Higher Education Abstracts*.
- Reduced rates for conferences.
- Extensive contacts and scope for facilitating initiatives.
- Reduced reciprocal memberships.

Corporate

Corporate members receive:

- All benefits of individual members, plus
- Free copies of *Studies in Higher Education*.
- Unlimited copies of the Society's publications at reduced rates.
- Special rates for its members e.g. to the Annual Conference.

Membership details: SRHE, 3, Devonshire Street, London WIN 2BA. Tel: 0171 637 2766 Fax: 0171 637 2781
Catalogue: SRHE & Open University Press, Celtic Court, 22 Ballmoor, Buckingham MK18 1XW. Tel: (01280) 823388

IMPROVING HIGHER EDUCATION
TOTAL QUALITY CARE

Ronald Barnett

This book provides the first systematic exploration of the topic of quality in higher education. Ronald Barnett examines the meaning of quality and its improvement at the levels of both the institution and the course – contemporary discussion having tended to focus on one or the other, without integrating the two perspectives. He argues against a simple identification of quality assessment with numerical perform- ance indicators *or* with academic audit *or* with the messages of the market. These are the contending definitions of the modern age, but they all contain interests tangential to the main business of higher education.

Dr Barnett offers an alternative approach which begins from a sense of educators attempting to promote an open-ended development in their students. It is this view of higher education which, he argues, should be at the heart of our thinking about quality. Quality cannot be managed, but it can be cared for. Building on the con- ceptual base he establishes, Dr Barnett offers proposals for action in assessing insti- tutional performance, in reviewing the quality of course programmes, and in improving the curriculum and the character of the student experience.

Contents

256pp   0 335 09984 X (Paperback)   0 335 09985 8 (Hardback)

LEARNING TO EFFECT

Ronald Barnett (ed.)

This book discusses contemporary issues of curriculum change in higher education, and examines various ideas and initiatives concerned with making student learning more effective. It addresses curriculum purpose, curriculum delivery, and curriculum impact on the wider society. It considers the ways in which the higher education curriculum is changing in response to the wider society, how a higher quality of curriculum delivery might be achieved, and how the necessary institutional change might be effected. It covers, for instance, experiential learning, skills and training, competence and outcomes, assessment, student control over learning, the quality of teaching and learning, curriculum theory, and the institutional context. More generally, it explores ways in which teaching approaches and the curriculum in higher education can be designed so as to have a demonstrably positive effect on the quality of student learning.

Contents

Contributors

Graham Badley, Ronald Barnett, Gaie Davidson, Roger Ellis, Michael Eraut, Norman Evans, Malcolm Frazer, Graham Gibbs, Sinclair Goodlad, John Hughes, Elisabeth Lillie, Diana Tribe, A.J. Tribe, Susan Weil and Peter W.G. Wright.

240pp   0 335 15759 9 (Hardback)